D1014840

LINES IN THE SAND

Desert Storm and the Remaking of the Arab World

DEBORAH AMOS

Simon & Schuster

New York   London   Toronto   Sydney   Tokyo   Singapore

SIMON & SCHUSTER
Simon & Schuster Building
Rockefeller Center
1230 Avenue of the Americas
New York, New York 10020

Copyright © 1992 by Deborah Amos

All rights reserved,
including the right of reproduction
in whole or in part in any form.

SIMON & SCHUSTER and colophon are registered
trademarks of Simon & Schuster Inc.

Designed by Richard Oriolo

Manufactured in the United States of America

10 9 8 7 6 5 4 3 2 1

Library of Congress Cataloging-in-Publication Data
Amos, Deborah.
Lines in the sand: Desert Storm and the remaking of the Arab world/Deborah Amos.
p.   cm.
Includes index.
1. Arab countries—Politics and government—1945– 2. Persian Gulf War, 1991–Mis-
cellanea.   I. Title.
DS63.1.A47   1992
956.704'3—dc20   92–10341
                                                                          CIP

ISBN 0-671-76068-8

Opposite page: Excerpt from "Be Angry at the Sun" by Robinson Jeffers. From *Selected Poems* by Robinson Jeffers © 1941 and renewed 1969 by Donnan Jeffers and Garth Jeffers. Reprinted by Permission of Random House Inc.

For Rick Davis, who understood more
than I about war and what comes next.

That public men publish falsehoods
Is nothing new. That America must accept
Like the historical republics corruption and empire
Has been known for years.

Be angry at the sun for setting
If these things anger you. Watch the wheel slope and
            turn,
They are all bound on the wheel, these people, those
            warriors,
This republic, Europe, Asia.

Observe them gesticulating,
Observe them going down. The gang serves lies, the
            passionate
Man plays his part; the cold passion for truth
Hunts in no pack.

—Robinson Jeffers

ACKNOWLEDGMENTS

This book was written with the help of many friends and colleagues. The opinions in the book are my own, but I had enormous help in seeing the region through a number of perspectives. Many people spent long hours on the phone with me and I am grateful for their help. Some read the manuscript in its early form. Others were my cultural guide in a region that does not proclaim itself easily, and saved me from making factual errors. The errors that remain are mine alone.

I'd like to thank the editors and producers of National Public Radio for allowing me to pursue a long story in the Middle East. Robert Siegel was my first guide in the region. Bill Drummond and Marty Kurcias were my colleagues during a difficult trip to Lebanon. Cadi Simon supported my intention to move to Amman, Jordan, where I was able to see the Arab world for myself. Looking back, the next five years were a preparation for the predawn call on August 2, 1990, with an assignment to cover the Iraqi invasion of Kuwait.

ACKNOWLEDGMENTS

I'd like to thank Karen DeYoung of *The Washington Post,* novelist Marianne Wiggins, and Tom McNaugher of Brookings Institution for their suggestions in the early stages of my writing. The many months in Saudi Arabia were shared with Carla Robbins of *U.S. News & World Report,* Juan O. Tomayo of *The Miami Herald,* and my colleagues Mike Shuster, Scott Simon, Neal Conan, and Deborah Wang. I am grateful to many extraordinary people who served with the American military during Desert Storm. I learned a great deal from Lt. Colonel Tom Sacks, General Walter Boomer, and Lt. Colonel Martin Semik. Adel al-Jubier was an invaluable guide to the desert Kingdom. His charm and humor were an antidote to the tensions of the long buildup of a shield that became a storm. While my impressions of the country are entirely my own, Adel's insights into the ways of his countrymen and women were important to my understanding of Saudi Arabia. Nathaniel Kern spent hours on the telephone after the war was over to help me sort out my impressions. Thanks as well to Eleanor Doumato, who gave time to explain the situation for Saudi women.

I want to thank Noah Adams for his encouragement to write this book and Johnathon Lazear for his hard work in finding a publisher. Thanks to Bill Buzenberg and John Dinges for giving me the time to write the book. My editors at Simon & Schuster, Paul Aron and Chuck Adams, helped me through the months of writing. Ken Jaques worked hard as a researcher and then checked the facts again. Samira Kawar and Jacob Dawani turned Arabic into English and were my cultural translators. They have been important instructors over the years and have trained my American eyes.

I'd like to thank Key Maleski and Rob Robinson for finding the details at the last minute. Stan Grossfeld made the book jacket better. I'd also like to thank Bill and Lynn Kovach and the Nieman class of 1992 for listening to my war stories. And finally thanks to John and Regina Amos.

C O N T E N T S

INTRODUCTION

On a gray Washington day at the Grand Hotel, another epic chapter in the history of the Middle East is played out to the tune of "Don't Get Around Much Anymore." The cocktail bar pianist strokes a restrained repertoire of 1930s tunes while Palestinian negotiators talk over the details of the morning's session at the U.S. State Department. A haze of blue cigarette smoke settles over the lounge as delegates drink endless cups of coffee.

The negotiations are carried out against the insistent tearing sounds of death. The impersonal carnage of Desert Storm has given way to the kind of violence that reaches out to claim "normal" lives. The warriors of the Storm killed at a distance, claiming a sense of military professionalism. That war is over. The haters have reclaimed the stage. On one side the weapons of choice—the machete, kitchen knife, the sharpened hoe—are the kind that require a slayer to look a victim in the eye. A forty-two-year-old woman, a recent immigrant from Russia, is knifed to death while shopping in Jerusalem. On another side, death comes at a remove. Political assassination in southern Lebanon is ordered by the Prime Minister of Israel. The event is so matter-of-fact that the controversy focuses on when the order was given rather than the fact that it was given at all.

The fate of two five-year-old children tells a story of a fury that refuses to acknowledge that there is a distinction between the innocent and the guilty. Hussein Musawi is not the target of the Israeli rockets that hit a Hezbollah convoy in southern Lebanon. His father, Sheikh Abbas Musawi, is the man marked for destruction. But a young boy burns to death along with his parents. The predictable retaliation claims more than thirty victims, most of them Lebanese. In a northern Israeli settlement, a young girl runs to greet her father, when shrapnel from a Katysha rocket pierces her skull.

Back in Washington, the Middle East peace process announces its intention with its name. Peace in the Middle East—a tall order for a region that has known little peace for the past half-century. Nevertheless for the first time in history a people under occupation face their occupiers across a negotiating table. They meet in the capitol city of the nation that has long supported the occupier. The delegates trade insults and accusations and at the same time exchange diplomatic hints that they are preparing to fundamentally change the way the region operates. There is a sense that there is something new here. It may not be the New World Order that the American president promised, but it is a change in a region that has always seen history through the prism of selective memory. Progress is slow, but hope rests in the details of personal encounters. The language of negotiations is beginning to replace the harangues of war.

There is at least some small irony in the fact that the man who made these meetings possible is not welcome in Washington. For the American administration, he is the Hitler of the Middle East. For the Israelis, he is the chief villain in a hostile Arab world. For the Syrians, he is the evil twin of their own political system. For the Palestinians, Saddam Hussein is an unsavory hero who had almost dragged them to the abyss of history. All of the participants in Washington are uncomfortable in acknowledging Saddam's role in bringing them to these talks, first to Madrid and then to Washington. With reluctance, however, all of the participants will admit that Saddam's decision to invade Kuwait on August 2, 1990, played some part in bringing them to the negotiating table.

Of course the collapse of the Soviet Union played an enormous role in changing the dynamics of Middle East politics. The end of the super power rivalry in the region has had practical results. Michael Gorbachev, as well as Saddam Hussein, was responsible for the shift in the order of the Middle East. But the Iraqi invasion of Kuwait has in effect accelerated history. It may be the only positive outcome of a war that was committed as a consequence of a decade of colossal miscalculation and misunderstanding, a process set in motion by a seemingly disjointed progression of events. This book is an attempt to understand that process.

I came to Washington to watch the Middle East peace negotiations with more than a journalist's curiosity. In fact, I wasn't reporting on the events at all. I was a Nieman Fellow at Harvard University. The year was supposed to be a break after more than ten years of reporting in the Middle East. Nevertheless, I followed the developments with a passion that had developed over a decade of living and working in the region. During the cold, dark, Cambridge winter I set my alarm to watch the predawn television pictures of the conference in Madrid. It was the first time that Israelis and Arabs faced each other at the negotiating table. The meeting had enormous symbolic importance, and I wanted to watch the faces of the people who sat at the table to see if they revealed intentions.

The Madrid conference and the meetings that followed in Washington were not pictures I could have imaged a decade earlier. In 1981 I boarded a plane from Washington for my first trip to the Middle East. At the time, the prognosis for the region was grim and about to take a turn for the worst. The Iran-Iraq war was simmering. The shock waves of the Islamic revolution continued to resonate in a region that was convinced of its impotence and embraced Islam in despair. While one hostage crisis in Tehran had been resolved, the precedent would lead to more kidnappings. In Lebanon, the uncivil war would soon bring the Palestine Liberation Organization and the Israeli military into direct and violent confrontation. The definition of terrorism was tainted by political perspective, and the battle lines blurred.

At the time of that first trip I hadn't given much thought to the complicated politics of the Middle East. I had been assigned to work as a radio producer for Robert Siegel, a National Public Radio colleague. We had come to cover the election campaign. The veteran Likud hardliner, Menachim Begin, was running for his second term as Prime Minister. It was my first foreign assignment for NPR, and the experience was to change my life.

The following year a trip to the Middle East was more complicated. This time a battered Cypriot freighter carried me to the shores of Lebanon. There was nothing in my life so far that had prepared me for what I would witness over the next two months. There was no particular courage that propelled me into the middle of the Israeli invasion of Lebanon but simply a lack of imagination for the reality of urban warfare. The scene at the port of Jouneh was the first sign of the contradictions of conflict, as I watched the morning sun sparkle off the waterskiers on the Mediterranean Sea while the dull thuds of death rumbled from another part of the capitol.

This was a war that mixed the smell of jasmine on the cool breeze of a Mediterranean summer night with the ominous creek of tank tracks on a tarmac road. This was a war that raised such fundamental questions about history and justice that I knew I had to live in the region to begin to understand.

I moved to Amman, Jordan, in 1985 and from this home base traveled to almost every part of the Arab and Islamic world. My first trip to Kuwait in those days taught me about the large Palestinian community in exile in the Gulf. This was a different refugee population than the one I'd encountered in Beirut, Amman, and in the camps of Gaza and the West Bank. These refugees defied the definition except in one important aspect: the community was the financial engine for much of the Palestinian population in the Arab diaspora. Yasser Arafat, the Chairman of the Palestine Liberation Organization, had made his fortune in Kuwait. However, these Palestinians shared the same statelessness and powerlessness of their brethren in the cramped concrete and tin shacks that house three generations of despair.

By that time the Palestinians had disappeared from the front pages of the newspapers, replaced by a war that raged at the "Eastern Gate" of the Arab world. The Iran-Iraq war introduced a new level of brutality as the combatants carried out an ancient dispute with twentieth-century weapons supplied by America, Europe, and the Soviet Union. There were no jasmine or cool breezes in the flat yellow killing grounds of southern Iraq. This was the place that I recorded an interview with an Iraqi commander who told us that the Iranians were no better than insects who had to be exterminated. A few hours later I watched as a group of Iraqi soldiers took great delight in turning over the blackened corpses of Iranian soldiers for a press corps who had come to report on the progress of the war.

I would soon mix with the "fundamentalists" of Iran in the enveloping black cloak of anonymity, my *chador* covering everything but my mind. In Pakistan I was the target of the believers' wrath after a book published in England made them forget the Koran and attack a woman. A gentle and charming Pakistani doctor apologized for them as he stitched up the tear in my scalp. The reaction to Salman Rushdie's *The Satanic Verses* caught me by surprise. It was a reminder of the deep gap between the world I had grown up in and the one that I was now trying to understand.

By the time of the Iraqi invasion of Kuwait I had traveled to just about every corner of a region that would be engulfed by the conflict. I had spent almost a decade of my life writing about the contradictions and the daily life of the Middle East. I had always made it a point to mix political analysis and war reporting with the personal stories of the people who lived in the region. I wanted to convey that there were people who washed the dishes, drove the children to school, ate dinner, and worried about the future. I had spent years trying to see the issues from their perspective. I couldn't help thinking about those people when the Iraqi tanks rolled over the border of Kuwait.

This book is in no way a complete history of Desert Storm. I only describe what I saw, which was a small segment of a campaign that began long before August 2, 1990. The lines in the sand have faded for those who watched from a distance. I wrote the book for those who remain close to the fault lines.

ONE

IN THE SHADOW OF THE PROPHET

"Goooooood Morning, Saudi Arabia. Navy Chief Journalist Rich
Jankoo kicking off Desert Shield network FM 107. We start off
Rocking the Casbah . . . with The Clash."
—The first broadcast of Desert Shield Radio
    in Dhahran, Saudi Arabia

There was no question that the Kuwaitis needed help. The Liberation
Brigade was armed as if they were going to a cocktail party in Beirut
rather than the "Mother of all Battles" in their own backyard. The
heaviest weapons were 50-caliber machine guns mounted on the
flatbeds of Toyota trucks. The vehicles were Japan's gift to the allies
in lieu of soldiers.

The creative adaption was a specialty of the Fifth Special Forces
group, Fort Campbell, Kentucky. They had dubbed the truck the Jed
Clampet model. The Kuwaitis had shared the joke.

The exiled government of Kuwait had ordered better weapons for
the brigade, but the shipment remained at the Saudi port of Jubail.
With liberation assured, the al Sabahs had reconsidered their options.
A well-armed and trained fighting force might turn against Kuwait's
returned rulers. The Liberation Brigade would have to fight with what
they had. The Americans were their guardian angels.

The brigade was recruited from the Kuwaiti refugees who fled Saddam Hussein's vice in late summer. It was a ragtag fighting force. The commander of the brigade had been an air defense officer. There were a couple of bedouins. One of the men had four wives back in Kuwait. There was a six-footer everyone called "Famous" because he'd been on Kuwait's international boxing team. Famous had earned his name again when he stole back into Kuwait City before the battle and brought back the winter clothes of the men in the brigade.

The Kuwaitis had been recruited because they knew the neighborhoods of Kuwait City. A U.S. Special Forces team trained them to fight as guerillas for the final act of liberation. They had practiced their new skills at Saudi Arabia's King Khalid Military City and in abandoned villages in the Saudi desert.

The Liberation Brigade was in daily contact with the resistance inside Kuwait. The cellular telephone was the resistance's link to the outside. Resistance groups had faxed daily intelligence reports since the early days of the occupation. The brigade's job was to root out the occupiers in a neighborhood-by-neighborhood sweep with the help of an American air force and special forces team. "We knew where all the roadblocks were, where the armory was. There was a constant flow of feedback," said U.S. Air Force Staff Sergeant Charlie O'Riordan.

"They would send pictures of the atrocities with the intelligence reports," said O'Riordan. "There were reports of families who had a member in the military. The Iraqis would find out about that and take the family out in the middle of the street and shoot them."

The resistance smuggled out pictures to Saudi Arabia. The Kuwaiti Liberation Brigade had a daily diet of the grotesque skills of Iraq's intelligence service. It was clear to the Americans who were training the Kuwaitis that the pictures were creating an irresistible climate for revenge.

"Even we would get real emotional about those pictures," said O'Riordan. "One day I asked the brigade commander, 'Are you going to act like an Iraqi when you confront these people?' " It was a question he asked again on the battlefield. About thirty hours into the ground war the Liberation Brigade encountered their first Iraqi soldiers.

"They were sitting in front of a tank with their hands up," said O'Riordan. "There was a Kuwaiti in a pickup truck who walked over to round up the Iraqi prisoners. He was blown apart by an explosive box wired to the top of the tank. Two other guys were wounded. The Kuwaitis would have gone crazy if the Americans had not been with them."

•   •   •

An hour before the cease-fire that officially ended the war the Liberation Brigade and the Americans were camped out on the western outskirts of Kuwait City. A thin sliver of sunlight struggled through the black oil clouds that hugged the city. There was light, but there was no heat to drive out the chill of the desert night.

A clutch of men from the army's Fifth Special Forces group talked as they huddled around the warmth of a coffee pot. A small pup they'd found in the desert nipped at their heels. The Kuwaitis were inside their tents, brewing up thick Arabic coffee and frying bread over a pit of open coals. The three Americans from the air force team were poking through the plastic packs of military rations. One had propped a mirror on the hood of a military vehicle for a morning shave.

It is a fleeting moment in warfare when victory has no politics and is measured by one simple question: Who got here alive? In this twilight between war and peace, Staff Sergeant Charlie O'Riordan relaxed for the first time. He was philosophical after his first war, comfortable with his new status as victor. He had nothing good to say about officers in general, special forces in particular, and the Iraqis, in that order. Charles Patrick O'Riordan was thirty-one years old. His thirteen years as a noncommissioned air force officer had honed a keen cynicism. Nevertheless, he'd been touched by the experiences of the past three months. The evidence was the joined American and Kuwaiti flag patch on the shoulder of his desert camouflage uniform. "It took a lot of tea and a lot of bullshit with them," he said, to get the Kuwaitis ready for combat.

The Americans had fought side by side with the Kuwaiti Liberation Brigade. The air force team, Captain David Halla, Staff Sergeant Charlie O'Riordan, and Air Force Specialist John Davis, had worked hard. The idea was to give the Arab brigades all of the advantages of the American forces: communication, firepower, and air cover. Americans all over the desert provided the same service for every Arab brigade. This team functioned as the Tactical Air Control Party (TACP) for the Liberation Brigade.

In 1990s high-tech warfare, the TACPs coordinated the intricate aerial ballet of jets that flew over the heads of the allies to kill the enemy. It was a complicated job. O'Riordan radioed the locations to a forward air controller (FAC) who swooped down over the battlefield. The FAC monitored the positions from the air and worked like a traffic cop to direct the A-10 pilots who fired the missiles. In this kind of close warfare a mistake could end in "friendly fire," the inappropriate term for killing your own men.

For the Liberation Brigade the fighting had stopped twelve hours earlier. The Kuwaiti commander, Colonel Khalid Rodeeni, ordered the slaughtering of a sheep for a victory dinner. The Americans and the Kuwaitis sat cross-legged on carpets in a military tent eating hot spiced meat and rice from a metal platter. The Americans had learned the custom of rolling the moist lamb and rice into neat balls that could be shot into the mouth with a flick of the thumb. It was a subdued evening. Rodeeni, a portly soldier, ate in silence. The battery light on the tent floor outlined his drawn and dirty face, revealing his anxiety over the fate of his family in Kuwait City and the future of his newly liberated country. What would Kuwait be like?

There were already some clues. The young princes of the al Sabah family had insisted on running loyalty checks on Kuwaiti soldiers three weeks before the ground war began. Those who failed the test had been purged from the forces. In the first hours of the ground assault the Kuwaiti royals ordered all communications cut with the resistance, which represented all segments of Kuwaiti society. Palestinians, Kuwaiti Shiite and Sunni Muslims, antiroyalists, all fighting together inside Kuwait, were not welcome in the new world order envisioned by the young al Sabahs.

On the morning of the cease-fire the intelligence reports showed that the Iraqis had already fled Kuwait City. The plan to use the Americans to back the Kuwaitis in house-to-house fighting had been scrapped. The Americans would stay behind in the desert while their Arab partners marched into the city. The idea was to make the victory a strictly Arab show.

"It's the Saudis," said Colonel Rodeeni, shaking his head. He was angry that the Saudis were still in control in his newly liberated country. The Kuwaiti brigades had been melded into the Saudi command structure and Rodeeni resented it. The Kuwaitis had grown close to the teams of young air force and special forces officers, and wanted them along for the march to the city.

Five minutes before the cease-fire, Lieutenant Colonel Martin Semik called on the tactical radio phone from King Khalid Military City in Saudi Arabia. Semik was the chief air force liaison officer for this project. He'd watched the war's progress from a bunker in Saudi Arabia, monitoring the work of his team in the field. Semik, a Vietnam veteran, was eager to bring his teams "home." The plan for the Americans to assist the Kuwaitis in the house-to-house searches had made him uneasy. If the Kuwaitis acted like the Iraqis he didn't want his air force team tainted.

The orders were broad enough for interpretation and O'Riordan had other plans. The Americans had risked their lives with these Kuwaitis. He was going to the liberated city. "We told Colonel Rodeeni we were staying with him all the way," said O'Riordan.

As the cold morning wind stirred the sand, Air Force Captain Greg Hawkes climbed into his Hummer. Hawkes was a few miles south of the Halla team when he got the same set of messages. The American military's 1990s jeep, officially called the "High Mobility Wheeled Vehicle," was the communications center for this air force team and had the look of a cramped college dormitory. The dashboard mirror was festooned with an American flag, a battery-powered fan, a box of "Wet Ones," green night-vision goggles, and a pair of women's sheer purple panties.

Hawkes was working with the Kuwaiti Shaheed (Martyr's) Brigade, a different kind of outfit than the Liberation Brigade. The Shaheed Brigade had been Kuwait's Thirtieth Brigade on the day of Iraqi invasion. They were chased across the border by the invading Iraqi army. Reconstituted and renamed in Saudi Arabia, the Shaheed Brigade drove up the desert in British-made Challenger tanks and fought to retake their old barracks on the second day of the war.

Hawkes was disappointed that he would miss the last moments of victory, but he knew he would see his friends again. He had invited the Kuwaitis of the Shaheed Brigade home to Alaska where he ran a fishing business during his off-hours from Elmendorf Air Force Base. They all promised they would make the trip. Hawkes was sure they would come.

"This isn't the war I thought it would be," said Hawkes. "There were no dead bodies—just guys with smiles on their faces and their hands up." It would be days before he knew of the carnage in other parts of the desert and the escape of two divisions of the Iraqi army.

Hawkes spent the last day of the war attending to Iraqi prisoners of war. There had been thousands of them, worn, hungry, and tired, popping up out of sand bunkers as the Americans and the Kuwaiti Shaheed Brigade rolled up the desert. It was a bizarre lesson in the strengths and weaknesses of the Iraqi army. There was plenty of ammunition in the Iraqi bunkers. There were also pigeon cages wrapped in burlap bags. Could this be an Iraqi dinner, an early warning system for poison gas, or a primitive form of command and control? Whatever the explanation, the Iraqi army was a different kind of enemy than the one envisioned by this young American air force officer one hundred hours earlier.

In the countdown to the cease-fire, the Kuwaitis of the Shaheed Brigade were organizing and cleaning the war booty in the desert 10 miles west of Kuwait City. There was time to take pictures in front of Soviet weapons captured from the Iraqis, souvenirs from this desert campaign. Lieutenant Yusef al Awadi had found a logbook in one of the bunkers. It had belonged to an Iraqi division commander. It looked like a crude high school yearbook with a black cardboard cover and white lined paper. On every page, in neat, handwritten Arabic script, a description of the career and personal details of each Iraqi officer had been penned by his commander. The small passport-size black and white photographs that accompanied each description were of young Iraqis who looked more like hopeful high school boys than soldiers.

A decade's worth of military history was contained in these pages. Some of the files showed that the officer had died in the Iran-Iraq War. The next lines described the man's ethnic origins, Arab or Kurd, Sunni Muslim, Shiite, Christian, and his position in Iraq's ruling Ba'th party. The most ominous detail was a long notation at the bottom of the page that included a list of relatives, brothers, sisters, their addresses, telephone numbers, and workplaces. The Iraqi army kept close tabs on the families of its soldiers. Punishment for a deserter could reach to the "4th degree"—down to the cousins of the family tree. This sinister form of control had kept many of the men from deserting despite the punishing air attacks of the past weeks. The men in the book were now prisoners of war, or they were dead, buried under the sand in nameless graves.

At Ali al Salem Air Base, about 40 miles west of Kuwait City, the oily clouds made the desert landscape look like a mean winter day in Fayetteville, North Carolina, Air Force Captain Russ Meyers' home base. When the rain came it was in greasy droplets that coated military vehicles and men's faces in a sheer gray film. This was man-made weather, a new feature of modern warfare. Meyers was the American air force liaison officer for the Saudi Twentieth Brigade. Meyers' war had ended on the third day of the fighting and he was waiting for further orders.

The Saudi Twentieth was part of the Arab coalition that swept up the heart of the battlefield. Meyers and this mechanized division had two missions. First they were to cross the mine fields and then head north to hold a road intersection, a possible escape route for Iraqi soldiers. The second objective was a barracks complex attached to the Ali al Salem Air Base.

The start of the ground war, "G Day," had been scheduled for 4 A.M. local time on February 24, 1990. G Day came earlier than expected for the Arab armies on the front line. The plan called for the Arab coalition to cross the Saudi border into occupied Kuwait twenty-four hours after the start of the ground war: G plus twenty-four. The schedule was revised after the U.S. Marines made lightening progress into Kuwait. The forces in the Arab sector had to scramble to close the gap on the marines' flank.

G plus nine hours was the new starting mark for the Arab coalition. On the afternoon of February 24, a task force of Egyptian, Saudi, Kuwaiti, and Syrian tanks and trucks assembled on the flat desert like an armada on a sea of sand. This was Joint Command West. The Syrians and Egyptians kicked off the campaign with a twenty-minute artillery barrage.

Saudi tankers stood in the open turrets of their mechanized machines. The green flag of Saudi Arabia fluttered from the tank tops emblazoned with Islam's statement of faith: "There is no God but God." There was a hitch in the plan from the first moment that the Arab armies crossed the border. The new start time put them in Kuwaiti territory as the desert light darkened to a fiery red across the sand. The Arab armies were not trained or equipped to fight at night.

The Saudi Twentieth Brigade stopped on the other side of the sand berm in the twilight. The Saudi tankers jumped out of their turrets, knelt in the sand facing Mecca, and touched the cold sand with their foreheads for the evening prayers. The brigade had stopped for the night. They didn't move for the next fourteen hours as the war went on around them. "The special forces advisors told 'em, 'If you sit here you're jamming everybody up. If they decide to use artillery on you, you're prime targets,' " said Meyers.

The Egyptian commanding general had impressed his American counterparts with his graphs and charts, anticipating all of war's surprises. In the twilight, the Egyptian army secured a police post, their first objective in the ground war. The commander had ordered his men to stop early, wary of crossing in front of Saudi artillery. The rest of the Arab front line stalled in the darkness.

The next day's progress was slow as well. For these Saudi soldiers, moving across the sand berm into Kuwait was a political point of no return. It was the end of the hope that war could be averted. Most of them believed that Saddam would never go this far, that Saddam would pull out at the last minute, that Saddam's army would simply collapse and come streaming across the border. They lived in a country that made a religion of inter-Arab consensus. War against an Arab neighbor went against a deep sense of Arab brotherhood and Islam. In the early days of the occupation they had shared their food with hungry Iraqi soldiers who had come from the other side of the berm. Even when the scuds started falling on Riyadh and Dhahran, they would ask their American liaison officers, "What will happen now?" "We are going to war" was the reply.

A week before the ground war, the special forces team rehearsed the breach of the mine field. There was training in tactics, in pulling the tanks forward, how it should look, the number of lanes. The timing was as precise as a wedding rehearsal. In the dress rehearsal it took thirty minutes to blow through the mine fields. On the second day of the ground war the job took four hours.

"When we got across the mine field, that's where the Iraqi resistance was," said Russ Meyers. "They had a couple of mortar pits and a lot of dug-in infantry positions on the other side." Now the situation was dangerous. The Saudi advance had halted with half of the brigade on one side of the mine field and half of the brigade on the other side. The Americans knew this was crazy. They were sitting ducks. If the artillery fire got bad enough, inexperienced troops would panic, scattering off the cleared paths into the mine fields as they scrambled for safety.

Meyers called back to Saudi Arabia for more air support. The forward air controllers circled the Iraqi positions in OV-10s, a slow-flying, Vietnam-vintage reconnaissance plane that enables the pilot to spot the enemy and then direct the jet pilots to their targets.

"The quote on the radio was, 'Hey, I think we kicked over a pile of ants,' because we had two hundred guys coming out of the ground sticking their hands up," said Meyers. The first Iraqi soldiers had surrendered to a jet plane and the pilot was calling Meyers for advice. "It was making him kinda nervous because he didn't know that those guys were even out there," said Meyers.

The forward air controller circled the prisoners. Mortar shells continued to drop with a thud in the sand. Meyers called back to the pilots and told them to lay down a couple of 30-millimeter strafing runs to scare whoever else was out there.

"That's when we had over a thousand—we ended up with 1400 hundred prisoners who gave up that instant. Now we were really nervous, because that's a lot of people," said Meyers. The mine field was forgotten as the Americans and the Saudis scrambled to deal with 1400 Iraqi prisoners of war.

"You can't just say to 1400 guys, 'Okay, sit in the desert while we go forward.' That's not smart. We had to secure them and get them out of there," Meyers explained. The Saudis began ordering buses on their field radios to haul this mob back to a high school sports stadium in the border town of Hafr alBatin. The Americans watched in amazement as the Saudis hugged the Iraqi officers and welcomed them back into the Arab fold.

Two weeks before the ground war I had spent a day and a night with a small unit of the Saudi Twentieth Brigade. I was a part of a media war combat pool assigned to report on the B-52 strikes on the Iraqi Republican Guards by the U.S. Air Force. In the cold black of the desert night the rumble of a B-52 strike could be felt before it was heard. At 3 A.M. the first blast shook the desert floor. There was a muffled boom, and then another, and then another. An awful white light spread behind the clouds on the horizon.

In the morning light, the empty desert became a crowded community of Saudi soldiers. They had tumbled out of the back of armored personnel carriers to brew morning coffee, smoke cigarettes, and investigate the visitors to their sector. They patrolled this part of the sand berm.

Desert hospitality dictated an invitation to breakfast at the commander's tent. The offering was sumptuous. There was fresh Arabic bread and wild honey, white cheese, a pot of melted butter, and scrambled eggs. We were invited back for dinner that night. The menu was obvious: Two sheep were tied to the back of a water truck.

That evening two Saudi officers sat on carpets in their tent, warmed by a pit of charcoal that smelled of the spices and lamb they were cooking. They wanted to talk about the constant stream of Iraqi defectors coming over the border. "I tell my people not to deal with them with weapons," said Captain Ibrahim al Hamed, the commander of a reconnaissance unit. "Their [Iraqi] hearts are broken already."

In the first weeks of the war there were a few deserters, but the constant bombing forced more to risk the crossing. Some Iraqis came holding white invitation cards dropped in the millions by allied bombers. Others waved ragged gray-white underpants over their heads. This company of the Saudi Twentieth Brigade had welcomed 420 Iraqi prisoners since the start of the air campaign.

The Americans saw the Iraqis as the enemy with a capital "E"; the Saudis saw them as errant Muslims. History and faith had made them part of the same family. It was a complicated emotion that was understood only by those Americans who had spent lots of time in the Arab world.

"Any vehicle is immediately bombed. No type of logistics is getting through. When they have not the necessities of life, they will all defect eventually," said Hamed.

That evening, as the darkness fell around the tent, an unexpected light show began on the other side of the sand berm. White balls of light made a high arc over the desert. There were dozens of them, dropping sparks that fell gracefully back to earth and brightening the desert with a ghastly daylight. There were muffled pops, but the light made it seem as if the flares were falling just a few miles away.

The Saudis were baffled. They had never seen a display like this before. The American liaison officers were excited because they could read the message of the light. This was the fire of a multiple launched rocket system (MLRS). Designed in the 1970s, the MLRS made its debut in Saudi Arabia as a high-tech artillery machine that shoots off twelve rockets a minute. The rockets are like metal melons carrying 260 bomblets that spray out at ground level over the length of three football fields, shredding anything in their path.

The American air force officers in our company knew something that the Saudis did not. The firing of the MLRS signaled the opening stages of the ground campaign. It was February 13, eleven days before the ground war. The American artillery gunners were "softening up" the Iraqis on the other side of the berm. As the night grew darker, the Saudis left the tent and went outside in the starlight for the evening prayer before supper.

"Allahu Akbar" cried the prayer leader, and the others answered in a muted response.

"God is great" they chanted again as they touched their heads to the white sand.

The prayer lasted for a long time. The Americans began to talk quietly among themselves, restless, as they waited for the Saudis to finish the prayer and start the dinner. But the praying continued. The prayer leader was reciting a long verse by heart from the Koran. His chant was growing louder now and had the ragged edge of a wail. The Saudi soldiers were praying and sobbing in response.

They had heard the news on the radio. In a Baghdad suburb four hundred civilians had been killed in an allied air raid. In Riyadh and

Washington, U.S. military spokesmen had said that Ameriyeh was a military command center, not a civilian bomb shelter. President Bush declared that it was Saddam Hussein who "kills civilians intentionally." For anyone listening to the news this night it was clear that the Americans killed civilians too.

The Saudis were distraught. They had been moved by the reports from Baghdad. They had prayed long and hard. I had been at dinner parties in Riyadh where wealthy, educated Saudis had said it was a shame to have infidels in the Saudi desert. These deeply religious soldiers from the small villages of Saudi Arabia felt the weight of that shame as they prayed in the night.

The Americans had developed a language that allowed a mental distance between the bombs and death. American pilots talked about collateral damage, about jets that killed tanks rather than people, about smart bombs. It was the kind of high-tech training that made young F-16 pilots describe a day of bombing raids like a day at a video arcade. The Saudi army scouts from the small villages of the hinterland didn't have this protective language. Their grandfathers had galloped to warfare on horseback.

The Saudis filed back into the tent for the dinner party. The Americans were baffled by this show of emotion. Hassan Gharebi understood what it meant. Gharebi was a master sergeant in the Royal Saudi Air Force. He was training with the U.S. Air Force to be a forward air controller. As a young Saudi soldier, he had gone to school in Texas and fallen into a pattern that many Saudis adopt when they go to the United States.

Gharebi had lived with an American girl, got into some fights, got drunk, and gone to parties. But when he came home he put those wild times behind him. He grew a beard and became a volunteer with the religious police. He returned to the certainties of his faith. The only remnant of his time in Texas was a strange slang that peppered his American English.

Gharebi stood up and addressed the Saudi soldiers. He launched into a long story about the courage and exploits of the bedouin fighters. His was a poetic tale of desert fighting on horseback in the days of Abd al-Aziz ibn Saud, Saudi Arabia's first warrior king. He entertained them for twenty minutes as the pieces of lamb wrapped in tinfoil sizzled on the fire. The mood lightened in the tent as Gharebi's voice reached through their gloom. The radio news was repeating the details of the bombing raid in Baghdad.

"Excuse the language, they're bitching. I think they're paid to make this news," said Gharebi in English. "They always talk about Yemen, Iraq, and Palestine and what they have done and who's against the coalition forces and all these things.

"You just hear bitching from this people, you know, saying, how *bad* were the coalition forces, and how *bad* it is that civilians were injured in Iraq . . . and all sort of things. *They are dead wrong!*" Gharebi abruptly ended his speech about the unfairness of all those who criticized the coalition and turned his attention to teaching the Americans to eat the lamb morsels with their fingers. In the shadow of the Prophet, there was no room for doubt.

Second Lieutenant Georgette Young had bet that the ground war would start on February 24. A short headline at the top of the list of air targets that came to her office each day from Riyadh proved her right: "Welcome to the ground war." The Air Support Operations Center—ASOC—at King Khalid Military City was in northeastern Saudi Arabia, about 300 miles from Riyadh, close to the Iraqi border. It was the communications center for the air support for the Arab armies. On the first night of the ground war the room was buzzing with a deep concentration of American adrenaline.

The offices were two floors below the Saudi desert. There were electric coffee pots, telephones, televisions, and desk chairs that had been designed to keep fatigue to a minimum. If this group of Americans had been working for American battalions they would have been out in the desert, the air force living rough with the army, in the cramped working space of an expando-van. A handwritten sign posted on the wall was the only war graffiti: "Don't look conspicuous, it draws fire. Never draw fire, it irritates everyone around you. Anything you do can get you shot, including nothing." There was little danger of getting shot here.

Earlier in the evening President Bush had delivered his final offer. Iraq was to withdraw from Kuwait by noon Washington time. The president said the withdrawal must be completed within one week. All prisoners of war must be released within forty-eight hours. The United States pledged not to attack withdrawing Iraqi forces.

About an hour after the deadline an Iraqi scud missile arched over King Khalid Military City. There was an explosion as the Patriot missiles shot up in the sky to meet the targets. The shrapnel rained on an airfield of British helicopters.

Georgette Young looked up at the map. "They're shooting out of Baghdad because that's where their SAMs are," she said. The surface-to-air missiles around Baghdad made the scud launchers a more dangerous target for the F-16 pilots assigned scud hunting duty.

Second Lieutenant Georgette Young sipped her coffee and studied the large map on the wall to her right. Young was the night-shift intelligence officer. She was twenty-eight years old and this was her first war. The map showed northern Kuwait and southern Iraq crowded with red squares. Each one represented the brigades, battalions, and regiments that made up the divisions of the Iraqi Republican Guards. In southern Kuwait, more boxes showed the positions of Iraqi army units. Across the map's border, the "friendlies" were marked and ready to go. What the map didn't show was the thousands of tons of fuel, ammunition, spare parts, water, and food that all the ground forces had on hand. In the past week, the French, British, and American armies had moved into positions along the southwestern border of Iraq in preparation for the surprise left hook, the punch of 270,000 troops that would sweep around the Iraqi flank. In the west, the French and the U.S. Eighty-Second Airborne were set to make the first cross into Iraq. The One Hundred First Airborne were poised to head for Iraq's two-lane highway eight to cut off the escape routes of Iraq's Republican Guards. In the East, the U.S. Marines were already moving into occupied Kuwait. The bulk of the Arab coalition was positioned along Saudi Arabia's northern border with Kuwait. The Arab armies would move straight up the heart of the Iraqi army. It was the one attack Saddam was expecting.

For the past few days the two-lane highway out of the northern Saudi town of Hafir al Batin had been jammed with tanks and trucks. It didn't take a military genius to figure out what this kind of massive movement meant. Had Saddam figured out what was coming next? Did he have "human intelligence" in the town? No one knew for sure.

A printed advisory was tacked to the intelligence map. The heading, in large type, said "Recognition Guide: Twenty-four U.S.-made recreational vehicles purchased by Iraq between 1982 and 1988 are known to be used exclusively by VIPs, flag-rank officers, and ministers as well as the president. All vehicles have a single rear axle." The advisory undermined the president's assertion that there was no targeting of the Iraqi leadership. It was also the only sign in the room of the colossal political failure that had brought all these people to this office bunker behind 2-inch-thick doors deep under the Saudi Arabian desert. If Saddam had indeed become Hitler, then the forces that created him were now preparing to destroy him.

Young watched the clock. The war for the Arab armies was still

hours away. There was nothing else to do but wait. Staff Sergeants
Wayne Gott and Mike Sager moved down the hall for a smoke. In air
force slang they were called "Romads," radio operators, maintainers,
and drivers. Their official title was tactical air command and control
specialists, and while they complained about the term "Romad," they
always used it themselves. When the Arab armies moved, they'd be in
the radio room, in touch with the American teams in the field, writing
down the requests for jet planes and updating positions on the battlefield every hour. They would pass the requests to the FIDO, or fighter
duty officer, who would work to match the jets with the targets. Gott
and Sager joked with the Saudis who brought them scalding hot glasses
of sugared tea. They had become popular with the Saudi officers.

"When we first got here the Saudis had no grasp of what we were
here for," said Gott. Gott and Sager had arrived on December 4 to
set up the radio network that would connect the forward air controllers
to the Air Support Operations Center. When that job was done they
used their skills to engage in a business as old as warfare: Gott and
Sager bartered a hook up to the armed forces television network for
Saudi desert boots and desert gear.

"They'd come to us and ask, 'Make TV?'" said Gott. It was a valuable
commodity for Saudi officers who had been brought up on Saudi Arabia's religious television programming. Armed forces television network carried CNN, American network news, and sports. American
culture was beaming into King Khalid Military City. The fashion programs on CNN were popular. They were practically pornographic in
a country where censors routinely inked out any picture showing a
woman's arms or legs.

The team assembled in this room came from Bergstrom Air Force
Base in Austin, Texas. Back in the states, they were trained to provide
the communications hub for close air support to the U.S. Army's Third
Corp. In this war, their clients were the Arab armies of the coalition.

"Some things are like designer functions—we draw as we go," explained Lieutenant Colonel Martin Semik. "We're not functioning
within our, quote, normal system. We've tailored some things."

They had been forced to improvise. As Arab troops arrived in the
desert, air force liaison teams had to be assigned to each Arab battalion.
When there were not enough air force personnel to work with the
coalition troops, Army Special Forces teams were trained to fill the
gap.

There were no training manuals to guide them. The operation had
been patched together over the past couple of months. No one in this

room was sure it would work. It was too late for worries now. Semik had gathered the dozen Americans and briefed them. This was G day. The First Marine Division and the Second Marine Division were launching attacks through the Iraqi mine fields in the east. The official start of the ground war was just hours away and soon the Arab armies would cross President Bush's "line in the sand" into Kuwait and the work here would begin.

More than a half million Americans had come halfway around the world to fight "Iraqi aggression." Only a handful of Americans would fight alongside the Arab armies. General Norman Schwarzkopf's war fighting plan called for the armies of the coalition to fight as separate units with separate objectives. In the last major war of the twentieth century, most of the Americans here would fight in a foreign land and return home with no more understanding of the people they had fought for than if the battle had taken place on the moon. For most Saudi civilians, they only knew of the presence of American troops through the media.

T W O

You Pay, We Fight

"I fully realize the power and the capacity of the United States, and I am not against establishing an honorable relationship with that nation if it will serve our interests without the U.S.A. exploiting our region for its purposes."
—Saddam Hussein, August 1979

"We committed a boner with regard to Iraq and our close friendship with Iraq."
—Ronald Reagan, February 15, 1991

Florida was the ideal setting for Central Command's 1990 summer exercise. Fort Walton Beach was as hot and humid in June as the eastern coast of Saudi Arabia. Operation Internal Look was a new name to test an old contingency plan. Plan 1002 had been written in the early 1980s for regional contingencies but was shelved as obsessive concerns with the Soviet threat overshadowed all others. In the past eighteen months Saddam's muscular army had taken center stage in the minds of Central Command's generals. Operation Plan 1002–90 outlined a deployment to counter an Iraqi invasion of Kuwait.

Operation Internal Look was a command post exercise. Known as a CPX, it meant there were no troops on the ground. It was a test of communication and a workshop for policy planning. This war game was fought on computers. The "controllers" of the game stayed in a hotel a few miles down the beach. They fed the moves of the forces into the computers and fed problems to the units to generate policy.

As in most games of this type, units huddled around the computer screen in their tents and responded to a set of situations as the war unfolded.

At about the same time as Central Command staff were gathering in Florida, the Kuwaiti cabinet was meeting to consider a list of demands by Saddam Hussein. The Iraqi leader had accused Kuwait of stealing more than 2 billion dollars worth of oil from an oil field that straddled both borders. Saddam's Revolution Day speech of July 17, 1990, was a furious attack on Kuwait and the United Arab Emirates. He said the Gulf states were trying to "undermine Iraq after its military triumph." He accused Kuwait and the United Arab Emirates of lowering the price of oil, "an evil act against Iraq." A day before the speech, Iraq sent a detailed list of grievances to the secretary general of the Arab League. It wasn't simply the oil, the Iraqis charged, but Kuwait had planted military posts inside Iraq and both states were part of "an imperialist-Zionist plot against the Arab nation." The Kuwaiti ministers argued among themselves about Saddam's intentions. Most thought he was bluffing and it was better to ignore his threats. The meeting ended with no clear decisions, then on July 18 the Kuwaitis dispatched diplomats to Arab capitals and put the country's 20,000-man armed forces on alert.

"We thought Internal Look was a waste of time; we never thought the plan would be executed," said Captain Brian R. Vines of the Fifth Special Forces group from Fort Campbell, Kentucky. "With the end of the Cold War we thought CENTCOM was going away. The only reason to do Internal Look was to justify Central Command." Captain Vines was in Florida as a controller. The Fifth Special Forces group commander, Colonel James Kraus, had only sent part of his force. It was expensive to mount these exercises at a time of military budget cuts in Washington. The Fifth Special Forces group, First Battalion, was in Amman, Jordan, in a joint exercise with the Jordanian Special Forces.

Captain Vines' job was to send messages on the computer to simulate the battle to special forces units in the exercise. Their assignment in the exercise was to work with the Arab forces stationed in Saudi Arabi

The scenario for Internal Look was what is called worst case. Th computers were programmed to show that the Iraqi army had roll over the border to invade its tiny oil-rich neighbor, Kuwait. In exercise, the invasion had been a lightening strike by the elite u of Iraq's Republican Guards. There had been little warning of the at as Saddam's army continued the march and swept down the coa

the eastern province of Saudi Arabia. In the computer game the Iraqi army used poison gas. Iran was threatening to make trouble for any Americans in the Persian Gulf and the Soviets were blocking American movements on the Red Sea.

Meanwhile, in the Middle East, Saddam really did move 30,000 troops to the border of Kuwait on July 21. At the U.S. State Department, reporters asked the State Department spokeswoman, Margaret Tutwiler, about the buildup. "We do not have any defense treaties with Kuwait and there are no defense or special security commitments to Kuwait." An OPEC (Organization of Petroleum Exporting Countries) meeting was scheduled in the next few days in Geneva. In Washington many policymakers believed that Saddam's sabers were rattling to raise the price of oil. There was a general agreement among Arab oil producers that the Kuwaitis and the United Arab Emirates (UAE) were cheating on their oil quotas. Saddam had warned them that this must stop. There was some pressure on Kuwait from the Saudis to meet Iraq's demands.

The participants of Internal Look listened to the news of trouble in the Gulf. "By the end of the second week, the intelligence guys were working half time on real time and half time on the game," said a senior officer who was a participant. The Iraqi buildup on Kuwait's northern border was a "real-life" replay of the early part of the exercise. Exercise and reality were coming together at a remarkable speed. "That was the funny part," said Navy Captain Ron Wildemuth, a public affairs officer for Central Command. "The scenario inputs were looking like the real stuff." Wildemuth returned to the "real stuff" soon enough. He was called out of the game to work on public affairs for the navy's exercise in the Gulf, Operation Ivory Justice.

On July 24, 7000 miles away from the exercise in Florida, Washington arranged a show of force in the southern part of the Gulf. Iraq's heated rhetoric had targeted the United Arab Emirates along with Kuwait. The UAE had decided to take out an insurance policy and requested a joint training exercise. It was quickly arranged. Six American navy combat ships patrolled the southern Gulf while the United States and the UAE conducted a joint refueling exercise. The exercise got Saddam's attention.

On July 25, Saddam summoned U.S. Ambassador April Glaspie to his office. It was one day before the OPEC meeting in Geneva and Saddam talked at length about Iraq's need for money. He was disturbed by the joint American UAE exercise and expressed his displeasure. The transcript released from the meeting released by the Iraqis show

that Saddam told Glaspie that the American exercise had encouraged Kuwait and the UAE to "disregard Iraqi rights."

Ambassador Glaspie told Saddam that the United States understood Iraq's desire for higher prices to strengthen the economy. She asked "in the spirit of friendship, not of confrontation," why Iraqi troops were massing on the border. Saddam said he had just talked to Egyptian President Hosni Mubarek on the telephone. Mubarek had said that the Kuwaitis were concerned with the buildup on their border. A meeting had been arranged between the Iraqis and the Kuwaitis in Saudi Arabia. The group would then go to Baghdad for "deeper discussions." Saddam said:

> I said to him that, regardless of what is there . . . assure the Kuwaitis and give them our word that we are not going to do anything until we meet with them. When we meet and when we see that there is hope, then nothing will happen. But if we are unable to find a solution, then it will be natural that Iraq will not accept death, even though wisdom is above everything else. There you have the good news.

What April Glaspie did not say will be debated by historians and policymakers for years to come. Ambassador Glaspie did not make it crystal clear that the United States would defend Kuwait if Iraq tanks rolled over the border. On that day, April Glaspie told Saddam: "We have no opinion on the Arab-Arab conflicts, like your border disagreement with Kuwait."

Meanwhile, at Hurlbert Field in Florida, the message traffic of the "practice" war continued to light up the screens of a reserve unit's computer. "In my game there was a message: You've got a bunch of civilian dead, how do you bury Muslims," said one reserve officer with a civil affairs unit. The chaplains were writing policy guidelines that would be used in a real war seven months later.

There were some differences between the war game and what was soon to become the real thing. One example was the beer and soft drink tent for the thirsty combatants of Operation Internal Look. In this worst-case scenario the Soviet Union and Iran were hostile to an American presence in the Gulf. In the Florida war game Saddam had sent his army to occupy Saudi Arabia's eastern province, denying U.S. forces the use of Saudi Arabia's ports and airfields in the eastern part of the country. In the exercise, Saddam was using poison gas. The other difference was that in the exercise the U.S. forces lost the game. Operation Internal Look ended on July 28, 1990. Over the weekend

Central Command's three-star generals were debriefed in what is called a "hot wash"—an after-action review.

"We knew we needed a heavier force," said one colonel involved in the meeting. The lessons learned in this summer exercise were incorporated into the plan. The stage was now set. Operation Plan 1002–90 was tested and ready. Saddam Hussein couldn't have picked a worse time to invade Kuwait. It is unlikely that Saddam Hussein was aware of the Central Command exercise in Florida. The American military umbrella built in the past ten years over the oil fields of Saudi Arabia had a serious flaw: The fact that it was based on secrecy meant it had no deterrence value at all.

"On July 29 I drove back to Fort Campbell, Kentucky, after the game," said Captain Vines. "The Iraqis were agitating. They were rattling their swords." Vines listened to the news as he made his way back home to Kentucky. He had just practiced a war in the Gulf and now he might have to put his training into practice. "In Florida there was a picture of Saddam in our tent. It came from a news magazine cover and it said he was the world's most dangerous man. It was the first time I really thought about it."

On July 30, Pentagon satellites showed that Saddam's force on the Kuwait border had grown to 100,000. While the force represented one tenth of Saddam's army, there was muted concern in Washington. Few were expecting an invasion. The intelligence reports showed that the Iraqi army sat on the border without the necessary logistical backup for an invasion. The communications, artillery, and munitions were missing. This looked like garden-variety Middle East saber rattling in preparation for a meeting the next day in Taif, Saudi Arabia. On August 1, Kuwaiti and Iraqi representatives met for what was to be the last time in the Saudi resort town.

The Kuwaitis faced their Iraqi counterparts believing that Saddam was bluffing. Kuwait's ambassador to France, Dr. Tariq Rassoukie, was a participant at the meeting in Taif, Saudi Arabia:

Izzat Ibrahim was reading from a paper. He started citing accusations. He said Kuwait had comported with the Americans against the security of Iraq, against their economy. He said we had to prove that we weren't doing that. It was, well, you know, it was a kind of accusation without foundation. We said, let's talk now, let's take these things problem by problem. We will answer. He didn't want to hear any comments. "You know what you've been doing, he insisted. You know what we spent on the Iran-Iraq War, 102 billion more than Kuwait and Saudi Arabia put together. You have to settle these things." It was really strange; we never heard these kind of things before from Iraq.

The meeting ended without the usual joint communiqué. The Iraqis requested that both parties make an individual declaration. The Kuwaiti party boarded the plane for home at 6:30 P.M. They talked among themselves about what might happen. They were all convinced that, at worst, Saddam would capture the Rumayla oil fields and occupy Bubiyan and Warba Islands. In a post-invasion interview, April Glaspie echoed that same notion in the only comments she made about her last days in Baghdad: "We never expected they would take all of Kuwait."

On that same day, Iraqi logistics units were moved toward the border. In Washington, General Norman Schwarzkopf, fresh from the exercise in Florida, gave a briefing on the situation in the Middle East. General Colin Powell, chairman of the joint chiefs of staff, had assembled a group in the "tank," the Pentagon's secure conference room. Within hours, Iraqi tanks had swarmed over the Kuwaiti border.

On the morning of August 8, Colonel Bandar bin Mohammed saw the first silver glint from the twenty-four F-15C jets of the Seventy-first Tactical Fighter Squadron. Six days after Iraqi tanks had crossed the border into Kuwait, the American jet fighters touched down in Saudi Arabia's eastern province, loudly drawing President Bush's line in the sand.

Colonel Bandar, a self-confident member of the younger generation of Saudi princes, welcomed the American arrival. He'd trained in the United States and walked with the swagger of a man who had mastered highly complex technology, and was sure of his position in the hierarchy of the country. Colonel Bandar was the commander of the Thirteenth Squadron, a team of F-15 fighter pilots of the Royal Saudi Air Force. His squadron had been flying combat air patrols since August 2, keeping watch on Saudi air space and the Iraqi Air Force.

Bandar supported King Fahd's decision to invite American troops into the kingdom. The first day of the invasion confirmed what he already knew. Although the Saudi Royal Air Force was a well-trained fighting force, his men had only one experience in combat. During the Iran-Iraq War a Saudi pilot had shot down an Iranian Phantom jet, but these pilots were no match for an Iraqi blitzkrieg if Saddam was still hungry. Despite the billions of dollars spent on defense, Bandar agreed that Saudi Arabia would need American protection.

The invasion of Kuwait showed that the systems put in place to defend the kingdom were inadequate. Arab forces of the Gulf Co-operation Council (GCC) had failed to confront the Iraqis. The GCC soldiers had stayed in their barracks at Hafr al Batin, a garrison town in northern Saudi Arabia. According to Western military attachés in Riyadh, it took two days for a battalion of the Saudi National Guard to move out of the town of Hofuf and head north to defend the border near the Saudi town of Khafji. The Saudi army followed a day later as the national guard was stationed along the coast.

The invasion had caused near panic in the eastern province cities of Dhahran, Dammam, and Khobar. People there had turned off their air conditioning in the brutal summer heat, afraid that poison gas would kill them in their sleep. Colonel Bandar was on the asphalt runway to greet the American commander, Lieutenant Colonel Pip Pope, and direct the tired American pilots to a bunkhouse he'd ordered set up in a concrete hangar.

These American jet pilots had scrambled in less than twenty-four hours halfway around the world. This first team had a grueling adren-aline-filled fifteen-hour flight. They had been through at least seven midair refuelings on the long trip. They had flown armed to fight if Saddam decided to order his army over the Saudi border. The F-15s were loaded with live ammunition. Each one carried four AIM-7 Spar-rows and four AIM-9 Sidewinder air-to-air missiles, 940 rounds for the 20-millimeter cannons. Over the next five weeks the tactical air power assembled in the Gulf region would grow to more than 400 combat and 250 support aircraft, roughly equivalent to the force de-ployed in Europe during the Cold War. Colonel Bandar told Pope that his Saudi pilots could handle combat air patrols for now while the Americans got some sleep. There was no immediate threat.

Saudi Arabia's state radio and the eleven privately owned but closely controlled newspapers had been silent about the invasion for the first three days of August. There were oblique references to a brief "summer storm," but no details of Saddam's ruthless grab for Kuwait. The Iraqi leader had assured the Saudi king he would not attack.

Only hours before the tanks rolled into Kuwait, King Fahd had been host to Iraqi and Kuwaiti officials at the conference palace in Taif, Saudi Arabia's resort town in the mountains of eastern Arabia. The Saudis had worked to head off this confrontation. King Fahd ibn Abd al Aziz al Saud was a master of the backroom deal underlined by the Saudi checkbook. But this conflict was about something larger than the Saudi pocketbook.

Fahd had urged the Kuwaitis to consider their situation. Saudi Arabia had forgiven Iraq's war debt and the Saudis advised the Kuwaitis to do the same. The atmosphere was tense at the meeting in Jeddah. According to the Kuwaiti version of events, they had agreed to write off Iraqi debts and lease two islands off the Kuwaiti coast to Baghdad. The Iraqi version was reported by Mohammed al Mashat, an Iraqi diplomat. He said the Kuwaitis came to the meeting in bad faith. "They were arrogant and conducting themselves like small-time grocery store keepers. The gap was irreconcilable, so the meeting collapsed."

The Saudis had assessed their strength and forged a policy of appeasement with Saddam. The Kuwaitis had followed an opposite policy. They had balked when Saddam wanted gratitude for fighting the Ayatollah, arguing that Saddam should be grateful for their large financial support. They had challenged Saddam with no notion of what they would do if he carried out his threats. On August 2, Kuwait and Saudi Arabia saw the results of the two policies: Kuwait was gone. Saudi Arabia decided to adopt Kuwait's strategy with one important addition. They would challenge Saddam but with the U.S. military at their side.

An American delegation arrived in Jeddah four days after the invasion. They came armed with maps, satellite photos, and a plan for the largest American deployment since Vietnam. According to Saudi sources, the king had already decided to invite the American forces to the kingdom. This was an unprecedented emergency. Saudi Arabia was well aware of U.S. military plans to protect American "vital interests" in the region. Saudi Arabia's vital interests were also at stake. The king would invite the Americans in, but the plan had to work. The future of the House of Saud depended on it.

The Washington delegation included U.S. Secretary of Defense Dick Cheney and General H. Norman Schwarzkopf, the cranky but capable commander and chief of U.S. Central Command. Since 1983, Central Command had been the Pentagon's rapid reaction force and the American main standard bearer of U.S. military policy in the Middle East.

Schwarzkopf had taken command of Central Command in 1989. His new friends called him "Stormin' Norman" for his part in the Panama invasion. His old friends called him "the Bear." He certainly looked the part. At 6 feet 3 inches, the big burly general was known for his temper. One subordinate officer spoke of leaving his office "with scratch marks on the back and further down." Schwarzkopf was also known for his intellect. He had done his homework before assuming the job of head of Central Command. He had attended lectures at the Foreign Service Institute in Washington, D.C. He sat in on seminars on the Middle East whenever he could. He approached the region as a political challenge as well as a military one.

Central Command had been created in the years of Washington's obsession with a Soviet takeover of the Iranian oil fields. In the Pentagon's eyes, Central Command's importance had dwindled with the decline of the Soviet threat to the region. More than a year earlier, Schwarzkopf had ordered a rethinking of Middle East strategy. In spring 1990, he told a Senate Armed Services committee, "The most probable near-term threat to the uninterrupted flow of oil would likely originate from a regional conflict." Schwarzkopf was either extremely smart or extremely lucky. Saddam's move had proved him right.

Central Command had filled in the blank spaces in the Soviet invasion scenario with Iraq, the country in the region with the largest military capability. In Central Command's view, the only likely culprit for an oil grab was Saddam. "The cease-fire with Iran has allowed Iraq to resume its bid for leadership and influence within the Arab world."

Schwarzkopf arrived in Saudi Arabia as the head of a military organization with ten years of experience in the region. As the dealer of U.S. military assistance to America's Arab allies in the region, Central Command had built up a wealth of information about the military strengths and weaknesses of the major players.

However, Schwarzkopf knew that he couldn't pull off a successful defense of the Saudi oil fields without King Fahd's approval to base U.S. ground forces on Saudi soil. All the exercises and computer models had shown that a trip wire force or a show of air power was not enough. It was the one issue that CENTCOM commanders wrestled with in making their plans and exercises. It was the essential issue. Central Command assumed that if the Saudis were really in trouble the answer would have to be yes. After that, all things were possible. But Schwarzkopf didn't know for sure.

King Fahd wasted little time in giving his approval. The Saudi resolve to allow twenty-four American pilots to land at the Dhahran Air Base was the first indication of how the politics in the region had shifted in just a few days.

For eight years, Saudi Arabia had backed Saddam's war against the Shiite Muslim radicals in Tehran. The kingdom had supplied cash almost from the beginning. In later phases of the war, Riyadh passed on important satellite intelligence from the Americans to the Iraqi regime. Saudi Arabia and Kuwait had coughed up 30 billion dollars in "loans" during the eight-year war that ended in August 1988. However, Riyadh had never been comfortable with the wartime ties to Baghdad. Ba'thism does not mix well with the values of conservative, religious Saudi Arabia, but the Saudis had concluded it was the price for guarding the eastern flank of the Arab world. They were also following the old Arabic saying: "Kiss the hand you can't cut off."

A few years earlier it was Saddam Hussein's air force pilots who were landing at Dhahran Air Base. Iraqi pilots had stopped at the Dhahran airfield for refueling missions on their way to bomb Kharg Island terminal on the Iranian coast. It was an open secret during the war that Riyadh had given landing rights to Baghdad and was housing Iraqi aircraft. Secret refueling privileges at the Dhahran Air Base for Iraqi pilots were a small gesture for Saudi Arabia, a country that shares a 500-mile border with Iraq. A hostile Iran was bad enough for Saudi Arabia; a hostile Iraq would be a disaster.

The Saudis kept an even deeper secret about the Americans. Few of the residents of Dhahran, Khobar, and Dammam, the sprawling tri-city area of the eastern province, were aware of the extent of the presence of Americans at this base.

The Dhahran Air Base had figured in Saudi-American relations since the 1940s. Its importance for America was its location. Dhahran is in Saudi Arabia's eastern province where Saudi Arabia's vast pool of oil reserves sit under a shallow covering of sand. The eastern province is the home of Aramco, the Arabian-American Oil Company. In 1948, Aramco was formed by Standard Oil of California, Texaco, and Standard Oil of New Jersey, to produce Saudi oil.

In the late 1940s, the United States signed its first lease with the kingdom that put an American military mission at the base to protect the country's "vital" asset. In time, the Dhahran Air Base would become part of the Strategic Air Command network as well as the largest U.S. installation between Germany and Korea. By the 1980s, the Dhahran Air Base figured in all of U.S. strategic planning to protect the Saudi oil fields and those in Iran from a Soviet invasion.

The Americans had spent billions of dollars over ten years to ensure that the beans, the bullets, the water purification systems, and the air conditioners were ready to go the moment there was trouble in the region. While it was President George Bush who had ordered the deployment, it was President Jimmy Carter who set the process in motion.

• • •

The last three months of 1979 had set the stage for ten years of turmoil in the Middle East that was to confound three American presidents. In December 1979, the Soviet Union invaded Afghanistan. The Iranian revolution was then in full swing. In the waning months of 1979, a band of Islamic students had climbed over the wall of the American Embassy in Tehran and held American diplomats hostage. Oil prices were rising in a way that raised questions in Washington about the continued availability of oil to the West at reasonable prices. At the same time the stability of Saudi Arabia was in dispute.

November 20, 1979, was the first day of Islam's fifteenth century. On that day, at the Grand Mosque in Mecca, Islam's holiest site, the faithful gathered for the dawn prayer. They were startled to hear a voice from the mosque's loudspeaker denounce the Saudi regime and proclaim the arrival of the mahdi (savior) "to cleanse a corrupt Arabia." A band of religious revolutionaries had disguised themselves as religious pilgrims. It was a terrifying two weeks for the House of Saud. The Saudi government called the revolt "The Blasphemy of the Age"; Saudi sympathizers called it "The Uprising in the Holy Places." Whatever it was called, it rocked the kingdom to its foundation.

The leader of the revolt, Juhaiman ibn Saif al-Utaiba, was a son of the Saudi desert, a former religious student and a follower of Saudi Arabia's most influential religious scholar. Al-Utaiba was an officer in Saudi Arabia's National Guard, the country's "second army" recruited from the kingdom's tribes. The national guard was the guardian of internal security; their unwritten mission was to protect the House of Saud.

The revolt appeared to take the government by surprise, although Juhaiman had made no secret of his movement. Juhaiman and his supporters had publicly distributed pamphlets, well-written tracts that railed against usury, royal corruption, and what Juhaiman saw as the licensed thievery by the legion of foreigners who were invading the country. The revolt came at a time when Saudi Arabia was experiencing unprecedented social disruptions. The oil embargo and then the oil boom of 1973 meant that Saudi Arabia was floating in oil money. Fortunes were made overnight. A Saudi produce salesman who bought his first car in 1976 bought his first plane in 1978.

King Faisal's far-reaching plan to modernize the country brought hordes of foreign contractors to parts of the country that had never seen a non-Muslim before, much less a Westerner. The tenuous balance between development and tradition was tipping. The most radical sym-

bol of Saudi religious discontent was Juhaiman al Utaiba and his band
of fanatical followers.

Juhaiman and his disciples were against the introduction of television
in Saudi Arabia. They were against the introduction of radio. Juhaiman's revolutionaries were against the foreign infidels who had brought
this technology to Saudi Arabia. This was *bid'a,* and *bid'a* was condemned in the Koran.

The rough English translation of the Arabic word is "innovation,"
but the word has a deeper meaning. Religious Muslims are not against
all innovations. Saudis drive cars, play video games, use computers,
and the religious police, known as the *Mutawaeen*, cruise for miscreants
in the latest model four-wheel-drive jeeps.

Bid'a describes an object or act created or invented after the time
of the Prophet that doesn't conform to Islamic values. It takes a religious ruling, a *Fatwa,* by religious scholars to remove the stigma. There
was a long debate among Muslim scholars over birth control pills.
Wristwatches were considered the work of magicians until religious
scholars in Saudi Arabia issued a Fatwa approving their use. Even cuff
links required a Fatwa to determine whether this piece of men's jewelry
was an unnecessary affectation alien to Islam. In Saudi Arabia, conservative religious scholars put a black mark on the modern inventions
of radio and television. It was the work of the devil, an instrument to
introduce Western culture into the homes of religious Saudis.

At the time of Juhaiman's revolt, the Saudi Fatwa against television
and radio was still on the books. *Bid'a* was causing social disruptions
in a country that had jumped from the fourteenth century to the
twentieth on the magic carpet of oil wealth.

"We have broken with the opportunists and other bureaucrats who
serve the government," wrote Juhaiman. "We know that one day we
will be strong enough to name among us a *Mahdi,* to take refuge at
this command in the Great Mosque of Mecca, where we will proclaim
the beginning of a new Islamic state."

It took more than two weeks to put down the rebellion in the Mecca
mosque. The revolutionaries had taken up positions in the labyrinth
of Islam's holiest place and fought a bloody battle with the Saudi army.
Juhaiman was killed before the army prevailed. Those revolutionaries
who survived the battle were executed. The public beheadings had a
wide audience. This was meant as an example for religious revolutionaries who were interested in undermining the House of Saud. The
revolt was a lesson for the royal family as well.

Across the Persian Gulf, in neighboring Iran, there were other lessons. Shah Mohammed Reza Pahlavi had left the country for his second and final exile on a cold January morning in 1979. The shah's replacement was a stern-faced, bearded, septigenarian with four wives.

Ayatollah Ruhollah Khomeini was an anti-Western, anti-American, Islamic revolutionary who was to define religious radicalism in the Middle East. His message was not that different from Juhaiman al Utaiba's. Khomeini preached the message of "Western detoxification." He appeared to reject democracy, equality, and material progress. For Washington, the success of the Iranian revolution put an end to an American policy that had shaped events in the region for ten years. America's "policeman" in the Gulf, the shah of Iran, had been forcibly retired.

The shah's departure meant the end of a doctrine that had defined American security policy in the region for a decade. The Nixon Doctrine was a security formula that had worked for Washington. In its simplest terms, the doctrine stated that the United States would provide military and economic assistance to any nation whose freedom was threatened, but those nations would be expected to take the responsibility for their own defense. The short form was coined years later as "We pay, you fight."

The strategy rested on the "two pillars:" Saudi Arabia, the world's largest oil producer, and Iran, the most populous country in the region. With Saudi Arabia's money and Iran's military might, the region was relatively safe from what Washington saw as the threat of Soviet adventurism. The events of 1979 and 1980 sent alarm bells ringing in Washington. One pillar had collapsed and the other pillar had been weakened by the convulsions in the region. Washington would have to dramatically rethink its Persian Gulf strategy.

In Washington's eyes it was increasingly clear that there was no workable policy for the region. Washington was at a logistical disadvantage. While the region was 7000 air miles or 12,000 sea miles from the east coast of the United States, it was adjacent to the Soviet Union. American forces could not get to the region fast enough if matters got out of control.

In this atmosphere, President Jimmy Carter delivered his State of the Union address on January 20, 1980. The president outlined American intentions with a blunt declaration. "Let our position be absolutely clear: An attempt by any outside force to gain control of the Persian Gulf region will be regarded as an assault on the vital interests of the United States. It will be repelled by use of any means necessary, including military force."

Carter said that the Soviet invasion of Afghanistan was "the most serious threat to peace" since World War II. Carter's "line in the sand" was as dramatic as the one laid down by President George Bush ten years later. Carter made it clear that the Persian Gulf region was a "vital interest" of the United States. This was an indisputable warning to the Soviet Union to stay out of the world's foremost oil-exporting region. The United States was willing to go to war for oil.

The problem was there was no force in the U.S. military that was specifically designated to carry out the policy. There were other problems as well. The United States had no access to bases in the region. Iran was out of the question. Iraq declared its opposition to the Carter Doctrine in the pan-Arab Charter. The president was unlikely to get that kind of commitment from Saudi Arabia where the royal family was still smarting from the anti-Western Juhaiman rebellion. Carter had committed the United States to repel Soviet aggression in the Persian Gulf, but Washington's military establishment argued that a conventional force based halfway around the world would have little chance against a Soviet army that could march into the Iranian oil fields within a few hours.

Defense Secretary Harold Brown began to define the solution in his department's annual report in 1980: "The president and I believe that the prospect of renewed turbulence in the Middle East, Caribbean, and elsewhere and the possibility of new demands on our nonnuclear posture require additional precautionary actions." The new Rapid Deployment Joint Task Force was born. The so-called Carter Doctrine now had a military arm.

The original plan placed the Rapid Deployment Joint Task Force under the command of a U.S. marine general. The marines had experience in this kind of operation. They had coordinated ground and air units. The marines had used ships as logistical bases. General P. X. Kelly was appointed the first commander of a force that was mostly on paper. He could call on the Marine Corps, the Army's Twenty-fourth Infantry Division, the Eighty-second Airborne, the One Hundred and First Air Assault Division, and some navy units in times of trouble. Kelly had 150,000 troops at his disposal. Headquartered at MacDill Air Force Base in Tampa, Florida, he started to map out scenarios to test what units would be necessary in case of war.

There were other problems to solve. This new commitment required more money for airlift and sealift. It was one thing to create the force and quite another to make sure the troops and equipment could get to the Persian Gulf in a big hurry.

At the same time, the Carter administration pursued the use of military bases in Oman, Somalia, Kenya, and Egypt. Military sales were increased to Saudi Arabia, Egypt, and Israel. Military aid to the region began to rise.

When Ronald Reagan took office in 1981, the belief in the "Soviet threat" was elevated to a state religion. The Rapid Deployment Joint Task Force (RDJTF) was seen in Washington as a tool in the Cold War arsenal.

But Reagan inherited the same contradictions that had plagued the Carter administration when it introduced the Rapid Deployment Force. There was no Middle East nation willing to host the RDJTF. The Camp David agreements had added a new element into inter-Arab politics. The Egypt–Israel peace treaty had polarized the region and isolated Egypt, the region's traditional Arab power center. The pact that launched a cold peace between Israel and its largest Middle East neighbor clouded all Arab agreements with the United States.

In spring 1981, U.S. Secretary of State Alexander Haig unveiled a new strategy. In testimony to a Senate hearing, Haig outlined a policy called Strategic Consensus. The key to the philosophy was a shared concern about the influence of the Soviet Union and its allies. Haig believed that Middle East leaders saw the Soviet Union with the same alarm as Washington. The concern could be used as a lever, along with arms sales, to wrap the region in a U.S. security blanket. The arms sales were not linked to Strategic Consensus, but were to be used as an inducement to join the club. The inducements were substantial. The administration introduced a 3.2-billion-dollar aid package to Pakistan and an 8.5-million-dollar military sale to Saudi Arabia. In April, the White House announced an arms package to Saudi Arabia that included five sophisticated AWACS, airborne early-warning control system radar planes. The administration argued it would enhance Saudi Arabia's ability to withstand the Soviet threat.

Robert G. Neumann, the former U.S. ambassador to Saudi Arabia, captured the contradictions at the time: "The trouble with a strategic conception as a guide for politics is that you look at a region as a piece of territory and you forget there are people living on that territory, and if those people do not share your perceptions, what good is it?"

Haig quickly found out that Robert Neumann was right. The regional players didn't quite share Washington's obsession. First of all, the Arab states saw Israel as their main threat rather than Moscow. Next on the list was the Iran-Iraq War. The Soviet Union might make a grab for the oil, but the Iranian revolution was appealing to the hearts and minds of the people.

While Saudi Arabia had taken a leading role in the campaign to reverse the Soviet invasion of Afghanistan, the policy had as much to do with Saudi domestic policy as a shared belief in the evil empire. The failed Islamic revolution at the mosque in Mecca had been a warning. Saudi Arabia had spent the last two decades resisting challenges from the Arab left. They had survived attacks from the radical socialism of the Ba'thist party and the Egyptian revolutionary Gamel Abdel Nasser's pan-Arabism from Cairo. The challenge from the right was more dangerous. The Islamic revolution scared its enemies. The Ayatollah Khomeini hit the House of Saud where it was vulnerable.

The Saudis were pleased that the administration was willing to sell them AWACS, but they were uncomfortable with a policy that would not only divide the region into American or Soviet camps but would move the Saudis toward a tacit approval of the Camp David accords. Iraq had made its opposition to the Carter Doctrine clear in a document called the Charter for pan-Arab Action. The Syrians were already suspicious of Saudi relations with the United States, and the Syrian/Saudi connection was important to Riyadh. The Syrians had sided with Iran in the Gulf War and Riyadh needed links to Damascus when the war tipped in favor of Iran.

The Gulf War outweighed Washington's global problems. The royal policymakers drew closer to Syria's radical rejection of Washington's plans, gave financial support to Iraq, and let Haig know that his Strategic Consensus was unwelcome in Riyadh.

"It was nonsense from the word go," said Robert Neumann. "It was a dream of Secretary Haig who saw everything in East-West quarrels. It was pure flimflam."

So Strategic Consensus was a bust. But the short era produced some concepts that would shape the development of the Rapid Deployment Force, Central Command, and Washington's strategic thinking about the region. Saudi Arabia got its five AWACS radar planes despite the objections of the Israelis and members of Congress who worried about introducing sophisticated weapons in the region. Part of the Saudi deal was an agreement to "overbuild" military facilities in the country. There were no written agreements to allow U.S. forces to use the facilities, but the intent was there. "No conceivable improvements in U.S. airlift or USAF rapid deployment and 'bare-basing' capability could come close to giving the United States this rapid and effective reinforcement capability," wrote military analyst Anthony Cordesman.

The Reagan administration also authorized the first joint combat exercises in the region. Shortly after the assassination of Egyptian President Anwar Sadat, the United States sent 6000 ground, air, and naval personnel for an exercise called "Bright Star." Oman and Somalia joined in the exercise. For the first time, American military personnel could test the sands of the Middle East for themselves. There were other tests as well. A small number of B-52s flew from North Dakota and dropped bombs on Egyptian test ranges and then flew back home.

President Reagan added an important corollary to the Carter Doctrine. He broadened the concept: "There is no way—as long as Saudi Arabia and OPEC nations provide the bulk of the energy that is needed to turn the wheels of industry in the Western world—there's no way we could stand by and see that taken over by anyone that would shut off the oil."

Carter had directed his warning to the Soviet Union. He said that any attack on the Gulf oil field was a threat to the vital interests of the United States and would be repulsed militarily. Reagan added that no one force could control the oil. This addition was directed at the regional powerhouses: Iran and Iraq.

The 1980s was a decade in which the American military learned more about the Middle East than American politicians. The developments of the decade had a direct bearing on the success of Operation Desert Storm.

In 1983, the Rapid Deployment Joint Task Force was upgraded and renamed. It became an independent multiservice organization called Central Command. Central Command was added to the other unified and specified commands in the U.S. military. There was a Central Command commander-in-chief, known as the CINC, for this new warfighting unit. Central Command's "area of responsibility" was designated as Southwest Asia, which included the Middle East, Pakistan, and parts of Africa. Central Command could call on of 300,000 troops, with two airborne and one mechanized division from the army; seven tactical fighter wings and two strategic bomber squadrons from the air force; a marine amphibious assault division; three navy aircraft carrier–led battle groups; and specialized counter insurgency units like the Rangers and the Green Berets.

Central Command watched over an area that focused on the Persian Gulf and stretched from the Horn of Africa to Pakistan. Israel and Syria had been hived off to another command. It was an important omission because it meant that CENTCOM commanders were spared the political balancing act performed at the State Department. Over time, Central Command would become the only unofficial Arab lobby in the U.S. government. The Arabs were Central Command's constituents. Central Command was a voice for the Gulf. These American military men were not Arabists in the Lawrence of Arabia mold; they were more like businessmen who learned to do their job and learned about their clients along the way. CENTCOM's commander-in-chief had to know how to do business with the Arabs. Joint exercises and regional visits gave him direct contact with his constituency.

Central Command's only permanent presence in the Gulf was in Bahrain. A small command post aboard the LaSalle, the flagship of the Middle East force, served as a forward headquarters. The restrictions meant that CENTCOM's doctrine had to evolve into one that didn't require land-based forces or official treaties. Central Command learned how to be an invisible "over-the-horizon force" to reduce the political embarrassment to the states it was designed to protect. The keys to CENTCOM's war-fighting ability were mobility and logistics.

The Reagan administration embarked on a huge military buildup in the Middle East to ensure CENTCOM's success. Over the years, the United States spent millions of defense dollars upgrading bases in Morocco, Oman, Kenya, Somalia, Turkey, Bahrain, and Egypt. American ships became floating arms and equipment warehouses. The Island of Diego Garcia, a rock outcropping 1000 miles off the coast of India, became a depot for tanks and ammunition. U.S. sailors stationed on the tiny island were ready to depart on twelve hours notice aboard more than a dozen ships that each carried enough equipment for a Marine Expeditionary Force of 32,000. The armaments were stored in the ship's air-conditioned, dehumidified hull.

Saudi Arabia remained the United States' most important ally in the region, but also the most reluctant to allow full use of military facilities to the United States. The region was littered with leaders who had fallen on the swords of nationalism sharpened over the issue of Western military bases. Saudi Arabia offered an alternative solution. It spent tens of millions of defense dollars to build a modern military infrastructure that could, in an extreme emergency, accommodate an American Rapid Deployment Force. Most of the facilities were planned and supervised by the U.S. Army Corp of Engineers to U.S. standards. Military equipment was purchased by Saudi Arabia for its compatibility with the equipment of an American intervention force. The Saudis housed a U.S. KC-10 aerial tanker so U.S. fighter bombers based on carriers could reach Iranian targets in the northern Gulf.

By the mid-1980s, the Reagan administration's defense budget reflected a particular bent for desert warfare with its request for 72 million dollars for water purification equipment and 32 million dollars for air conditioners. The commitment was unspoken but clear: If the threat was big enough, the war would be conducted from the Middle East.

The Carter Doctrine had evolved into a regional defense system with an invisible U.S. backbone. The policy had been driven by the concern of two U.S. administrations that troops from the Soviet Union would one day cross Iran's northern border and capture the oil fields. The military literature of the 1980s is filled with such talk. It was a decade where a frenzy of military activity was barely noticed by the average American as the Carter administration and then the Reagan administration built a platform to cast a large American shadow of military power over the southern borders of the Soviet Union.

Two events in the late 1980s began a process that sent Central Command hunting for a new mission. The Iran-Iraq War ended in the final months of the Reagan administration. The Ayatollah Khomeini surprised the world with his announcement that he would "drink the poison cup" of defeat. The longest war of the century was over. The cost had been staggering: eight years of war and a million dead. While the regional players were reassessing the implications of the peace, Washington was focused on events in the Soviet Union. *Perestroika* was introduced into the world's vocabulary and Washington policymakers were learning to use the word in complex sentences.

The Soviet withdrawal from Afghanistan was the first chapter in the book that closed the Cold War. A generation of Americans was riveted by television pictures of East German refugees boarding trains for freedom in the West from a rail platform in Prague. As Soviet troops boarded trains heading east from garrison towns in Czechoslovakia, Hungary, and East Germany, American military hardliners could no longer argue that the Soviet Union was a credible threat in the Gulf. The Reagan administration had spent billions of dollars and political capital to build a safety net to protect U.S. vital interests in the Gulf from an enemy that had packed up the hardware and gone home leaving the United States alone on the playing field.

Central Command needed a new enemy and Iraq fit the bill. It was a gradual reassessment of the threat in the region. Its most important convert, General H. Norman Schwarzkopf, studied Iraq's military position in the aftermath of the Gulf War as he assumed his new duties as the commander-in-chief of Central Command.

It wasn't so much that Iraq was posing a threat to the region, but the country fit a category at a time when the Soviet Union left a blank spot in U.S. military plans. While Iran might intend to pose a threat, the Iranians were hardly in a position to carry it out. The Gulf War had devastated Iran's military capability. The country would be hard-pressed to defend its own borders. Meanwhile the Baghdad government emerged from the war militarily strong but economically weak, a prescription for trouble. Saddam had made no efforts to cut the swelled ranks of the military. In the final two years of the war, Saddam's generals had transformed the country's fighting force into the fourth largest army in the world. It appeared as if Saddam intended to keep it that way.

There were arguments in Pentagon circles about replacing the Soviet Union with Iraq as the threat to the region. There were those who wanted to keep the threat generic. They argued that although Iraq did have the largest army in the region, there was no indication that the Iraqis had designs on their neighbors. The meaning of the designation as the fourth largest army had to be compared with the world's fifth largest army—Vietnam.

"Those who argued for filling in the blank won the day," said one official. "The guys who have to count the beans and know where the tanks go need to know who the specific threat is. You can't do that without filling in the blank. You have to plan against something."

By 1989, the Central Command planners had turned their full attention to Iraq. It was argued that Iraq had the force posture to make the country a credible threat. Central Command had a new mission. Iraq answered the "what ifs" for the military planners. There were computer war games and simulations played out against the Iraqi army. At Fort Irwin, in California's Mohave Desert, the National Training Center offered exercises against Saddam's fighting doctrine. The National Training Center, opened in 1982, offered the closest thing to actual desert combat on a training field the size of Rhode Island.

Fort Irwin was the home of the best "Russian regiment" in the world, according to military commanders who have trained there. Known as OPFOR, or opposing force, it offered American soldiers the opportunity to hone their skills against a real enemy featuring six video cameras to record the practice battles. By the late 1980s, the National

Training Center was reflecting the American military's new thinking. OPFOR fought using a tactical doctrine employed by the Iraqis.

While the Warsaw Pact countries were practitioners of Soviet doctrine with Soviet equipment, the Iraqis were more flexible. Saddam's army employed what the U.S. military dubbed the "Sumerian Doctrine." The Iraqis bought military hardware from all over the world and their military evolved a hodgepodge war-fighting doctrine borrowed from their suppliers and trainers. The Iraqis used techniques from the Soviets, the British, and the Indian army. The National Training Center offered the closest thing to actually fighting the Iraqi army. With Soviet T-72 tanks captured in Jordan, the Sinai, and the Golan Heights, OPFOR taught the lessons of desert warfare.

Saddam Hussein hadn't always been an enemy. Washington's first flirtation with Saddam came in the last years of the Carter administration. There were no illusions about the Iraqi dictator. The intelligence reports had shown a consistent analysis: Saddam was a thug and an assassin. Saddam had just come to power after a brutal and bloody struggle in Baghdad. However, he was the dictator of choice at a time when Washington was reeling from the twin setbacks of a Soviet invasion of Afghanistan and the Islamic Revolution in Iran. If Saddam was bad, the Ayatollah was worse. In April 1980, a public statement by Carter's national security advisor, Zbigniew Bzezinski, reflected the administration's tilt: "We see no fundamental incompatibility of interests between the United States and Iraq." That statement would define the policy of three administrations toward Iraq until Baghdad's tanks rolled over the Kuwaiti border ten years later.

The Reagan administration deepened the relationship. For Washington, an Iranian victory in the Iran-Iraq War was unthinkable. The 444-day hostage nightmare in Tehran had already undermined one president. An Iranian victory in the war with Saddam would make the Mullahs the ruling power in the region with control of Iraq's vast oil reserves. Washington's conservative Gulf allies were also at risk. Saddam's record on human rights was brutal, but it was weighed against a visceral fear of the black-garbed clerics of Tehran.

The Iraqi tilt was most evident in Washington's response to the outbreak of the Iran-Iraq War. The United States, with the rest of the Security Council at the United Nations, voted to condemn the Iraqi invasion of Iranian territory and yet the Security Council didn't call for a withdrawal. The message was clear: The Iraqis were the favored belligerent in the war. The following year, when Israeli pilots bombed

Iraq's Osirak nuclear reactor, Jeanne Kirkpatrick (the U.S. United Nation's representative) and Iraq's foreign minister, Saadoun Hammadi, worked closely together to work out a compromise resolution at the United Nations to condemn Israel.

Washington professed to be neutral in the war, but a series of policies showed that Washington was prepared to put a thumb on the balance scales when necessary. The first public sign of the policy surfaced in 1982 when the State Department removed Iraq from the list of countries that supported terrorism, despite evidence that Iraq still harbored the Palestinian terrorist Abu Nidal.

In the same year, the Iraqi government bought American helicopters for "civilian" use. Soon afterward, General Electric was permitted to sell Iraqi engines manufactured in Italy for Iraqi warplanes. The House Foreign Affairs Committee passed a resolution criticizing the Reagan policy, but even when Abu Nidal was implicated in the 1982 assassination attempt of Israel's ambassador to London, an act that served as the Israeli pretext to invade Lebanon, the administration imposed no punishment on Iraq.

In 1983, the Reagan administration embarked on a foreign policy initiative that would marry the Iraqi regime with American agro-business as well as one of the most powerful lobbies in the United States. It was a policy that was in keeping with the philosophy of the Reagan years: capitalism in the service of foreign relations. The instrument was a loan guarantee program run by the U.S. Department of Agriculture (USDA). The program allowed the Baghdad regime to buy American commodities with loans from American banks guaranteed by the USDA. In the years that Iraq bought and borrowed with the help of the Commodity Credit Corporation, the Baghdad regime became one of the major importers of U.S. grain. Iraq was the largest buyer of American rice in the world.

On November 26, 1984, Washington restored diplomatic relations with Iraq after a seventeen-year break. There was a small party that day at the embassy in Baghdad. In Washington, Tareq Aziz, Iraq's foreign minister, met with President Reagan. In the same year, the export-import bank began to extend short-term loan guarantees to the Iraqi regime to buy manufactured goods. American business followed the money trail to Baghdad. In 1985, the U.S.-Iraq Business Forum was formed. It was a self-styled chamber of commerce with seventy members. Government loan guarantees removed much of the risk of doing business with a country that was deeply in debt. The U.S. Department of Commerce approved 500 million dollars worth of high-technology equipment to Iraq despite protests from the Pentagon. Much of that equipment was used to build Saddam's war machine. When the U.S. Congress considered sanctions against the Baghdad regime, Saddam's human rights record was weighed against the damage to U.S. business and farming interests.

Saddam Hussein enjoyed an eight-year honeymoon with Washington. His relations with Washington were matched by his relations with European governments. The research and development center for Saddam's missile program, known as Saad 16 near Mosul, was built by Germans, Austrians, Brazilians, and Egyptians. Saddam was an excellent arms cutomer for French companies. German companies sold him chemicals for his weapons program. Reports after the Gulf War showed that the British government contributed to the Iraqi war machine as well. A House of Commons committee report revealed that until 1990 the British Department of Trade and Industry approved the export of a chemical used in the production of mustard gas. The shipments violated a 1985 international agreement to stop the spread of chemical weapons.

Saddam saw his human rights record as a public relations problem. The West complained about his behavior but rarely took action. The postwar reconstruction of Iraq promised to be an excellent market for American business. There was a large American turnout in 1989 for the Baghdad International Trade Fair. In a brochure welcoming visitors to the U.S. pavilion, U.S. Ambassador April Glaspie wrote that the embassy "places the highest priority on promoting communication and friendship between our two nations." It wasn't a policy that Glaspie invented; it was the evolution of a policy pursued by three administrations. Six days before the Iraqi invasion of Kuwait, the U.S. Congress voted to gut an amendment that would cut off one billion dollars in annual U.S. farm credits to Iraq. By late summer 1990, communications were so degraded by a decade of inconsistent carrot-and-sticks that only the clearest message of American intentions would have altered Saddam's march to war.

Watching the last years of the Iran-Iraq War was like watching two reckless gamblers in the game of their lives. The Ayatollah Khomeini pored over his cards and wagered that he could dismantle the Ba'thist regime, set up an Islamic republic in Iraq, and put Saddam Hussein on trial as a war criminal. In 1986, the cards were in his favor. In February, Khomeini's Islamic shock troops, the Pasdaran, seized Faw, an empty city on Iraq's southern peninsula. The crossing of the Shatt al Arab by 85,000 Iranian soldiers and the capture of Faw was a dev-astating blow to Iraq. Western military attachés in Baghdad reported at the time that Iraqi soldiers had "downed tools and run" as the Iranian irregulars stormed over their positions. The next week the Baghdad regime was so convinced that the recapture of Faw was within their grasp that they invited foreign correspondents to the southern port city of Basra to wait. It was my first trip to Iraq and it was a lesson in the workings of Saddam's regime.

Baghdad was a capital remarkably free from the trappings of war. The bus ride to Basra was a trip to the heartland of the combat. On the flat modern highway that connects the capital to the south, taxi cabs with flag-draped coffins tied on the roof roared past our bus. Nearer the city the landscape had been converted to the business of killing. Iraqi tanks were buried in dirt on the road shoulder facing east. The long trunks of artillery guns pointed the way to Iran. Basra had the frantic energy of a city under siege. Sandbags hid storefronts and the ground floors of apartment houses.

Saddam's face stared benevolently from giant posters all over the city. There was a joke in the country that the population of Iraq was 36 million: 18 million Iraqis and 18 million pictures of Saddam Hussein. In Basra, like Baghdad, there were few streets or walls free of Saddam's smiling face. He appeared as a benevolent president with a little girl beaming on his lap. He was a military general in an olive drab uniform. He was a diplomat in a shiny blue suit with aviator glasses. He was a white-robed Arab warrior on horseback in the seventh-century battle with the Persians. The modern version of this contest was being played out in a small uninhabited city on Iraq's southern peninsula. Basra was the closest place to wait.

As the days passed, our "minders" from the Ministry of Information ran out of ways to pass the time. There had been a tightly controlled tour of Basra and a visit to an Iraqi bunker where Iraqi soldiers had a steady supply of cold Pepsi Cola. Large television sets in field bunkers showed Japanese, German, and American war films dubbed into Arabic. The programming between the movies was a chorus of Iraqi singers warbling the praises of their great leader.

As the days dragged on, it was clear that the Iranians were in Faw to stay. They had burrowed into the Iraqi-built fortifications in the city. Iraqi efforts to dislodge them were in vain. From Basra, the battle was a series of dull thuds on the horizon. Our requests to visit the front were repeatedly rejected. The press corp was herded back on the buses for the eight-hour drive to Baghdad where our visas were not renewed. We were left to draw our own conclusions about the victory in Faw.

The capture of Faw showed a fundamental flaw in Saddam's military strategy. Saddam had insisted to his main financial backers, Saudi Arabia and Kuwait, that Iran would eventually run out of steam and petition for peace. Baghdad's strategy had been one of static defense. Saddam had ordered his generals to sit tight and keep casualties to a minimum. In Baghdad, Saddam pursued a strategy of guns, butter, and video tape. The state grocery stores were full and Baghdadis could buy the latest in Western consumer technology.

However, there was a darker side to the story. Western diplomats told of the combat dead stored in giant freezers to be dispersed in small lots to dull the shocks of loss. Saddam had banned public funerals. Family gatherings for burials at Baghdad cemeteries were off-limits to reporters; to attend was an invitation for arrest by the local police as the government sought to downplay the death toll.

The Iranian victory in Faw made Saddam's frightened Gulf allies wonder if they shouldn't hedge their bets and rethink their options. The Pasdaran added to their worries by building Silkworm missile sites on Faw and lobbing shells into nearby Kuwait City.

Another shock to Baghdad came in 1986. On November 3, a Lebanese magazine published what seemed to be a fantastic story. American officials had carried a bible, a cake, and a revolver to Tehran. There were more shocks to come. The Irangate revelations showed that the Reagan administration, with Israel's help, had been secretly funneling arms to the Islamic republic. Publicly, Washington stood for a negotiated settlement and had given support to Baghdad. Privately, Washington was driven by concern over American hostages in Lebanon and funding the contra rebels in Central America.

Israel's exact role in the deal remains unclear. The Israeli relationship with Iran dated to the shah's time when Tel Aviv bought oil from the Persians. Parts of the partnership had survived the Islamic Revolution. It gave the Israelis insights and contacts with Tehran that the Americans didn't have. In strategic terms, Baghdad was seen as more dangerous to Tel Aviv than Tehran. The Ayatollah, while not particularly friendly to the Jewish state, was seen as a counterweight to the Iraqi regime.

In addition, Israeli arms sales were crucial to the economy. Washington's Operation Staunch prohibited arms sales to Iran. Israel couldn't sell arms to Iran without violating Washington's arms embargo. The American hostage crisis presented an opportunity. For the Iranian government, the hostages were becoming worthless, except as a bargaining chip for arms. Israel became the middle man in a deal that looked to make everyone happy—except Saddam.

Saddam Hussein looked over his cards and saw a desperate hand. Armed with American hardware, the Iranians had pushed to within artillery range of Basra. Saddam took the gamble of his political career: He let his generals take over the war. Saddam still appeared on Iraqi T.V. in his crisp green military uniform, but for the first time since the war's beginning Iraq's military professionals took charge. The character and the nature of the war changed dramatically. With the loosening of controls from Baghdad, the generals could conduct a mobile defense that employed flexibility and required decision making in the field.

Saddam's days of micro-managing the military campaign from Baghdad were over. For the first time, student deferments were canceled as the country wagered its future on victory. The Republican Guards, Saddam's elite corp, opened its ranks to bright university boys who came from villages other than Saddam's own hometown of Takrit. In the same year, Iraq bought advanced computers from a New Jersey firm for a ballistic missile facility known as Saad 16 in Mosul. Brazilian military officers were supplying rocket technology in a program that was known to the U.S. government.

If the 1986 Irangate scandal showed that Washington appeared to favor Iran, the next year Washington swung the other way. In May 1987, President Reagan answered Kuwait's request to reflag Kuwaiti tankers against Iranian attacks. Saddam Hussein had kicked off the tanker war in 1984 to prevent Iran from enjoying its oil revenues. Saddam's oil was shipped out of the country by land through pipelines built in Saudi Arabia and Turkey. The rest was shipped on Kuwaiti tankers. At first, Washington hesitated to play the role of Kuwait's protector, but when the Kuwaitis let it be known that Moscow was interested in the job, Washington quickly agreed to the reflagging exercise. Operation Ernest Will went some way to restore Washington's credibility in Baghdad and patch the tattered friendship between Iraq and the United States. It was a successful Central Command exercise that meant a large U.S. presence in the Persian Gulf with no large-scale local repercussions. By midyear, the U.S. Navy was in a head-to-head confrontation with Iran.

By spring 1988, the Iran-Iraq War had become the war of the cities. Baghdad launched missile attacks on major population centers and prime economic targets. Iran returned the fire. I arrived in Tehran in

July 1988. The war of the cities was over and the Iranian government had issued journalists visas to cover another event in the war. On July 3, an Iranian airbus had taken off from the Bandar Abbas Airport bound for Dubai when a missile ripped through the metal skin of Iran Flight 655. The commander of the *U.S.S. Vincennes* had ordered the attack, convinced that the airliner was about to attack. Two hundred and ninety civilian passengers had fallen from the sky. The *U.S.S. Vincennes* was part of Operation Ernest Will and the accidental shooting and the reaction in the United States was in part a result of the anti-Iran hysteria of the time.

There were Americans who believed that the Iranians had sent the civilian airliner on a suicide mission. The theorists claimed that the Iranians had packed a plane with dead bodies and then used the incident to embarrass the Reagan administration. They used it as an excuse to dismiss with little sympathy the deaths of the 290 passengers.

I flew to Tehran on an Iran flight out of London. The Iran Air staff were in mourning for their dead friends. Many had worked for the airline before the Islamic revolution. Their uniforms, dark navy gabardine dresses with pants and a head scarf, reflected the Islamic government requirements, but these women were not fervent revolutionaries. It was impossible to imagine that their colleagues had agreed to strap dead bodies in these seats and then fly to their deaths.

The funerals in Tehran were somber. In a downtown mosque, female relatives and close friends stood on a balcony wrapped in the white robes of mourning, while in the courtyard another troop of mourners carried large posters with pictures of the dead. The city was focused on the immediate tragedy, but the Iran-Iraq War dominated the conversations in Tehran. In the southern suburbs of the capital, in the revolution's heartland, there were public complaints about the government's pursuit of the conflict. It was the one difference between these two ugly regimes. In Tehran it was possible to criticize government policy. The complaints came in two categories. The poor of Tehran had taken the worst of the war of the cities. They watched as government officials fled the capital and left them behind to cope with the destruction. Food prices were soaring. The Islamic revoltion was in danger of collapsing under the weight of a senseless war.

While the war of the cities had been devastating to the morale of Iran's civilian population, the battle for the city of Halabja practically halted Iran's recruitment drive. In March, the Iraqi army had targeted Kurdish insurgents in a small town in northern Iraq. The weapon was poison gas. The Iranians had recaptured the town shortly after the attack and brought worldwide attention to the Iraqi atrocities. Over the next few months, the Iranian military used the horrifying pictures of Halabja as a propaganda film for recruitment. The film had the opposite effect. Although young Iranian revolutionaries might be willing to walk aross Saddam's mine fields for a chance at martyrdom, they were not prepared for the grisly death by poison gas.

When the Ayatollah Khomeini next talked of poison, it was the poison chalice of defeat. "Taking this decision was more deadly than taking poison. I submitted myself to God's will and drank this drink for His satisfaction." On July 18, United Nations Secretary General Perez de Cuellar received Iran's acceptance of U.N. Resolution 598, a cease-fire and withdrawal of troops to the internationally recognized borders. Khomeini died eleven months later.

With the war's end, Saddam turned his attention to internal matters. Twenty-five days after Iran accepted the U.N. cease-fire, Saddam Hussein's army launched what he called the "final offensive," a chemical attack on Kurdish villages in northern Iraq. The first reports reached the West through eyewitness accounts from those Iraqi Kurds forced to flee to southern Turkey. A staff report to the U.S. Senate Committee on Foreign Relations includes this eyewitness account:

> Bashir Shemseddin and his father from Vermil village: Four planes came over on August 25 and dropped bombs. We did not know what happened. We ran outside. We got dizzy and could not see. We fell down and threw up. In our village, 200 to 300 people died. All the animals and birds died. All the trees dried up. It smelled like something burned. The whole world turned yellow.

On September 9, the U.S. Senate passed the most drastic sanctions bill in the history of relations between the United States and Iraq. The Prevention of Genocide Act of 1988 would bar imports of Iraqi oil, curtail further borrowing at the International Monetary Fund, eliminate Commodity Credit Corporation (CCC) guarantees worth 500 million dollars, and end any Iraqi purchases that required an export license. In short, the Senate bill would have stopped all U.S. business with Iraq.

The next day the Iraqi government mounted the largest anti-American demonstration ever in front of the U.S. Embassy in Baghdad. More than 100,000 Iraqis marched past the American Embassy doors that had opened four years earlier. Over the next five weeks the two chambers of the American Congress wrestled with a variety of versions of the sanctions bill. The Reagan administration argued against the measures. Administration spokesmen stressed that Iraqi behavior could only be modified if the United States maintained "solid, businesslike relations." At the same time, grain exporters, oil companies, and the exporters of high-technology equipment launched a campaign to sabotage the bill. American chemical companies flooded congressional offices with complaints.

In the end, pressure from the White House, the weight of special-interest groups, and the chaos and infighting at the end of a legislative session combined to sink any efforts to take a stand against Saddam's use of chemical weapons. Peter Galbraith, a senior aid on the Senate Foreign Relations Committee, had helped to shape the original Senate bill. "Basically the policy for eight years was one of appeasement. The Reagan administration said it was against sanctions. They worked to water them down. What kind of message does Iraq get? You have oral statements of toughness combined with inaction."

"The defining moment of American policy came in September 1988," said Peter Galbraith. "There was no strategic rationale for the poison gas attack, unlike the use of gas against the Iranians. This was pure barbarity. The world did nothing."

The Prevention of Genocide Act of 1988 died with the One Hundredth Congress. It was the last serious effort to send Saddam Hussein a clear message from the American Congress.

The Iran-Iraq War ended just as events in the Soviet Union and in eastern Europe shoved the Middle East to the back burner for top American policymakers. The Bush administration took nine months to complete a policy review of the region. In October 1989, George Bush put his signature on National Security Directive 26. It read like a replay of the Carter and Reagan years: "Access to the Persian Gulf and the key friendly states in the area is vital to U.S. national security. The United States remains committed to defend its vital interest in the region, if necessary and appropriate through the use of U.S. military force against the Soviet Union or any other regional power with interests inimical to our own." It was a signal for business as usual with the Iraqi regime as the new president and his secretary of state, James Baker, focused their energy on Moscow and eastern Europe.

The Reagan administration had done all it could to support the Iraqis in their campaign against Tehran and they could point to some political dividends. After the September chemical attacks, there were no more incidents of this kind. On the Middle East peace process, the Iraqis were saying publicly that they would support the PLO's policy of a two-state solution. In February 1989, Saddam joined with Jordan, Egypt, and (then) North Yemen in the Arab Cooperation Council. Saddam appeared to have suppressed his regional ambitions.

Saddam sent messages to Washington that he wanted to continue the relations that had brought the two countries together during the Iran-Iraq War. Saddam's economy was now more closely tied to the West than to the Soviet Union. The CCC credits program meant the Iraqi government continued to buy rice and grain from American farmers.

There were requests from Iraqi military bureaucrats for unclassified American military training manuals. Iraq wanted to upgrade the relationship established during the war and send doctors to the United States for training in battlefield casualties. (Both requests were turned down.)

At the same time, Saddam launched his first postwar foreign adventure in Lebanon with a shipment of arms to the renegade Christian general, Michael Aoun. His treatment of the Kurds in northern Iraq showed he was as ruthless as ever with internal opponents. His weapons program proceeded at a remarkable pace.

Saddam's policies challenged the accepted wisdom in Washington and Europe that he was a man to do business with. In March 1990, Iraq's secret police had arrested Farzad Bazoft, an Iranian-born British journalist, at the Baghdad Airport. Bazoft had openly collected soil samples at the gates of an Iraqi munitions factory where a mysterious explosion had reportedly killed 700. On March 10, Bazoft was condemned to death by an Iraqi court, and despite appeals for his release, he was executed five days later. In February an Iraqi diplomat at the United Nations hired a man who worked as a chauffeur to assassinate two Iraqi dissidents in California. The plot came to light when the hired killer went to the FBI instead and gave testimony.

In the meantime, Saddam continued to send signals to Washington that he wanted friendly relations. On February 11, 1990, Assistant Secretary of State John Kelly paid a visit to the Iraqi leader in the Bush administration's first high-level meeting in Baghdad. Iraqi Foreign Minister Tariq Azziz was warm in his greetings and repeated Baghdad's wish for improved relations. In a two-and-a-half-hour meeting Saddam spoke of the declining power of the Soviet Union and the implications for the United States. It was a theme he was to take up again with a different twist at a meeting in Amman, Jordan.

The first anniversary celebration of the Arab Cooperation Council (ACC) had ended one day early in Amman. Egyptian President Hosni

Mubarek had left the meeting abruptly, disturbed by the tone of Saddam Hussein's speech broadcast on Jordanian television. Saddam had expanded on his theme of American power in the Middle East. With the collapse of the Soviet Union, Saddam told his audience the United States would have a free hand to maneuver in the region for the next five years. The United States would use this power to the detriment of the Arabs.

"This will mean that if the Gulf people, along with all of the Arabs, are not careful, the Arab Gulf region will be governed by the wishes of the United States. . . . [Oil] prices would be fixed in line with a special perspective benefiting American interests and ignoring the interests of others." Saddam suggested it might be better to withdraw Arab investments in the West and place them in the Soviet Union or eastern Europe to force a policy change. In Saddam's view there was a "real possibility" that Israel would engage in "new stupidities" in the area encouraged by new American power.

The following day, Iraq's ambassador to Washington, Mohammad Mashat, was called to the State Department to explain the speech. "It's a strange way to do business," said John Kelly to the Iraqi representative in Washington. "As soon as we leave Baghdad, the president makes this speech." Mashat said he had no instructions from Baghdad and would get back to Kelly. He never did.

Word filtered back to the State Department from the other Arab participants at the meeting that Saddam had been enraged by an editorial that had been broadcast on the Voice of America four days after Kelly's meeting with Saddam. The broadcast stated, "It reflected the views of the U.S. government." The broadcast criticized the practices of the secret police in eight countries, including Iraq, and came at a time of excitement over the developments in eastern Europe. "The rulers of these countries hold power by force and fear, not by the consent of the governed . . . the tide of history is against such rulers. The 1990s should belong not to the dictators and secret police, but to the people," the editorial said.

Saddam was convinced that Washington was out to get him and Israel was about to attack him. Azziz told Secretary of State James Baker as much when they met for the first time in October 1989. He accused the Bush administration of "mounting a campaign" against his country. Saddam raised the issue again at an Arab summit meeting in May that was called to denounce the influx of Soviet Jews to Israel and support Saddam's speech threatening to "burn half of Israel." In this meeting

Saddam talked of economic warfare. He accused some Gulf states of lowering the price of oil by pumping too much of it.

When five American senators came to see Saddam in the Iraqi city of Mosul, he again raised the issue of an American "campaign." Senator Robert Dole, who represents a state (Kansas) that exported grain to Iraq, told Saddam that the Voice of America journalist responsible for the editorial had been fired. (He hadn't.) Senator Alan Simpson told the Iraqi leader that his problem was not with the American people but with its "haughty and pampered press." Saddam continued to believe that the news reports of his human rights record, the reports of the arrest of Iraqi agents for attempting to smuggle nuclear triggers out of England, and the coverage of the Bazoft affair were all part of an administration attempt to undermine him.

In the first five months of 1990, Saddam Hussein had called on Arab states to withdraw their investments in the West, called on the American Navy to leave the Gulf, threatened to burn half of Israel, and equated America with imperialism. While Saddam was convinced of a "campaign," in fact the White House was paying little attention to him.

Foreign policy in the Bush White House was run by a small, tight circle of men who had focused their attention elsewhere, leaving the middle ranks of government to continue a policy already in place. There was grumbling about Saddam's strange behavior, but those warnings did not alert top policymakers in the administration to take a second look. The agricultural credits were suspended. The loans from the import-export bank continued. The policy to argue against sanctions continued.

During the Reagan administration the credits were a prop to help Saddam win a war against Iran. When George Bush took office, the credits were a reward to keep Saddam from slipping back to his prewar policy. But for Saddam the stakes had changed. He was no longer fighting a war, but trying to rebuild the country. He could buy rice with American agricultural credits. He could buy high technology and chemicals for his war machines from Europe and the United States. But in postwar Iraq, Saddam could not repay his war debts or rebuild the country for a population that had rising expectations of a better life following the peace. Washington's carrots had grown smaller as Saddam's economic problems grew larger. Other regional factors, like the falling price of oil, were the sticks that now drove him.

In Saddam's eyes, his former wartime allies were ungrateful. Iraq had sacrificed for them and they were unwilling to continue their financial support. They were enjoying the peace while his people paid the price. He was convinced of an American "campaign" and convinced by the tone of rhetoric coming out of Tel Aviv that the Israelis were getting ready to target him again. He began to see enemies all around him, and in Saddam's Iraq, no one could tell him he was wrong.

THREE

THE ARABS

"Fight in the way of Allah against those who fight against you, but begin not hostilities. Lo! Allah loveth not agressors."
—The holy Qur'an, Surah 11, verse 190

"Is it just my imagination or does Yasser Arafat look like Ringo Starr?"
—Comedian Robin Williams New Year's special broadcast on Armed Forces Radio Network for American troops in Saudi Arabia

The border between Saudi Arabia and Kuwait is marked by a gentle embankment that slopes out of the flat desert floor like a giant dune. The sand berm traces a straight border that could only have been mapped with pencil and ruler. The bedouins use the stars to track the trails that zigzag through the wastelands. The earth is speckled with the steps of camels, sheep, and their human herders. Before August 2, neither Saudi Arabia nor Kuwait needed tanks on this border. The last time armed men prowled here was over a half century before.

Abd al-Aziz Ibn Saud, Arabia's warrior king, found the border drawn out by the British and the Ottoman Turks unacceptable. It made him forget Kuwaiti generosity. At the turn of the century Kuwait's emir, Mubarak Ibn Sabah, had provided Abd al-Aziz refuge while he and his band of Muslim warriors plotted their conquest of the heartland of Arabia.

Twenty years later, Abd al-Aziz was the king of a country that carried his name. He had visions of a grander kingdom and was disturbed by what he saw as an arbitrary border. While the Saudi king was stewing over the power of Englishmen, his fanatical Muslim warriors, known as the Ikhwan, had their own scores to settle with Kuwait. Compared to the ascetic puritans of Arabia the Kuwaitis were unbearably lax in their practice of Islam. The Ikhwan had already proved that they were excellent defenders of the faith at home. Charged with religious zeal and the exhilaration of conquest, in the fall of 1920 the Ikhwan declared war on their neighbors.

Kuwait's emir, Mubarak's son Salim, rallied his troops and met the Ikhwan at the Red Fort, at Jahrah, 30 miles west of Kuwait City. The Kuwaitis were no match for the militant Ikhwan, but the Kuwaitis had an important advantage. The Kuwaitis had British protection. The emir's men held out long enough for British warships and British marines to land on the Gulf coast. Until August 1990, this was to be a pattern repeated by the Kuwaitis whenever they were in trouble. The arrival of the British convinced the Ikhwan that, at least in this battle, it was best to let a higher authority tend to Kuwaiti souls.

Britain was to play another important role two years later. To satisfy Abd al-Aziz's claims, the British added a chunk of southern Kuwait to his kingdom and set up a neutral zone between the two states where bedouin tribes had free access for grazing. To appease the Kuwaitis, Sir Percy Cox, the British government agent, guaranteed the old Ottoman demarcation assigning the islands of Warba and Bubiyan to Kuwait. However, by the 1930s, Iraq was an independent state and the British legacy—a border that gave Iraq a narrow window on the Persian Gulf—was already a festering conflict between the two states.

On the first day of August 1990, one of Ibn Saud's grandsons was cooking rice on his farm about 100 miles outside the Saudi capital of Riyadh. A prince by birth, a military man by training, Khalid bin Sultan was a burly, gregarious chain smoker. He was the eldest son of Saudi Arabia's defense minister, Sultan bin Abd al-Aziz.

Khalid loved spending time at his 3000-acre farm. He talked more about his irrigated wheat fields, his herds of sheep, the flocks of quail, and his date trees than he did about the Saudi military. On August 2, a telephone ring woke Khalid at the farm. It was 3 A.M. and a calm voice from the military command center in Riyadh said, "We have proof that Iraq has invaded Kuwait." At first, Khalid didn't believe it. A second call five minutes later sent a spurt of adrenaline through Saudi Arabia's air defense commander.

The Air Defense Command is the fourth branch of the Saudi armed forces. Prince Khalid had built the institution over the past seven years from a force of 3000 men to a force of over 15,000. The Air Defense Command is the backbone of the country's military shield, an expensive, high-tech alternative to a large ground force. Saudi Arabia is about one quarter of the size of the United States with only a fraction of the population. There are no official census figures for the kingdom, but it's generally agreed that there are about 9 million Saudis in a population of about 14 million. The rest are expatriot workers imported to serve the Saudis.

With a quarter of the world's oil reserves, Saudi Arabia is a rich prize in a rough neighborhood. Over the past ten years Riyadh bought about eight hundred short-range surface-to-surface missiles from the United States and Europe. The Saudis concluded a secret deal with the Chinese for dozens of CSS-2 long-range ballistic missiles when the U.S. Congress turned down their requests for F-15s.

In 1989, about a year after the end of the Iran-Iraq War, Saddam had surprised Khalid's uncle, King Fahd, with a proposal for a non-aggression pact. Saddam had suddenly proposed the treaty while the king was on a visit to Baghdad and he urged the Saudi monarch to sign right away. Fahd could hardly turn down the deal, but he later made it clear to his ministers that he didn't put much faith in Saddam's pledges. The agreement had raised eyebrows among Saudi Arabia's Gulf neighbors. It was an odd move for Saddam at a time when the rest of the Gulf was mending fences.

The Saudis didn't publicize the details of the agreement, but Saddam was unusually open about the conditions, which included a statement of "the non-use of force and armies between the two states." It was as if the United States and Canada had just announced they would not fight each other. A Western diplomat at the time wondered if the nonaggression pact was a way of soothing Iraq's neighbor or if it was an implied threat to force similar pledges from Gulf war allies. At the time, Kuwait and the other states in the Gulf were mending frayed relations with Iran.

In the early hours of Saddam's invasion, Riyadh hoped that Saddam would remember the commitment. However, there were a number of incidents that raised questions about Iraqi intentions. A day after the invasion, Iraqi Vice-President Izzat Ibrahim came to Riyadh armed with assurances for the Saudi king. However, one day after the meeting, Iraqi troops crossed into the neutral zone, a diamond-shaped spit of sand on the Saudi-Kuwait border. What were the Iraqis up to? Was this a violation of the nonaggression pact? Riyadh was not sure, and this was no time for guessing games.

There were three border incursions that day. On the last trip back to occupied Kuwait the Iraqis blew up a Saudi overpass. If Saddam had meant to intimidate the House of Saud, the political message delivered by the Iraqi soldiers had the opposite effect. If Saddam had bet on Saudi Arabia's longstanding sensitivity to the presence of American troops on Saudi soil, he had bet wrong.

Four days after the Iraqi invasion of Kuwait, Prince Khalid bin Sultan attended a meeting with U.S. Secretary of State Dick Cheney and General H. Norman Schwarzkopf, the commander of U.S. Central Command. The prince knew that both men had met with his uncle, King Fahd, a day earlier in Jeddah. He knew that the king had invited American ground troops into Saudi Arabia. He backed the decision "with no hesitations." Khalid knew that the Americans had brought satellite pictures of Iraqi positions in Kuwait. "The satellite stuff, yes, I heard about it, but I already knew what happened," said Khalid.

This was the first meeting between the man that would command the Western forces of Desert Shield, and the Saudi prince who would command the Arab and Muslim armies. "We just said hello, politely," said Khalid. "To tell you the truth, I didn't know Schwarzkopf's name." Khalid was more familiar with Lieutenant General John J. Yeosock who also attended the meeting.

Yeosock had spent two years in the early 1980s as the American advisor to the Saudi National Guard. Yeosock knew his way around MODA, Saudi Arabia's Ministry of Defense and Aviation. He was a Pennsylvania coal country boy. He smoked cigars at breakfast and he had made it his business to understand the tribal traditions of Saudi Arabia. He had friends in Riyadh and they welcomed him back.

Yeosock was now the commander of the U.S. Army branch of Central Command. The Saudi king's decision would bring 280,000 American troops to Saudi Arabia. The Central Command timetable for deployment had already been worked out. Yeosock and the other commanders had finished the briefings on a Central Command summer training exerise two days before the Iraqi invasion. Central Command could not have been more prepared for the job ahead. They had "war-gamed" an Iraqi occupation of Kuwait and the American defense of the oil fields of Saudi Arabia. The blueprint for the next steps were contained in a three-ring notebook. The classified operation plan, 1002-90, laid it all out.

In the months ahead Central Command would test the plans and training of a decade. There would be 6 billion pounds of gear shipped halfway around the world. Central Command would use "host nation support" and depend on military supplies quietly stockpiled in Saudi Arabia, Bahrain, and Oman over the last ten years.

Two days after the meeting with the Americans, Prince Khalid was told he'd be in charge of the *joint forces,* a name and concept he had suggested to Saudi Arabia's chief military officer, Saleh al Hammad. Khalid was the logical choice to head the effort. He was the most senior prince serving in the Saudi armed forces. By all accounts he was a capable officer, with a direct connection to the minister of defense. An operation as delicate and important as this one clearly required a personal link to the royal family. The House of Saud was risking a lot, perhaps its very identity. The decision to allow American soldiers to set up bases in Saudi Arabia was unprecedented.

Saudi Arabia has a history of close relations with the United States that dates back to the meetings between Franklin Roosevelt and King Ibn Saud during World War II. King Fahd was particularly known for his warm feelings toward the Americans. There were rumors of Fahd's self-imposed exile when he was crown prince, contending that he had stalked out of the country when his brother refused to support the American-brokered peace treaty between Israel and Egypt.

These were the stories that were traded among journalists and diplomats. In public, however, the Saudis had learned to keep the relationship with Washington a private affair. There was a national trick of mind that allowed the House of Saud to have a close connection but at the same time deny that it existed.

It was an open secret that American advisors had trained mechanized and artillery battalions of the Saudi National Guard. Most taxi drivers in Riyadh knew the location of the U.S. Military Training Mission. The U.S. Corp of Engineers planned and supervised the building of Saudi military bases, and the 1982 sale of AWACS, the Advanced Air Warning Communications Support radar planes, came with a built-in dependence on American software. At the same time, Saudi newspaper editors printed endless editorials critiquing "Zionist-directed" U.S. policy.

The U.S.-Saudi relationship was now out of the closet and the implications were enormous. For years radical Arab states had chastised Saudi Arabia for its close connections with Washington. Radical Muslims at home and abroad were likely to mount a campaign against the decision. King Fahd had put his throne on the line.

The chief religious authority in the country had given his blessing

to King Fahd's decision in a religious ruling called a Fatwa. Shaikh
'Abdallah bin 'Abd al-'Aziz bin Baz, the chief of the Supreme Council
of Islamic Research, Ruling, Call and Guidance, had proclaimed the
virtue of the invitation. He praised King Fahd for "fulfilling a duty
sustained by shari'a law which instructs the ruler to seek assistance
from those capable to providing it." Bin Baz, a civil servant in the
Saudi state, had found precedent in Islamic law for the American
deployment. Other religious scholars found justification for their anger
in different parts of the holy texts: "O ye who believe! Take not the
Jews and the Christians for patrons. They are patrons to one another.
He among you who takes them for friends is of them. Lo! God guideth
not those who do wrong."

King Fahd had been a playboy in his youth. He had gambled and
drank in the best clubs of Europe, but when he settled into his royal
duties the king had become a born-again Muslim. Fahd was known for
his flexibility and his intelligence. In the kingdom, he preferred the
title "Custodian of the Two Holy Mosques" to any royal designations.
King Fahd was also a man who understood the realities of modern
geopolitics. The Custodian of the Two Holy Mosques had now invited
American soldiers to protect what some Muslims considered holy soil.

The Americans would stay well away from the two holy sites of
Mecca and Medina—the king had made sure of that. The Saudis knew
how to isolate the American soldiers in the vast desert. They had
learned the technique from separating thousands of Western development workers from the Saudi population in specially built housing
compounds. The House of Saud could limit the taint of Western contamination, but there was no predicting the reaction of the religious
radicals at home and in the region to the presence of infidels in the
sands of Saudi Arabia's desert. The very fact of the American deployment raised questions in some Arab minds about whether Fahd was
the servant of America rather than Islam.

Prince Khalid was a good choice to ward off the most immediate
criticisms inside the Saudi military. He was senior enough to handle
the doubts of his officers. He had been trained almost exclusively in
the West. He was a graduate of Sandhurst, England's top military school
and had spent time in Fort Leavenworth and the Air War College in
Alabama. He had a master's degree in political science and had completed postgraduate work in Monterey, California. He enjoyed American television and kept a supply of video tapes of "The Golden Girls,"
"The Cosby Show," and "Murphy Brown." He knew more about the

culture of the Americans, British, and French than they knew about Arabia.

Within twenty-four hours of his appointment, Khalid chose twenty officers for his staff. "For the Americans, there is already a system in the computer. You push a button and the system is there," said Khalid. The Saudis had to start from scratch. This was a whole new command.

The first American F-15s were scheduled to arrive on August 8. This was the easy part. Saudi Arabian airfields had been overbuilt in the past ten years to accommodate the size of this deployment. However, the arrival of more than 200,000 American ground troops over the next few months was going to take an enormous amount of work. Saudi Arabia had the infrastructure to handle the mass of Americans, but their care and comfort would require massive amounts of water, gasoline, food, and housing. Khalid's logistics staff would soon start work on renting helicopters and water purification systems, contracting for the construction of extra runways, and building prisoner-of-war camps. There were contracts to award for food, air conditioners, and apartments.

Syria, Egypt, and Morocco also pledged to send troops to Saudi Arabia. With the defense of the kingdom ensured, Khalid considered the larger problem: Would Syria, Egypt, or Morocco agree to fight Iraq? The Arab allies signed on for a defensive operation, but who would be on board if Saddam presented a more difficult problem and chose to test the political strength of this new coalition by waiting it out in Kuwait?

"We didn't know anybody who was going to do anything except the Saudi armed forces and the U.S. armed forces," said Khalid. Arab leaders made a public distinction between defending Saudi Arabia and attacking Iraq.

While President George Bush was conjuring up images of Hitler for a Western audience, images of the Christian crusaders marched into the minds of Arab intellectuals as well as the Arabs of the street. For many Arabs, even those who supported the deployment, the presence of Western troops in the Gulf evoked powerful memories of past impotence. Saddam Hussein compared himself to a twelfth-century Muslim hero who had been born near his hometown of Takrit. Salah Ad-din Yusuf Ibn Ayyub—Saladin in the West—had fought and won against Europe's Christian crusaders.

Hitler was an inappropriate parallel. The Western powers had tolerated aggression in the Arab world when it suited their interests, and Arab leaders understood that all too well. Washington was quick to condemn the Iraqi annexation of Kuwait, but did nothing to reverse the Israeli occupation of Arab lands. Saddam's human rights record was well known to Western leaders when he was useful to Western powers worried about Iranian power.

Saddam was an Arab hero in the minds of many, the new Saladin. He was a proponent of pan-Arabism. He championed the mythical entity known as the "Arab nation." He believed in standing up against Israel. It is what they all said they believed. Defending Saudi Arabia was one thing; attacking Saddam Hussein's army, an Arab brother, was quite a different matter.

Khalid put off the discussion of an offensive operation for the first weeks of the deployment. "Out of politeness, I didn't ask them," said Khalid. "We were hoping for the sanctions, hoping the sanctions would work. We were hoping that all the United Nations resolutions would relieve the pressure. After twenty days or thirty days the U.N. produced no change in Baghdad. So we had to analyze. Who is willing to attack?"

The question needed an answer by the end of September. The war planners on General Schwarzkopf's staff were discussing the offensive plan by the second month of the Iraqi occupation. By that time they already knew they needed a second American corps to bring the war to Iraq and they were getting strong indications from Washington that the request would be approved.

The Gulf War started for me with a telephone call at 3 A.M. on August 2. "Saddam's army has crossed the border," said Audrey Wynn, my editor in Washington. It was still dark in London, but I had spent enough time in the Middle East's only city-state to imagine Iraqi tanks driving at lightening speed toward the austere skyscrapers of Kuwait City on a clear summer day.

Another war in the Middle East. I had been in Baghdad at the end of the last one. Iraq's capital city had been in a frenzy of celebration. The war's cost was more than 750,000 Iraqi dead and wounded. The country's economy was in shambles. I had watched the fireworks display at the sports stadium from the window of my hotel. Iraqi familes strolled along the banks of the Tigris River bathed in the glow of headlights from the parade of cars that circled the city. I was kept awake by the celebrations of young Iraqi men. They formed small street bands. They would stop playing for a few moments to hug and kiss each other, overjoyed because they'd been spared the call-up for the front line.

Yet even in this joyous atmosphere there were reminders that Saddam's men were always watching. I had opened the wooden shutters of the hotel to take a picture of the Baghdad skyline. There were fireworks and lights over the sports stadium. Baghdad seemed liberated from the dark gloom that had blanketed this city in my previous visit. Within moments of snapping the flash there was a knock on my door. The man was in plain clothes, but it was clear he was an officer in one of Iraq's security services. "You must come with me now," he said. As if on cue, the phone rang. It was a man I knew from the Ministry of Information. He picked up the conversation as if he'd been in the room. "They say you've been taking pictures of the president's palace. They want the film and the camera," he said.

It had only taken a few minutes for them to see the flash of light from the watching post across the river from the hotel. They were at the right room within moments. I protested. I was indignant. I didn't know where the president's palace was! I was taking pictures of the stadium. It took the rest of the night to sort out the trouble. I got to keep my camera and the film, but I left Baghdad with a healthy respect for the thoroughness of Saddam's protectors.

By the time I reached the office in London a few hours after my editor's call, it was clear the Iraqi invasion of Kuwait was a success. The Iraqi army had thundered down the six-lane highway that connects Basra to Kuwait City. It had been an incredible show of naked force, far larger than was needed to subdue the Kuwaitis. Soviet-made T-72 tanks and armored fighting vehicles had spread out around the city. Dasman Palace had been captured. The emir's younger half-brother killed, his body run over by an Iraqi tank. The U.S. Embassy was surrounded. The top members of Kuwait's ruling family, the al Sabahs, had fled across the border to Saudi Arabia in a caravan of air-conditioned armor-plated luxury cars. The defense minister, Nawwaf al Sabah, had abandoned the Kuwaiti military and joined the royal exodus to save his own skin. The al Sabahs left everything behind, including their own people.

When the reports of the mass looting in Kuwait began I wondered what the marauding Iraqi army would make of Kuwait City's fabulous wealth. I was thinking in particular about the SafeWay. The American grocery store chain was as well stocked as any in a wealthy American suburb. The gleaming rows of stainless-steel freezer cabinets offered Sara Lee cheese cake, Lender's egg bagels, and Aunt Jemima frozen waffles. The large array of fresh fruits and vegetables flown in each day from Europe glimmered with a fine mist of water.

I imagined Iraqi soldiers in squat helmets riding the wide escalator to the second-floor sports department. There they would encounter the large display of black-topped Weber barbecue grills and plastic packages of mesquite and hickory wood chips. What would these conscripts from rural villages make of Kuwait's acquired taste for American barbecue cuisine? Eight years of the Iran-Iraq War and Saddam's relentless pursuit of weaponry had transformed one of the richest countries in the Gulf into an Arab have-not. Kuwait was the top of the line of the Arab-haves. The country was now one giant shopping mall for Iraqi looters.

Fuad al Ghanim watched the Iraqi invasion of his country from the deck of his 48-foot fishing boat, *Reema*. Ghanim spent the first night of August first fishing in the shallow waters of the Gulf. It's one of the few ways, short of flying to Paris (as many Kuwaitis did), to escape the paralyzing August heat. The boat's telephone rang before dawn. It was his brother calling. "The Iraqis are here," he said. As the pink summer light broke over Kuwait City, Fuad could see the Iraqi helicopter gunships sweeping over the capital. He quickly headed for home.

Ghanim was a successful Kuwaiti businessman, a member of one of Kuwait's merchant families who'd made his money in the construction business. Most of his work was done in Iraq. He had built water reservoirs and imported oil refinery equipment for the Iraqis. He'd believed in Saddam's crusade against the Islamic revolution in Tehran. Ghanim had contributed 5 million dollars of his own money to the Iraq war chest. He'd bailed out his Iraqi partners when money was tight in the war years. "When they didn't have a check for the equipment, I bought it for them," he said. He had contributed gold bars when the Iraqi government had gone door to door asking women to donate their gold jewelry for the fight against the Ayatollah. Six months before the invasion, Ghanim had formed the Iraqi-Kuwait Electro-Mechanical Contracting Company.

For Ghanim, the invasion of Kuwait was an outrage. His anger came in part because he had been betrayed by a friend. Al Ghanim was also angry at his country's response. There was no counterattack. The al Sabah family allowed the Iraqi army to take the country without a fight. There were more surprises waiting at home.

An Iraqi battalion had surrounded al Ghanim's house. Saddam needed a new Kuwaiti government to legitimate his conquest. Baghdad had nominated Fuad al Ghanim. "I thought they were looking for the minister of interior—he lived next door," said Ghanim. "Then the news came that they were looking for me."

As the United Nations Security Council condemned the invasion in New York, Baghdad radio announced that Iraq had sent troops to support a coup. A group calling itself the *transitional free government* announced on Kuwaiti radio that the emir had been deposed, the National Assembly dissolved. However, the transitional free government didn't exist. At a local hotel, Kuwaitis who were known to be active in Kuwait's opposition movement were being pressured to join.

Before the invasion, Saddam kept a close watch on the dissidents in Kuwait. He invited opposition figures to Baghdad in the months before the invasion. They talked with the Iraqis about their dissatisfaction with the al Sabah regime. But while Saddam may have known much about the Kuwaiti opposition, he had understood nothing about their loyalties. The dissatisfaction with the al Sabahs didn't translate into support for Iraq.

"The commander of the brigade didn't have a picture of me so I went outside and told them that Fuad al Ghanim had left the country," Fuad al Ghanim said. He waited in his house for four days and then went underground to join a resistance movement that was organizing neighborhood by neighborhood.

Resistance meetings were held in local mosques and cemeteries. The resisters armed themselves with the most useful weapon against those intent on dismantling their state: the satellite telephone. It gave the resistance movement a voice to the outside world. They talked to Kuwaiti exiles in Saudi Arabia and faxed intelligence reports on the deployment of the Iraqi army.

"We smuggled in more phones through Saudi Arabia and Jordan," al Ghanim said. The same route that produced telephones was used to bring in cash. Some of the money came from Iraq—more than 7 million Iraqi dinars for the Kuwaiti resistance. "This story I can't tell until Saddam is gone," said al Ghanim.

Fuad al Ghanim turned the skills that had made his family successful traders toward organizing the distribution of food and money for Kuwaiti neighborhoods. "We were the civil administration in the first six weeks of the occupation in our neighborhood," he said.

There was a military arm of the resistance as well. Teenagers joined in armed bands, shopkeepers hid weapons in the basement, and military officers raided the country's arsenals. The Iraqi occupation of residential areas was not complete until the last week of August. The resistance had more than three weeks to organize and begin harassing attacks on the occupation army.

In those first weeks rumors circulated among the resistance groups that an unlikely group of men had joined the movement. They were offering to share their knowledge of unconventional warfare. In the first hours of the invasion, Kuwait's jails were opened, releasing sixteen of the best bomb experts in Kuwait.

Three years earlier, the sixteen had worked to undermine the Kuwaiti state. They were the sons of Kuwaiti Shiite Muslims. They had embraced the call for militancy from the Shiite Muslim revolutionaries across the Gulf in Tehran. They abhorred their government's support for Saddam in the Iran-Iraq War. There was evidence that they had trained in Iran and Lebanon. In January 1987, the group placed a small bomb in a Kuwait police station and in an oil installation. That year Kuwait City was the site of an Organization of Islamic Conference meeting. Iran had boycotted the conference and demanded that other states do the same. The young Kuwaiti bombers put muscle in the Iranian threat. In the first weeks of the Iraqi occupation three members of the group joined the Kuwaiti resistance and shared their knowledge of plastic explosives and car bombs with Kuwaitis who were new to this kind of warfare.

For eight years most Kuwaitis gave their full support to Saddam's war against Iran. Many Kuwaiti families had pictures of the Iraqi leader displayed in their living rooms. The conflict cost Kuwait in domestic tensions between its own Shiite minority and the Sunni Muslim majority. Kuwaiti newspapers carried more articles in praise of Saddam than of the al Sabahs. While the ruling family ran the affairs of state, Saddam spoke to Kuwait's dreams. August 2, 1990, jolted Kuwait to reality.

I was in Kuwait when the sixteen bombers were arrested in 1987. I had come to cover the meeting of the Islamic Conference Organization. The Kuwaitis had built a 400-million-dollar conference center for the meeting that covered nearly 100 acres. It was a testament to oil wealth and the protection it could buy. The delegates were there to find an end to the Iran-Iraq War. The Palestine Liberation Organization (PLO) chairman, Yasser Arafat, offered to serve as a negotiator between the two warring states. The Palestinian leader had good relations with the Iraqis and was still welcome in Tehran.

One evening I made an appointment to see a top-ranking PLO official. His office was in a palatial suite in one of Kuwait City's grander hotels. I was ushered into the living room of the suite and told to wait. The meeting had been postponed for about a half hour. I was not alone.

On the couch, a group of Palestinian journalists were engrossed in a cartoon show on Kuwaiti television. For what seemed like an hour, these men watched, in rapt silence, the "Tom and Jerry" show, a cartoon war of cat and mouse. The show was rumored to be the favorite of the PLO chairman, Yasser Arafat. As the cartoon concluded, one of the journalists noticed for the first time that I was in the room. He took a long draw on his cigarette and asked, "Who are you for, Tom or Jerry?"

It was a serious question. I thought about it for a moment. Who was I for? Tom or Jerry? I had no answer. I didn't watch cartoons this way. But for these Palestinians, the never-ending war between the cat and the mouse was a symbol of how the region worked. Palestinians and other Arabs were used to watching their leaders fight and make up. They were used to corrupt Arab governments fighting among themselves. Sometimes you were up and sometimes you were down, but the battle was endless.

The year 1990 was a rare year in Arab history. It was the year that Arab leaders had to decide who they were for, Tom or Jerry. For the Arab people it was a rare year too. For the first time they were not just passive observers to the regional fights among their leaders. Everyone had to choose who they were for and they knew it was a choice that would mark a generation.

Events that brought the Middle East from the margins of historical change began with the Soviet withdrawal from Afghanistan in 1988. Arab leaders were surprised by the weakness of the USSR. Arab regimes depended, in part, for their survival on playing the Soviet or the American card.

The collapse of eastern Europe was an additional shock to Middle Eastern dictators wise enough to grasp the implication. There were rumors that Syria's Revolutionary Command Council watched video tapes of the last days of Romania's dictator, Nicolae Ceausescu. Other reports said Saddam had shown the video tape to his Revolutionary Command Council. Arab leftists scrambled for a new definition of their political stands.

Saddam recalled his ambassadors in Cuba, Albania, and Vietnam for a firsthand assessment of the implications. He argued publicly that Arabs should invest petrodollars in the USSR to keep Moscow interested in the region, but Moscow was more interested in the West.

Saddam lost an important plank in a policy that had served him throughout the Gulf War. He was a master at playing the superpower game. He bought arms from the Soviets for his war against Tehran; Washington came to his aid when it looked like he was in danger of losing to the Ayatollah. The old system of superpower rivalry in the Middle East had ended and no one was sure about the rules of the new game.

Saddam courted the Middle East moderates during the Iran-Iraq War. The wartime relationship with Washington and the conservative Gulf Arab states shaved the hard edges from Baghdad's radical rhetoric. Saddam had shelved his call for a Gulf free of outside powers when he needed U.S. warships to confront the Iranians in the oil shipping lanes of the Gulf. His stand on a solution to the Arab-Israeli conflict was in keeping with the moderate position of a "Two-State Solution" proposed by the PLO and backed by Cairo, Amman, and Riyadh. However, his proclaimed victory in the Iran-Iraq War was a watershed. His "victory" over Iran fueled his dreams of power beyond the borders of his birthplace. Saddam saw his rightful province as the leader of the Arab world. He had sacrificed Iraq's wealth and mobilized his country to guard the eastern flank of the Arab world from the Persian clerics. The military collapse and political disarray in Tehran gave him confidence that his destiny was ordained. After all, he had been funded by the Gulf states, armed by Europe, South America, and the Soviet Union, and befriended by Washington.

In 1980, Iraq's military was an untested force of less than 200,000 men. In the summer of 1988, Saddam was the commander and chief of a million-man battle-hardened army, the largest force in the Middle East, the fourth largest army in the world.

At the same time, Iraq's economy was in shambles. The regime was 80 billion dollars in debt. There were no jobs for the returning veterans, no way to demobilize the military. While the Arabs who had bankrolled his military campaign might be squeezed to forgive his wartime debt, Western bankers wanted their money back on time.

Saddam had enough oil to finance his ambitions, but he needed cash to develop the resource. The Kuwaitis and other Gulf oil producers were making his position more difficult by pumping too much oil and driving down the price of oil at precisely the time that Saddam needed the hard currency.

In less than a year after the war, Saddam's rhetoric began to change. He started to offer an alternative to the moderate landscape staked out by the Egyptians, Jordanians, and Saudis. He began to appeal to popular sentiments at a time when two trends gave the message extra spin. Arab governments such as Egypt, Jordan, Algeria, and Morocco were loosening the controls over their populations. It was a time of democratic experiments and the Islamic movements, with their pan-Arab nationalism dressed up with Islamic credentials, were gaining power in a number of Arab countries.

Saddam always told his people that the revolution chooses its enemies. He played that card in 1969 when the regime claimed to have discovered an underground pro-Israel spy ring. Fourteen "spies" were condemned to death, ten of them Jews, the others Christians and Muslims. The day of the hanging was a public holiday and Saddam rode through Baghdad's public square in an open car seated next to the president, al Bakr.

He had chosen his enemy again in 1989. An Iranian-born English journalist, Farzad Bazoft, was tried after he confessed to spying for Israel. Bazoft's death by hanging on March 20, 1990, outraged the West. Bazoft's "crime" appears to have been his bad timing and his place of birth.

Bazoft was arrested after he was caught investigating a mysterious explosion at the Al Qa'qa weapons plant, an hour's drive from Baghdad. He wasn't the first journalist to make the journey to Al Qa'qa. A day earlier a British television team arrived at the front gate only to be turned back by Iraqi authorities. Bazoft was open about his quest. He told Iraqi officials he was going to make the trip and he talked about his plans with his editor in London on a phone line that was surely bugged.

Most Arab governments supported Saddam's decision to hang Bazoft. The Kuwaiti press was particularly harsh in condemning the journalist. The Iraqis were dismissive of British complaints. In the past, the Europeans had shown that business was more important than moral considerations when dealing with Iraq.

Two days after the death of Farzad Bazoft, another murder, this time in Brussels, raised the temperature in Baghdad. Gerald Bull, a Canadian-born scientist, was said to be working on a "super gun" for Saddam's regime. His death, an assassination-style killing on March 22, was widely reported to have been the work of the Israelis.

In May 1990, Saddam spoke at a conference of Islamic clerics about Bazoft. "They attack us from different directions. They say we shouldn't hang the spy, Farzad Bazoft. But what they really want is to control Iraq and make it a backwater place where all the spies can go

free and Iraq will be destroyed from within. And then they will just
take Iraq's strength away."

By the late summer of 1990, Saddam Hussein had enlarged his
enemies list. He spoke out against American power at a meeting in
Amman. He threatened to burn half of Israel in a speech in Baghdad.
At an Arab summit Saddam demanded concessions from Kuwait and
revived a long-standing border dispute with his southern neighbors.
Saddam presented his case and in a way predicted his own hostility.
The warnings went unheard in Washington until the early hours of
August 2, 1990.

In a kind of schoolyard logic, few Arabs regretted what they saw as
the end of the al Sabah regime. The Kuwaitis were not popular in the
Arab world. They flaunted their money in places like Beirut, Cairo,
and London. Their sons drove fancy cars and were considered politically empty by the Palestinians who ran their affairs. The word arrogant
was often used to describe the rich sheikhs who cared more about race
horses than the Arab poor.

A non-Kuwaiti Arab could spend his whole working career in Kuwait
and find himself chucked out of the country two weeks after his re-
tirement. Kuwaiti citizenship worked like a membership to an exclusive
country club. A noncitizen could not own property and had limited
legal rights. Nevertheless, Kuwait offered good jobs with good pay
and the Arabs who went there, mostly Palestinians, swallowed their
resentments and banked their checks.

The ruling families of the Gulf were seen as squanderers of the oil
wealth. A generation reared on the romantic notions of pan-Arabism
regarded Gulf oil as a resource to restore the power of all the Arabs.
The Kuwaitis were like rich relatives who had made a fortune from
the family's savings and wondered why all the other relatives were still
eating hamburger.

That Saddam's invasion was cruel was understood by the majority
of Arabs who followed the events, but the invasion also tapped a well
of popular support for the Iraqi dictator. It wasn't so much that the
Arabs of the street were endorsing this brutal tyrant. They were supporting his challenge to the established order of the Arab world—the
hardened arteries of power.

After the invasion it was open season on established order. Even
Tunisia, the most democratic and moderate of the Arab states, was
swept along with the tide. The middle ground was fast disappearing as
the major Arab players were called upon to take sides.

On August 10, Arab kings, emirs, and dictators arrived at the Cairo airport for an Arab summit in the stifling humidity of an Egyptian summer. An Egyptian military band played the accompaniment to embraces of public friendship while inside the conference hall in Nasser City there was an atmosphere of animosity and intrigue. These men had ruled the Arab world for years. They supported each other. They plotted against each other, but while their conflicts were temporary, their unity was permanent. Or so it seemed.

They believed in Arab unity, "the one Arab nation with an immortal mission." They preached it as a daily code of inter-Arab politics. It worked like the dynamics of the Arab family: I against my brother; I and my brother against my cousin; I and my cousin against the world. The trouble was, over the past decade the realities of national interests and the differences in national ambitions had undermined the workings of this family. In Cairo "the family" was on the brink of fratricide.

Saddam had called for an Arab solution; his appeal was to Arab self-determination. However, his stand was based on a colossal miscalculation. While his Arab brothers had little sympathy for Kuwait, they moved against him because he threatened them. Saddam assumed that the Arab haves and the Arab have-nots would find no common ground, but Saddam was wrong.

For the Syrian leader, Hafez al Asad, Saddam not only represented a rival wing of the Ba'th party but he had challenged Syria's role in Lebanon by arming Maronite Christian General Michael Aoun. It had been payback time. Al Asad's support of Tehran during the Gulf War had enraged the Iraqi leader. Meddling in what Syria considered its backyard was a way to even the score. Now, it was payback time again.

Saddam's invasion of Kuwait was seen as an enormous blunder in Damascus. Al Asad was one of the first Arab leaders to condemn the occupation and call for an Arab summit. The stakes were in Syria's favor. With Saddam tied down in Kuwait, al Asad would have a free hand in Lebanon. The Syrian economy was in trouble and the prospect of Saudi aid was appealing. Perhaps the most compelling consideration was the chance to jump start better relations with the United States and Europe.

For Egyptian President Hosni Mubarek there was domestic enmity against the Baghdad regime. After the Iran-Iraq War, planes out of Baghdad were always brimming with Egyptian workers returning from their work contracts in Iraq. Many had been dragooned into front-line duty in the Gulf War. Others had been dismissed to make room for returning Iraqi veterans. Some were cheated out of their pay. More and more Egyptians came home from Baghdad in coffins, the victims of violent crimes dismissed by the Baghdad regimes as "accidents."

Much of Cairo's leftist intellectual elite were opposed to Mubarek's support for American forces in Saudi Arabia. For them, Saddam was a distant tyrant, and the notions of pan-Arabism shaped their response. However, the Egyptian street and important religious leaders backed Mubarek's decision to join the American-led coalition. Many of Egypt's workers had experienced the brutality of the Iraqi regime up close and had a better measure of the man. A leading sheikh wrote a Fatwa justifying Mubarek's stand: "The tyranny has to be contained lest his tyranny spread." Later a significant number of the religious community, the ulema, rejected invitations to a religious gathering in Baghdad.

At the time of the Arab summit, the *U.S.S. Eisenhower* was already cruising through the Suez Canal with the permission of the Egyptian government. Mubarek had been in close consultation with the Bush administration from the early hours of the crisis.

The Arab summit opened as American combat troops and American warplanes were speeding toward the region. There were two issues on the table in Cairo: the invasion and the first massive American deployment in the Arab world. The Bush administration sent a letter to each Arab leader to say that the United States expected a clear-cut condemnation of the invasion. Meanwhile, Baghdad radio was broadcasting a steady stream of justifications for the invasion. Saddam invaded Kuwait in the name of all "zealous Arabs who believe the Arab nation is one nation." He was Robin Hood, stealing from the rich Kuwaitis to help the poor. After all, he argued, the oil belonged to all of the Arabs. When American troops arrived in Saudi Arabia, Saddam coupled his pan-Arab appeals with Islamic arguments. The American military presence in the holy places was a desecration. "Unbelievers and Jews" controlled the Prophet's tomb.

Saddam had put the Kuwaitis in their place. He was defying the moral and military might of the United States. In the minds of many Arabs, that meant he was defying Israel. Saddam was like a game show host offering fabulous prizes to a population that desperately wanted a new deal. All he was asking in return was a leap of faith and a denial of reality.

At the Cairo summit the Libyan leader Muammar Qaddafi, clad from head to toe in a white robe, was the last to enter the conference room. Qaddafi was the Arab world's best performance artist. His antics at Arab summits were often an indicator of the tensions behind closed doors. In an Arab summit in Algeria in 1988, Qaddafi had worn one white glove to show his displeasure at touching the hand of King Hassan of Morocco. There were reports at the time that Hassan had met secretly with Israel's Labor leader, Shimon Peres. Qaddafi smoked a fat Cuban cigar throughout the meeting to annoy Saudi Arabia's King Fahd, an "American lackey" in Qaddafi's eyes.

Qaddafi was subdued for this gathering. He dampened his public anti-American rhetoric for the summit. The precedent of a large, but poor, neighbor gobbling up a small oil-rich country was not lost on the Libyan leader. In the months preceeding the invasion his relations with his pro-American neighbors in Cairo were improving. This meeting was too important for dramatic gestures, even for Qaddafi.

Jordan's King Hussein warned that intimidation would not work on Saddam. The Jordanian monarch called on the Arab world to resolve the occupation within the Arab family. Colonel Qaddafi came with his own peace plan, a call for Saddam's withdrawal from Kuwait coupled with an Arab peacekeeping force to replace the Americans. PLO Chairman Yasser Arafat had another plan. He suggested sending six Arab leaders to Baghdad to negotiate withdrawal with the Iraqi leader. Arafat proposed that Hosni Mubarek lead the delegation.

It's unlikely that the Saudis would have accepted an "Arab solution" even if these Arab leaders had been able to bury their differences and agree to send an Arab replacement for the U.S. forces. From the first hours of the crisis, two Saudi officials, one an aristocratic bedouin, the other a diplomatic street fighter, were defining their country's strategy. While the older generation of the House of Saud had set the tone, the younger generations of princes were running the show.

Saudi Arabia's Minister of State for Foreign Affairs Saud al Faisal had worked hard a week earlier to get a meeting of Arab foreign ministers in Cairo to endorse a strong condemnation of Saddam's invasion despite a warning from Saddam that a condemnation would prolong the occupation of Kuwait. The Saudis released their own English translation of the foreign minister's statement in Washington. The translation eliminated the ambiguities of the Arabic, and contained a clear condemnation of Saddam's invasion.

The Egyptian leader closed the circle at the Arab summit. Hosni Mubarek, the most pro-American of the participants, tabled only one resolution. As the summit chairman, Mubarek allowed no alternative proposals to come to a vote. Mubarek's resolution combined the two most important issues of the conference: condemnation of the Iraqi invasion and support for Saudi Arabia's invitation to American forces.

The summit was hot-tempered and unpredictable, like a knife fight in Los Angeles. There had never been an Arab summit quite like this one. In one session the Libyan leader, Colonel Qaddafi, had screamed at Mubarek in an uncontrollable rage that Mubarek was a "tool of the Americans." Syria's President Hafez al Asad had smoothed the tempers of the two men. Asad's diplomacy prompted Mubarek to extend to the colonel an invitation to lunch.

The encounters between the Kuwaiti and Iraqi delegations were electric. A day before the summit Iraq had announced the annexation of Kuwait as its nineteenth province. In one encounter, Iraqi Foreign Minister Tariq Aziz confronted the Kuwait prime minister and told him he had "the tapes." Apparently these were personal video tapes that Iraqi soldiers had collected at the prime minister's quarters in Kuwait. Prime Minister Sheikh Saad al Sabah was known to have exotic tastes and the news of the "tapes" made him apoplectic.

Saad al Sabah responded by making a reference to the fact that Aziz is a Christian, a remark intended as a slur. Aziz heaved an ashtray at him. The atmosphere was too much for Kuwait's foreign minister, who fainted, to be revived by Yasser Abed Rabbo, a member of the PLO delegation.

The wrangling inside the summit was reflected in the outside world. The Arab world divided itself in Cairo. For the first time ever an Arab summit ended with a majority vote rather than a consensus as twelve out of twenty-one Arab government officials decided to support the Egyptian resolution. The next day the first contingent of Egyptian troops arrived in Saudi Arabia. Morocco and Syria announced they would be sending troops as well.

The decision at the Arab summit amounted to a declaration of a civil war. The Cairo summit defined a broad alliance for the future. The new axis in the Arab world put Saudi Arabia, Egypt, Morocco, and Syria on the side of the powerful Western coalition. It was the same coalition that dominated Arab politics in the 1970s. Jordan, the PLO, Libya, and Yemen tilted toward Iraq.

The first battles were conducted over the airwaves of the Arab world. Saudi Arabian television broadcast bedouin poets condemning Saddam in the flowery language of the Arabian desert. Saddam countered with Iraqi poets recounting the tales of immorality among the sheikhs of the conservative Gulf states.

In Jordan, news commentators lashed out at the Saudis for inviting American troops: "We don't ask for the impossible. We only ask in hope and fear and confidence that you not allow your mustache to be used as a shoestring in the enemy's boots."

In a Saudi Arabian–financed newspaper, an article entitled "What does the Iraqi President's Gibberish Mean?" said that Saddam had the "nerve" to claim he was a direct descendant of Prophet Mohammad, "a claim that was unheard of until ten years ago."

Salah Muntaser, an Egyptian commentator, said, "the saddest and most painful site" was television footage of Palestine Liberation Chairman Yasser Arafat and Saddam Hussein embracing in the Iraqi capital of Baghdad. "We find you engaged in quite another strategy, the strategy of who pays, who transfers [funds] and who signs the checks. Enjoy your new deity, oh symbol of Palestinians struggle . . . God save this nation from its heroes!"

For years, Yasser Arafat had played Arab politics like musical chairs. When the music stopped on August 2, he found himself sharing a seat with Saddam Hussein. Arafat broke the cardinal rule of Palestinian politics: He had gotten too close to one Arab leader at the expense of relations with other Arab backers.

There is an old Palestinian political joke. It concerns a trip by Arafat and his executive committee to the Hajj in Mecca. Part of the tradition of the Muslim pilgrimage includes a ceremony of throwing stones at the devil. Arafat is missing from the ceremony and one of the members of his delegation inquires about where he is. "He's not here because he never breaks relations with anyone, not even the devil." Now Arafat had limited his flexibility.

Arafat made the best of the situation. He pressed the Iraqi leader to link his occupation of Kuwait with Israel's occupation of the West Bank and Gaza. Arafat's lieutenants insisted until the day of the ground war that Arafat had stayed close to Saddam to talk reason to the Iraqi leader. The French, the Italians, and even the Pope had sent messages through the PLO to Baghdad. There was reason to believe in Tunis that a successful PLO peace initiative could change the fortunes of the Palestinians.

Arafat had the burden of satisfying a number of Palestinian constituencies with conflicting interests. Arafat was a canny assessor of the trends in these communities and responded in a more democratic way than most of his Arab brothers. While there were 400,000 Palestinians in Kuwait with their lives and fortunes in ruins, Arafat's largest and most important constituencies lived in Jordan and in Israeli-occupied territories.

The Palestinian uprising was three years old and desperate. Saddam's stance over the past few months made sense to the young Palestinians on the streets of Nablus and Gaza. Saddam preached what day-to-day life had taught them: As long as the Arabs were militarily and economically weak, there was no way to oust the Israelis from the occupied territories and establish a Palestinian state. Saddam's creed was to harness Arab wealth under the banner of pan-Arabism. Arab wealth must be invested in the Arab world rather than abroad to serve a pan-Arab military buildup, he said. He called for a special fund to support the uprising.

In early April, Saddam threatened to burn half of Israel if Israel attacked him with nuclear weapons. He proposed that, "If any aggression is committed against an Arab and that Arab seeks our assistance from afar, we won't fail to come to his assistance." The speech received wide support from Palestinians in Israel's occupied territories. Saddam was seen as an Arab leader with the guts to stand up to Israel. Saddam, like other Arab leaders before him, was playing the "Palestinian card." It became available in the spring of 1990.

Time had not been kind to the Palestinians. The winter of 1989 had been a time of hope. The Bush administration opened a dialogue with the Palestine Liberation Organization after a thirteen-year break. The Israeli response had been to offer an election proposal: Palestinians from the West Bank and Gaza would elect representatives who would begin a dialogue with the Israelis on peace negotiations.

Washington was working with Egypt to broker the proposal with the PLO. With quiet prodding from the Saudis and the Egyptians, Yasser Arafat signed on. At the news, local Palestinian leaders began to squabble over a seat at the proposed Palestinian-Israeli peace talks in Cairo. Optimism led to visions of positions in the local governments in Nablus and Hebron.

By early spring, hope turned to bitter disappointment. Israel's Prime Minister Yitzhak Shamir had rejected his own proposal for limited Palestinian rule. It was clear he would block even preliminary Israeli-Palestinian meetings. When Washington applied pressure to Israel's coalition government it collapsed. In the scramble to put together a new government two events sealed the fate of the peace talks.

In May a deranged Israeli soldier opened fire on Palestinian workers, killing seven. The PLO leader pressed for a meeting of the United Nations Security Council to discuss the murders. As the United Nations met in Geneva, the second event changed the course of the proceedings. An armed group of Palestinians based in Baghdad and funded by Libya mounted a failed boat attack on a beach near Tel

Aviv. The group's leader, Abul Abbas, was well known. He had orig-
inated the attack on the Italian cruise liner the *Achille Lauro.*

The next day the United States voted against a United Nations
resolution to protect the Palestinians. Washington called on Arafat to
condemn the Tel Aviv attack and threatened to close the door on
future dialogue with the PLO. A PLO spokesman said it was impossible
to condemn the attack in light of the U.S. veto. The dialogue with the
PLO was suspended on May 20, 1990.

By early summer, there was palpable despair among the Palestinian
community. In Washington, both houses of Congress had supported
a resolution to move the American Embassy to Jerusalem, a tacit recognition of Israel's annexation of the city. The immigration of thousands of Soviet Jews to Israel threatened to deprive the Palestinians
of jobs and ultimately their homeland.

Moderate Palestinians admitted they were losing all credibility. A
hunger strike by Palestinian notables in Jerusalem mounted on the day
of the United Nations vote got little support. It wasn't so much that
the moderates were seen as traitors by the increasingly radical youth;
they were seen as fools. The mood of the street was: There was no
moderation moderate enough for this Israeli government. There was
nothing that the Palestinians could do to make a deal. Saddam offered an alternative strategy. He offered exactly what the Palestinians
lacked: power and a patron with a strong army to force Israel to the
table.

It was impossible for Palestinians living in squalid refugee camps
under Israeli occupation to identify with rich Kuwaitis now under Iraqi
occupation. Palestinian intellectuals were cowed into silence by the
emotions of the crowd. Any savior, even the devil himself, was a strand
of hope.

Like other Arab leaders before him, Saddam knew how to use the
Palestinian card. Saddam trumpeted the American double standard in
the crisis. The U.S. president had said he was sending American troops
to Saudi Arabia to "oppose aggression." The Palestinians felt they were
living examples of that lie. When Israel invaded Lebanon in 1982, the
United States had called it an "unprovoked aggression" but then
blocked United Nations sanctions.

Arafat appeared to be betting there would be a diplomatic resolution
to the conflict. After an interview in Tunis with an NBC television
reporter, Arafat argued that the United States would not go to war.
He was counting on U.S. fears of entanglement in a long drawn-out

war in a distant land and a low tolerance for American casualties. "Remember Vietnam," said Arafat. "Remember Afghanistan."

But Baghdad was not Afghanistan or Vietnam. Baghdad embraced a conventional approach to combat. Iraq decided to discard the unconventional system of battle and adopt the Western and Soviet models. Saddam bought conventional weapon systems or manufactured his own. His army's fighting doctrine was borrowed from Moscow. His tanks were bought there, too. His army had nothing in common with the lean guerilla fighting forces of Vietnam and Afghanistan.

Iraq and Saudi Arabia are, in part, vast deserts. It is perfect tank country. There is too much open space for guerilla warfare. The British had proved in the 1920s that superior air power could halt a desert ground attack. They had used biplanes to stop the desert legions of Saudi Arabia from overtaking Kuwait.

President George Bush said the confrontation with Iraq would not be another Vietnam. What he meant could be found in the American military journals published over the past decade. U.S. military officials had examined their military doctrine in Southeast Asia and reached a conclusion. There would be no "incremental escalation." The next war would be swift, massive, and incredibly violent. Arafat had drawn the wrong conclusions from Vietnam. His mistake would cost his people dearly.

In the first weeks of the Iraqi invasion television executives in the United Arab Emirates banned all television coverage of the Palestinian uprising. It was the first concrete sign that the Gulf states would turn against the Palestinians. Pictures of Palestinian teenagers confronting Israeli soldiers had been a daily staple of television news programs in the Gulf. The uprising was a touchstone of Arab sentiments. While the Western media had grown tired of the struggle, T.V. viewers in the Gulf saw the shabby streets of Nablus, Hebron, and Gaza every night. The uprising was the center of the news universe.

There was no official announcement of the end of "Palestinian" programming. The Palestinian uprising simply disappeared from the television screens. It was replaced by the news of another occupation and the nightly patriotic call for military volunteers.

In Dubai, it was the Kuwaitis who were learning firsthand what it meant to be a refugee. In the first weeks after the invasion this port city on the south edge of the Gulf became a refugee camp with the old and the newly dispossessed sharing the same space. The Palestinians had come years before. They had waited for a reversal of their fortunes and suppressed their rage and settled here. They helped to build Dubai and Abu Dhabi. They were Dubai's doctors and government administrators. They were another constituency for the PLO leadership and were public in their criticism of the Arafat policy.

The Kuwaitis weren't here to work. Unlike the Palestinians, they had the backing of the world community. They were here to wait as the world responded to their plight. They settled according to their status back home. Some checked into Dubai's five-star hotels; others found living accommodations in Dubai's shabbier offerings. The rich and the poor spilled into the hotel lobbies to drink coffee and monitor the news.

Kuwaiti "resistance" radio was on the air in the first weeks after the invasion. The station was strong on hope but sparse in details. The coverage was mostly patriotic songs and appeals to resist. Saudi Arabia and Dubai television broadcast special programs each night. The themes were the same: newly arrived refugees from Kuwait with fresh tales of Iraqi perfidy. The programs served as a locator service. In Dubai, the fifteen-minute nightly program was recorded in the lobby of a local hotel. Kuwaitis stood in front of the camera, one after another, and recited their names and hotel room numbers. Some looked like they had wandered into a police lineup. They blinked vacantly into the camera and recited their names in the hope that a missing relative would see them. The children were flustered by the adventure and reeled off their names and hotel room numbers with nervous energy.

Hussain Ishmail arrived in Dubai on the fourth of August. He had been on vacation with his family in Switzerland when Iraqi tanks rolled into his neighborhood. "It was like somebody hit me on the head with a hammer," he said. He took the family to Kuwait airlines in Geneva to buy a ticket home. He was told the airport in Kuwait City was closed and there were no flights available to Bahrain. Ishmail picked Dubai for his refuge. He had worked as a petro engineer at Kuwait's oil company. He had a master's degree from the University of Wisconsin and his English was flawless.

It was hard to think of him as a refugee. He rarely wore the white dishdasha, Kuwait's traditional white flowing robe. Hussain looked more comfortable in well-cut sports clothes. He wore designer tortoise-shell glasses and the small round frames gave him the look of an

American academic. He spent his days listening to the radio, watching the television news, and walking to the Intercontinental Hotel to read the Reuters wire. He carried with him the dull anger that Kuwaitis would carry home as the legacy of their exile.

"Our cities look modern; we drive modern cars," Ishmail lamented. "But the mentality, it's still the old mentality. We worship our leaders without question. Our destiny is still ruled by these individuals."

Ishmail sat with other Kuwaiti men in a hotel coffee shop and talked about democracy. Democracy was the answer. It was all so simple. I wondered why Ishmail hadn't thought of it before the invasion. The reason was clear enough. The al Sabahs had ensured prosperity. Life had been good in Kuwait. There were few complaints when the government had dissolved Kuwait's parliament in 1986 and then in 1990 had installed a hand-picked council just a few weeks before the Iraqi invasion.

Ishmail argued that now that Kuwaitis had sacrificed for their country they would demand a say in its future. It was his theme and his mantra in the free moments between tracking down the news from home and watching events unfold on television.

In the 1960s, after Kuwait won its independence from the British, the al Sabahs had established the first constitutional government in the Gulf. The country was known for its lively parliament and the most open press in the region. Kuwaitis were proud of their experiment in democracy and were contemptuous of their "backward" neighbors in the Gulf. The Iran-Iraq War sent doubts through the population about whether their democracy could protect them from the forces unleashed by the war. The fury of the fighting was right next door. The battles for Faw and Basra were so close to the Kuwait border that the glow from the explosions could be seen from northern Kuwait. The blast from the battles rattled windows in Kuwait City. Assassination attempts on the emir were the beginning of the end of Kuwait's experiments with democracy.

By the end of the war, the al Sabahs were comfortable with their role as unquestioned monarchs. They discounted the protests of Kuwait's small but well-organized pro-democracy groups. The younger Sabahs supported the moves of the older generation of rulers. Democracy could only dilute their heritage, prestige, and power. Most of the country was relieved that the Iran-Iraq War was over and the future belonged to those who could seize the postwar markets. The economies of the Gulf states turned Western notions of politics upside down. The slogan "No taxation without representation" was meaningless in an oil-financed total welfare state. There was money to be made and democracy could wait.

In the first weeks of the Iraqi invasion the al Sabahs sent family representatives to take charge of every important embassy. Trusted family members watched over the workings of the national airlines, Kuwait Air. The visions of Hussain Ishmail seemed idealistic in the face of the reality of the al Sabahs.

F O U R

THE SAUDIS

"My kingdom will survive only insofar as it remains a country difficult of access, where the foreigner will have no other aim, with his task fulfilled, but to get out."
—Abd al-aziz Ibn Saud

"The Saudi Doodie Show, the Saudi Doodie Show, come on and join the fun, the Saudi Doodie Show."
—Theme song for "The Wizard," a radio program
  broadcast on FM 106 Armed Forces Radio

"Let's go kick some Iraqi butt," said Captain Prince Fahd, an instructor at Tabuk Air Base. Fahd had done his military training at Fort Benning, Georgia. He had trained with the U.S. Rangers and the special forces. Fahd was also a prince in the House of Saud. This was the ticket that bought him a break from his job in Tabuk to drive south to King Fahd International Airport to look up some old American friends from school, American Special Forces officers Captain Brian Vines and Captain Randolf Binford. They were part of the Fifth Special Forces group from Fort Campbell, Kentucky.

Forward Operating Base 51 opened at King Fahd International Airport on September 4, 1990. Captain Prince Fahd's visit would be the best thing that had happened to Vines and Binford since they started their work in Saudi Arabia. The reunion would be instructive in how things got done in the Kingdom.

General H. Norman Schwarzkopf had a problem in the early days of Operation Desert Shield. He didn't know where the Arab armies were. Arab troops had disembarked at the Saudi port of Yanbu on the western coast, or had flown into one of Saudi Arabia's international airports. There was a welcoming ceremony and then the units were dispatched to set up camps in the northern desert plain between Riyadh and the Kuwait border.

The first few weeks brought the Egyptians, the Forty-fifth Syrian Commandos, and a Moroccan mechanized unit. Remnants of the Kuwaiti military had crossed the border to Saudi Arabia and were reorganizing, but there was no grand plan for their deployment in the desert. The first assignment for the Americans who trained for secret missions was to find the Arab front line.

The special forces team fanned out over the desert and discovered that the Arab armies had built their camps 20 kilometers from Saudi Arabia's northern border. Their report caused some concern with the Central Command generals. This was 20 kilometers of free territory if the Iraqi army chose to take it.

Schwarzkopf wanted the special forces teams up on the border running reconnaissance missions. He wanted an early warning system in place. The Saudi commander, Prince Khalid bin Sultan, balked. The border was a sensitive issue. For one thing, Saddam had moved his troops back 20 kilometers from the border, leaving 40 kilometers of free space for Kuwaitis who were moving in and out of the country. On more than one occasion, hungry Iraqi soldiers had strayed across this undefended territory to share a meal with their Saudi counterparts. The Saudis fed them and sent them back into occupied Kuwait with the acquiescence of General Khalid. "I told my troops, let them have lunch or dinner. I believe this will demoralize them when they see what kind of food we have for our troops."

In early September when a company of Iraqis were found wandering near the Saudi town of Kafji, Khalid ordered his commander to pack them a sumptuous meal and send them back to occupied Kuwait well fed. Saudis are hospitable by nature and Khalid had no grudge against the Iraqi army. His problems were with Saddam Hussein.

Khalid didn't want to risk an "incident" with Baghdad that would raise the more difficult question of fighting Iraq, and the 40-kilometer free zone lessened the chances of a stray artillery shell that forced a response. It appeared that the issue was closed until Captain Prince Fahd appeared.

"Captain Prince Fahd wanted to work out a joint reconnaissance team," said Captain Vines. "He told us, 'I can get 124 guys. I'll buy the radios and the trucks and be back in a couple of weeks.' " Vines and Binford acted on this stroke of good luck and arranged a meeting with Colonel Gerald Thompson, the First Battalion commander. After listening to the proposal, Thompson told Fahd that they couldn't get anyone in Riyadh to consider it. Captain Prince Fahd said he'd go talk to General Khalid himself.

"Fahd went to General Khalid bin Sultan, the Saudi commander of the joint forces. He laid out the plan," said Vines. In Saudi Arabia, a prince, even one who is a captain in the military, carries enough weight to get in to see the top brass. The Saudi general stonewalled the plan for the first few weeks, but Captain Fahd was persistent. He bought the trucks and the radios and he rounded up 124 Saudis. Then General Khalid made a bargain that was to be the model for much of the joint operations in the months to come: telling Fahd that he could mount a joint reconnaissance mission if the American Special Forces agreed to train the Saudis for thirty days. By mid-September the training was complete.

"We gave him six special forces teams to pair with his guys," said Vines. "We had border posts from Khafji to Rooqi, sixteen border stations. For the first time we could provide a six-hour early-warning system if the Iraqis came over the border. They were in place by the first week of October." The reconnaissance teams transformed the atmosphere on the border and marked one of the first steps toward the American management of the crisis. The special forces teams tightened the rules on the border, allowing Kuwaiti civilians to cross only with passports. The free dinners for Iraqi soldiers ended. Those who crossed the border were declared prisoners of war and were taken to the port of Jubail for processing.

For some of America's secret warriors, Desert Storm presented the kind of assignment that is described in the trade as the "snake-eating" variety. In the weeks of the air campaign against Iraq, special forces teams would fly helicopters behind Iraqi lines to rescue downed pilots. There were reports of special forces units in Baghdad armed with laser targeters to guide the American smart bombs to very particular targets. These assignments were in the future. In the early months of Operation Desert Shield, army special forces teams performed much more mundane duties. The Fifth Special Forces group were the chief instructors for the Arab armies, an extension of their years of training in the region.

The assignment was not as glamorous as blowing things up or creeping behind enemy lines, but it was a significant contribution to the success of the coalition. The 1990s version of the hearts and minds campaign of the Vietnam era was now called Foreign Internal Defense. "We promote stability by supporting local government. We help them gain credibility with their own people," explained a special forces colonel. For a number of years, these secret warriors had cultivated relationships with Arab armies, learned the language, and lived with their Arab counterparts during training exercises. In Operation Desert Shield, they had as many months as Saddam would give them to organize training plans for the Arab forces arrayed against him. As vital as the training in the Saudi desert was for the conduct of the war, these early days also served another purpose.

At the end of August, President George Bush had pledged, "Whatever else we do, we are not going to do it the Vietnam way." It was a short declarative sentence that left room for interpretation. For Colin Powell, his staff, and the Central Command field commanders, all decorated veterans of Vietnam, it had one important meaning. For years they had analyzed and reanalyzed the lessons of Vietnam and had come to the conclusion that gradual escalation had cost them the war. This time it would be different. This time Central Command would estimate, and it was shown later, overestimate, the manpower and equipment needed to get the job done. There would be no "show of force" in Saudi Arabia. A similar lesson had been learned in 1982 in Lebanon when President Reagan's policy of "establishing a presence" had disastrous consequences. As far as the Commanders of CENTCOM were concerned, this policy led to the deaths of 241 marines as they slept in their barracks in Beirut. "This time we're going to do it right," said Marine General Walter Boomer. It meant there would be a combined military and political operation in confronting Saddam Hussein.

By late September, Central Command planners were sketching out the details of the military part of the equation, the offensive campaign against the Iraqi army in occupied Kuwait. Army Brigadier General Steve Arnold arrived in Saudi Arabia on September 7, 1990, part of the Central Command planning staff. "By late September, we were discussing the offensive plan and we shifted from a single corps to a double corps," said Arnold. "We had a strong signal from Washington that we would get the second corps and we could help to define how it would be used. The reason we wanted the second corps was because

of the 'mother of all obstacles,' Saddam's mine fields, but the closer
we got to the ground war, the more we realized that we were going
out west and he hadn't built the mine fields out there."

President Bush kept the news from the American public until two
days after congressional elections. On November 8, he announced the
addition of 250,000 troops and 1000 tanks to the Gulf theater. It was
a surprise twist in the second act of a drama that had gripped the world
for three months, but for the military men in Riyadh who helped to
write the script the announcement came as no surprise. Bush portrayed
the second deployment as a defensive strategy. "The mission of our
troops is wholly defensive," he said in an address to the nation. "Hope-
fully they will not be needed long. They will not initiate hostilities,
but they will defend themselves, the kingdom of Saudi Arabia, and
other friends in the Gulf."

The November 8 announcement was a political watershed that fundamentally changed the debate in the United States. In the summer
and early fall, President Bush made stirring speeches telling Americans
that "aggression does not pay." He used the imagery of World War II
to proclaim his refusal to be "blackmailed" and spoke of the consequences of "appeasement." This package was like the nonalcoholic beer
that American soldiers were drinking in the sweltering Saudi desert:
a lot of foam but no kick. On November 8, President Bush publicly
switched the brew. Despite the president's pledge that Desert Shield
was a defensive operation, the stage was set to back up his words with
force.

"General Khalid was the first to be briefed on the American plan,"
said Army Brigadier General Steve Arnold. "There was only a handful
of people who knew the details in the Arab coalition. After Khalid
was briefed he kept the information in a closed circle. Then there was
work on a combined plan. A plan that included the Arab coalition and
the United States. It was more detailed because of the participation
of the Arab armies. Let me make a guess, this work started in November, right before the announcement in Washington of the additional troops. You'll recall we said they were coming for defense and
everybody believed that . . . sure they did."

For the Pentagon the second deployment fulfilled a political re-
quirement that grew out of the experience of Vietnam. Bush's announcement prompted the largest call-up of military reservists since
the Tet offensive in 1968. The American military had eliminated the
draft and in doing so had diminished the effect of public opinion on
American military campaigns. The call-up of reservists was built in to

correct the balance. The gathering storm in Saudi Arabia touched American families across the country as insurance salesmen, dry cleaners, office workers, and executives put on their desert camouflage and boarded military transport planes for Saudi Arabia. The officers of Desert Shield expected and welcomed the reaction at home. Saddam was an acceptable villain. This time the military would not be hung out to dry. There would be a consensus among the American people one way or the other. The ghost of Vietnam was exorcised on television screens across the United States as Americans became a debating society over the merits of a war with a third world dictator. Or that's how it seemed for those who were watching the reflections of the country on the television screens carrying CNN.

On the other side of the globe, 7000 miles away, Lieutenant Colonel Daniel Brownlee of the Fifth Special Forces group had a very special job. The public pronouncements of the Arab leaders of the coalition made a distinction between defending Saudi Arabia and attacking a fellow Arab country. The American planning staff in Riyadh had to cut through the Arab rhetoric to know which Arab armies would join the attack on Saddam's army.

"We were supposed to say who would fight. All during the defensive phase we were responding to one question, who was where and what were their intentions. Even General Khalid didn't know. He didn't want to ask directly. It was our job to ask the question," said Brownlee. Brownlee's men were in the right place to do the polling. Fifth Special Forces group units were assigned to every Arab battalion in the theater. They asked the question each week and sent the answers to Riyadh.

"There was never any question about the Kuwaitis," said Brownlee. The Fifth Special Forces group helped to reorganize the Kuwaiti units in disarray after the Iraqi invasion. It was not a simple job. The Kuwaiti Commandos, a battalion of more than 500 men, had recruits that were former frog missile commanders, policemen, and royal palace guards. The Forty-third Kuwaiti Brigade was a Soviet-trained, Soviet-equipped unit, the result of a Kuwaiti military and foreign policy that balanced relations between the two superpowers. Warrant Officer Jeffrey King, assigned to train the Forty-third, had to tailor American fighting doctrine for a Kuwaiti unit that had radios from Czechoslovakia, armored personnel carriers from the Soviet Union, and fifteen different brands of machine guns.

"The Egyptians said, 'We'll go tomorrow'," said Brownlee. "They were enthusiastic enough to say, 'Let's go to Baghdad.' They had one caveat: They'd only go under the direction of U.S. command and control." The Egyptian army had trained with the Americans for years in the exercises known as Bright Star. The coalition organizational chart placed the Egyptian army under the control of General Khalid ibn Sultan, the Saudi commander. The war-fighting plan placed the Egyptians on the right flank of the American Seventh Corps.

"The Syrian answer was straightforward," said Brownlee. "They said they wouldn't go over the Saudi border under any circumstances. It was party line." President Hafez al Asad had made the political distinction between defending Saudi Arabia and an offensive war against another Arab country, a position in keeping with his pan-Arab rhetoric. His army followed the rules until the second day of the ground war when the victory was clear.

"Nobody knew what the Moroccans would do," said Brownlee. King Hassan of Morocco was one of the first Arab leaders to condemn the Iraqi invasion and he pledged troops to defend Saudi Arabia at the Arab summit in August. Hassan sent an elite motorized brigade and they were attached to Joint Forces East under the Saudi command, but Iraq's defiance was popular in Morocco. In December, a twenty-four-hour strike by two of Morocco's main trade unions ended in the deaths of at least five people. The unrest in Morocco was reflected in the Moroccan army's attitude in the Saudi desert. "When the plan shifted from defense to offense, we still didn't know what the Moroccans would do," said Brownlee.

In the Saudi Arabian capital, Riyadh, the Akariyeh Shopping Mall was a testament to the comfortable marriage of religion and materialism. The American T.V. evangelists who preach the gospel of guilt-free material well being would have felt at home in Saudi Arabia. Their counterparts, the mutoween, Saudi Arabia's religious police, patrolled the marble shopping arcade for sinners, but the sin of overspending was not on their list. The mall and others like it were Saudi Arabia's version of the traditional Arab souk with track lighting and marble replacing the long dark corridors of stalls and spicy smells. The sound of shoppers was hushed by the steady stream of falling water from the decorative fountains that graced the walkways. Among the displays of gold jewelry, sporting equipment, perfumes, and fabrics, Armed Force Radio 107 blared from the black walnut veneer display speakers in the hi-fi shop: "This goes out to Tina from the Sixteenth Aerial Force squadron and to the MPs from the secret cop, Phil Collins, and I don't care anymore."

The mutoween, assigned to watch over the customers in this shop, scowled and stayed close to the speaker lest some contamination from the heathen army in the desert befall his flock. It was a hopeless gesture. In a country where the American rap group Two Live Crew sells well and teenage Saudis sported one white glove at the peak of Michael Jackson's popularity, FM 107 was a hit. Car radios in the capital were tuned to Saudi Arabia's first rock-and-roll station. Professors at King Saud University listened to every word of the American newscasts on the hour. In Saudi Arabia's eastern province, CNN could be snatched out of the air from stations in Bahrain.

Saudi Arabia's hawks and doves were a different breed than their American counterparts. They listened patiently to the president's arguments about appeasement and the parallels with World War II, but they understood Saddam Hussein better than Bush's American audience. For them it had little to do with World War II and everything to do with regional politics with its roots in the distinction between the Gulf Peninsula Arabs and those of the Levant and Fertile Crescent.

For the Saudis on both sides of the debate, Saddam Hussein's invasion represented a monumental failure of the Arab system. His military conquest of Kuwait meant that the Arab world had lost control of its sovereign affairs. In the eyes of most Saudis, the Iraqi leader was to blame for the decision that brought American soldiers to pitch their tents on Saudi soil. The Americans were in the desert not because Saudi Arabia loved the U.S. military but because the Saudis hated and feared Saddam Hussein.

In the Saudi perception, the fault also rested with those progressive Arabs who had bankrupted the region with their "progressive" ideologies. It was the urban Arabs, the city dwellers, who had brought on this calamity. They had looked down on their "backward" desert cousins as simple bedouins or rich religious fanatics who were ruled by feudal monarchs. It was the more "advanced" Arabs who had written the agenda of the Arab world. Although Saudis had complaints about the House of Saud, it was far preferable to anything offered in Baghdad, Beirut, or Damascus. Saudis saw that Iraq's invasion of Kuwait was a symptom of a larger disease that they were now free to talk about. In October, the *Wall Street Journal* published an article by Abdulazziz H. Fahad, a young Saudi lawyer:

> The Arab intellectual spared no effort to construct impressive theoretical rationales for the unification of the disparate Arab countries. Yet most of these constructs managed to be oblivious to the stubborn facts of Arab diversity. The most dangerous aspect of this

exercise, however, was the intellectuals' failure to integrate democratic concepts in their ideas.

Yes, there were obsequious references to "democracy" and "freedom" as well as "Arab" socialism. . . . Those intellectuals waxed el-
oquent about democratic centralism and other nonsensical ideas. As
a result, the world is undergoing revolutionary democratic changes,
while many Arabs seem to be marching to a different discordant
tune.

For Saudi hawks and doves, the Iraqi invasion was a great political
awakening. All camps began to shed the inferiority complex that had
marked the Gulf Arabs as they made critical judgments of their so-
called advanced Arab brothers. Saddam Hussein charged that the Saudi
royal family had squandered millions of unearned oil wealth. While
Saudis admitted the truth of that statement, they also pointed out that
the House of Saud had also spent millions on education, health care,
infrastructure, and services. The government was unquestionably liberal in economic matters. Compared with Syria's 92 percent tax on
profits, the Saudis were unrestricted in their ability to make money.
The government proved the point in the first panicky days after the
August invasion when Saudis transferred billions out of the country.
When it was clear that the government would place no restrictions on
the transfers, many Saudis confidently brought their money back home.

In late summer 1990, Saudi Arabians looked around and saw that
they lived in a country materially better off than most of their neighbors, with a prosperous, educated middle class who preferred to stay
at home rather than emigrate to the West. While political dissidents
in the kingdom found that their passports were revoked, and Saudi
Arabia's Shiite minority did not always share equally with the country's
Sunni majority, most Saudis were free of what Abdul Azziz H. Fahad
called "the government of midnight visitors," the late-night knock on
the door from the secret police that was a regular feature of life in
Damascus or Baghdad. Saudi liberals complained about the limits of
their local newspapers. They grumbled when foreign papers hit the
newsstands with articles edited by government censors, but most had
fax machines and had a regular flow of the edited articles. For Saudi
men, travel abroad was unrestricted.

In Egypt, Arab intellectuals had argued that the Americans were
shoring up a corpse. They predicted that Saddam's invasion was the
beginning of the end of the feudal Gulf Arab regimes. It was a view
shared by Saddam Hussein. In September, a respected Egyptian in-

tellectual, Mohamed Heikal, wrote an editorial in the *Times* of London arguing that the heart of the crisis was the conflict between the desert people and the city people; the issue was one of the gap between the rich and the poor, not the lack of democracy.

The borders of the Gulf countries sprang from the British genius for creating situations which could provide reasons to keep return-ing. We in the Arab world accepted those borders as a means to bring the imperial era to an end. . . . The struggle for independence and ownership of the oil was conducted in the cities Cairo, Baghdad, Damascus, Beirut, but ultimately it was the tribal leaders who gained the oil. The cities were deprived of the fruits of their struggle.

After the departure of the British the first generation of tribal leaders behaved responsibly, respecting the implied contract of trust with the cities. Their children, however, grew up believing they had a right to rule. As each family grew in size it came to form the entire administration. In Saudi Arabia the royal family consists of 6500 to 7000 people: They take everything.

A new world order is emerging, but Arabs are at risk of being excluded. As West and East have come together, the fossilization of Arab authority has become worse while the extravagance of certain individuals has fueled mass resentments.

Yet the issue of the rich and poor Arabs was not on the agenda in Saudi Arabia. Saudis focused on what they saw as the political failure of the "advanced" Arabs. They argued that the other arabs had not come to their aid in the days before oil. "Saudis were once the have-nots," said Adel al Jubeir, a young Saudi diplomat. "Forty years ago the major source of protein in my country was locust. I've never heard any stories from my grandfather about Arab food trucks coming to help us then. The 'Arab agenda' was an ethnocentric one," he said. "It was the Syrians, the Egyptians, or the Palestinians' agenda, and then the hillbillies struck oil."

Saudis rallied around their king. They volunteered for the army and the national guard in record numbers in a wave of patriotism that appeared to come from all corners of the kingdom—the Shiite Muslim minority as well as the Sunni Muslim majority.

The new awakening was matched by a new foreign policy. It would still be backed with a large oil-enriched checkbook, but the checks would now go to proven friends. Saudi officials had a succinct phrase to describe their post-invasion approach: "No more Mr. Nice Guy." They had given millions to the Jordanians, Palestinians, and Yemenis.

They had funded religious parties in Algeria and Sudan. They had built mosques, schools, and hospitals as foreign aid, but now they saw that in a crisis the money brought no loyalty. For Saudi Arabia, the Arab world had suddenly grown much simpler. There were two categories of Arabs after August 2: friends and enemies, those who were for and those who were against the Iraqi invasion.

One of the first to be measured was Yasser Arafat, chairman of the Palestine Liberation Organization. Tensions between the House of Saud and the PLO had been growing even before the Iraqi invasion. The Palestinian leader had complained that the Saudis had not delivered promised funds to support the uprising in Israeli-occupied territories.

However, his tilt toward Baghdad cost him more than Saudi funds. It also freed Saudis from the issue that had tied them to the Arabs of the Levant and made them blind to the argument of American double standards that was fueling anger and support for Saddam in Algiers, Rabat, Tunis, and Amman.

"Jordan is Palestine," said a young Saudi official, dismissing the Palestine question with an answer that would have warmed the heart of an Israel hardliner. "I grew up giving a riyal for Palestine every time I took an exam. Palestinians were our teachers. The Palestine issue shaped our politics; it set the agenda. Now it's our turn to set the agenda for the Arab world."

It was a declaration of independence and went deeper than the surface tensions created by Yasser Arafat's public embrace of the Iraqi leader. "Don't talk to my father about the Palestinians," said Nuha, a young professional woman in her office in Riyadh. "If you say Palestinian to him, it's like saying the devil. The feelings here have changed. We don't mind Israel. We've been spoon-fed all these years and look what those Palestinians did. The Palestinian cause is nothing. If they want to fight, let them fight for themselves."

Many Saudis felt that the Palestinian leader had taken their money and then betrayed them, a feeling so strong that it didn't take into account the longstanding grievances of the Palestinians or make a distinction between the leader and his people. In the view of most Saudis, they had supported the Palestinians. They felt great guilt over the loss of Palestine. They had sympathy for the Palestinian refugees. After the 1973 war, King Faisal opened an office in Riyadh for al Fatah, the main PLO faction. The Saudis opened an embassy for the state of Palestine near the diplomatic quarter in the capital. But at the same time, Saudis had always been uncomfortable with the confrontational nature of Palestinian politics.

The rage of the dispossessed had frightened this insular country and the Palestinian cause had complicated relations with the United States and other Arab states. By arguing Saddam's case, Arafat allowed Saudis to say out loud what they had said privately for years. They didn't really like the Palestinians. To Saudis, they were the most arrogant of the urbanized Arabs. Palestinians snickered at the "black-eyed Arabs of the Gulf" as Abu Jihad, a leading member of the PLO, had once called them.

The Palestinian community in Saudi Arabia was quite large, more than 200,000, and some of its members were finding out that the withdrawal of funds was not the only punishment that would be handed out in the new atmosphere of Saudi Arabia's militant self-interest. Palestinians soon discovered that some work permits had been canceled. Those who had been in Jordan at the start of the invasion found they were not allowed to return to Saudi Arabia. Palestinian drivers were banished from work that had anything to do with the American military deployment. The only Palestinian group that was still blessed by Saudi largess was the Islamic Resistance Movement, harakat al-muquawama al-Islamiya (Hamas). Hamas was the fighting wing of the radical Muslim group known as the Muslim Brothers. Its largest following was in the Israeli-occupied Gaza Strip, where Hamas called for the return of all of Palestine for an Islamic Palestinian state. Hamas had two appeals for the Saudis. It was an Islamic movement, and in the first weeks after the invasion Hamas had broken with the secular wings of the Palestine Liberation Organization and condemned Saddam's invasion.

"There are some Saudis, the pragmatics I would say, they think it's time to change the system," said Othman al Rawath, a political science professor at King Saud University. "They think it was all wrong from the beginning, Arab solidarity, it was all romance. The previous system was built on romance and didn't take into account different interests."

We were sitting in the coffee shop of Riyadh's International Hotel. The Filipino waiters in their starched white coats brought small cups of Arabic coffee to the restaurant's family section, the only space where men and women can sit together. The hotel was one of the few places in the capital that was free from the prying eyes of the mutawaeen. The hotel is government-owned and somehow off-limits to Saudi Arabia's Islamic police force. Othman adjusted the folds of his white headdress.

"Some think it's better that we come out of this mess and we build a new system that's more realistic," he said. The Iraqi invasion unleashed a great political debate. The hawks in Saudi Arabia had a simple solution. A decisive war. A war that would cut Saddam's army into a size that could fit in the neighborhood again. It was the only way to cleanse the system, they argued. It was the only way to ensure that the Americans would go home. Saudi Arabia could then afford to go it alone in the Arab world, they argued. Saddam's invasion shattered the myths of pan-Arabism; it was now so much excessive baggage, they said. In the privacy of their homes they said they didn't think of themselves as Arabs anymore.

The hawks wanted to wipe the slate clean, to rebuild the system with ties to the West rather than the Arab world. They talked of more common interests with Washington than with Arabs. Saudi hawks said things like, "We're going to sock it to Saddam." They said things like, "We're going to bop him one." They said things like that knowing full well that the majority of the socking and bopping would be done by American troops.

For Saudi hawks, the world was not only simpler but it was more dangerous. The Iraqi invasion proved there were unexpected perils and a return to the status quo ante was not good enough. If Saddam heeded the United Nations resolutions and withdrew from Kuwait, he would leave with his power intact. Saudis would then have to confront the real prospect of a Saddam who had faced down an international coalition and returned home with his arsenal of chemical and biological weapons untouched. The Americans had come to defend the kingdom. Without a war how long would they stay? Through the first terrorist attack? Through the second?

In November, when Israeli police opened fire on Palestinian demonstrators in Jerusalem at Islam's second holiest site, the news had shaken the coalition. How many more shocks would it take in this volatile region to change the focus of Desert Shield's Arab coalition from Baghdad to Jerusalem?

Prince Bandar bin Sultan, an American-trained jet pilot, was Saudi Arabia's most public hawk. The young, flamboyant ambassador to Washington had been a high-profile figure in the U.S. capital even before the invasion. He had easy access to the White House and to the Pentagon. General Colin Powell, chairman of the joint chiefs of staff, had called him the Arab Gatsby; Bandar was more like an Arab Kissinger. In late July, as CIA (Central Intelligence Agency) analysts dismissed the Iraqi buildup on the Kuwaiti border as saber rattling, the Saudi Embassy in Washington leaked the details of the Iraqi buildup to the press. Bandar's office forced attention on Iraq, and as the alarm bells in Washington rang over the invasion, Bandar was one of the first visitors to the Oval Office.

Bandar, like his brother General Khalid bin Sultan, took advantage of the opening that the older generation of the House of Saud had given them. The marching orders were simply, "Do what works." Saudi Arabia's young princes stole the show. The moment would not last past the crisis and Bandar made the most of it by becoming the public face of Saudi Arabia. Bandar went to Moscow when the Soviets seemed to be wavering over their Gulf policy, wooing them with loans and renewed diplomatic relations after a break of more than forty years. Bandar went to China. He appeared on CNN. He was a glib performer polished by a lifetime of luxury and privilege.

Away from the public eye, Bandar stepped up his lobbying efforts. He established links with like-minded constituencies. He met with congressional hawks over breakfast. He lunched with conservative newspaper columnists known for their support of Israel. At dinners he met openly with American Jewish leaders.

American Jewish groups were more hawkish than mainstream American opinion and were as keen as Saudi Arabia to see the Iraqi leader defeated. American Jewish leaders also worried about a return to the status quo ante. Saddam had already threatened to "burn half of Israel," and telegraphed his intentions in the current crisis by moving scud missile launchers to the northwestern desert of Iraq. The Saudi prince invited members of the American Jewish Congress (AJC) to his palatial home in McLean, Virginia.

"He was very anxious to meet with American Jews," said Henry Seigman, president of the AJC. "We spent several hours with him. He wanted to generate as much support for a showdown with Iraq as he could. I think he was successful."

The Saudi prince was warm and charming to his Jewish dinner guests as he outlined his views on the war that he was sure was coming. "He ridiculed the Iraqi military," said Seigman. "He said to us, 'We know these generals because we were paying their salaries.' He was convinced that the Iraqi military would collapse immediately, that the Americans and other forces would not face resistance." Seigman explained:

> Bandar was one of the few people who early on called the shots more accurately than any other Middle Eastern expert. He said from the beginning that Saddam was going to go to the limit. Bandar

explained that Saddam was a man who didn't know what's going on. He would go to the brink and into war. This was at a time when everyone was certain that Saddam was bluffing. Bandar was convinced there would be a war.

In Saudi Arabia more than 300,000 Kuwaiti refugees were housed throughout the kingdom. They told their tales of rape and pillage to every community. There was open access to the Saudi media, and special programs about the crisis were broadcast each evening. The House of Saud made sure that the Saudi public knew the gruesome details of the behavior of the Iraqi army. With domestic opinion secure, the international message of Saudi determination to see the battle to the end was in the hands of a young Saudi diplomat sent home for the job.

In Dhahran, Saudi Arabia, the Bandar line was reinforced to the international news media by Adel al-Jubeir, Bandar's special assistant in Washington. The twenty-nine-year-old Saudi diplomat had been dispatched home to work as an alternative to Saudi Arabia's official Information Ministry. Prince Bandar knew enough about the American news media to know that the usual Saudi bureaucracy would be inadequate to manage Saudi Arabia's image.

The Dhahran International Hotel, whose blue-domed swimming-pool changing rooms became a familiar backdrop for T.V. reports, was the home of the international press corp during the Gulf crisis. Al Jubeir was the hotel's most peripatetic resident. This young Saudi diplomat was Bandar's alter ego, providing background briefings in his tennis whites or jeans. For official on-camera interviews Al Jubeir donned the traditional white thobe and headdress. The Kuwaitis had hired two Washington public relations firms at a cost of more than a million dollars to massage Kuwait's public image. But Al Jubeir proved as able as any Washington spin doctor in marketing Saudi Arabia's hawkish outlook, clocking more hours of television and radio time than any other Saudi official. His message was consistent: There would be no last-minute deals from Riyadh. He charmed the press with his disarming honesty about the inner workings of the Saudi system. Although a commoner, Al Jubeir was part of the mafia of young Saudi princes who were defining Saudi policy.

Not all Saudis were comfortable with the hawks' march to war. In Riyadh and in Jeddah, the business community were militant doves. They had grown up and prospered in a country that had followed, not led, events in the region. Saudi Arabia stayed out of all five Arab-

Israeli wars. They were old enough to remember the days of poverty and hardship before the oil boom. A war, with its unpredictable nature, could destroy everything they had built. The hawks of the country were the post-oil generation, and the change in the course was making Saudi doves uneasy. The doves argued that the Arab system had been wounded but was not beyond repair.

"We have been besieged by dictatorship and human rights abuses, but this doesn't mean that we believe in that. I know Iraqi people are against everything that Saddam does," said Jawaher al-Abdul Jabber, a psychiatrist at King Faisal Specialist Hospital in Riyadh. She was angry as she answered my questions. She was also afraid. Saudi Arabia had never been in a war before. Her children had their first drill with gas masks at a private school in Riyadh. She had not found a satisfactory way to explain to them why Saddam was a hero in Saudi Arabia and was now an enemy.

"I've explained to them about the Palestinians and the Israelis; they know what that means. I only told them that the Kuwaitis were kicked out of their country." Parents all over Saudi Arabia were having to explain to their children and to themselves why the comfortable certainty of the Arab world had changed overnight. Some were angry at their own government for saying nothing about the Iraqi invasion for the first three days. Shortwave radios had disappeared from the shelves as news-starved Saudis sought other channels of information. Others were angry about the aggressive media campaign directed at the Arabs in Saddam's coalition. Al Jabber shared their concern.

Saudi Arabia's doves asked if it was necessary to make more enemies than they already had. What if it all went wrong with Saddam? Iraq was a permanent neighbor and the conflict was taking on the flavor of an Arab civil war. While the Americans could fight and go home, Saudi doves argued that they had to live in this neighborhood. It was particularly hard to imagine Saudi Arabia living in harmony with Yemen after the crisis was over.

Yemenis held a special place in the hierarchy of workers in the kingdom. Unlike all other foreign workers, they did not have to secure entry visas before arrival or, once there, find a Saudi sponsor or partner for any independent business. This explained why there were 1.5 million Yemenis in Saudi Arabia, the largest single component of the foreign work force in the country. Yemenis were Saudi Arabia's mechanics, electricians, and shopkeepers. They maintained military vehicles for the army and sold Desert Storm T-shirts at the Shula Mall in Dhahran. Most had lived in Saudi Arabia for decades and some married into Saudi families. Yet in late August 1990, a small announcement on the front page of Saudi newspapers changed their status in the country and led to the exodus of more than half of the population.

The Saudi government denied it was expelling the Yemenis and officials said they were merely applying the same regulations that covered the rest of the work force. But the new decree meant that Yemenis had to find a Saudi sponsor to keep their business open. Most of those who left were unwilling to face the humiliation of selling half of their business interests to a Saudi partner who would do nothing but give his name and take half of the profits.

The Yemeni community had done nothing to displease their Saudi hosts—there had been no demonstration against the American deployment and no hint of sabotage. But Yemeni President ali Abdullah Saleh argued that Saddam could be forced to leave Kuwait without war. His position put him at odds with the Saudi government and Saudi Arabia was simply taking a page from American foreign policy.

At the United Nations, U.S. Secretary of State James Baker remarked that the Yemeni vote against U.S.-sponsored resolutions would be the most expensive vote the country had ever taken. In Saudi Arabia, the payment was extracted from the Yemeni community and Saudi T.V. broadcast the images of Yemeni families crossing the southern frontier in trucks. In interviews at the border, Yemeni families thanked their Saudi hosts for their "hospitality" as they crossed into their poor and populous nation. The Saudis made no secret of their desire to stir tribal rebellion to topple Salih. The exodus of unemployed, and in the Saudi view, bitter Yemenis, would add an economic burden to an "enemy" government. Saudi newspapers were filled with grand regional conspiracy theories that put ali Abdullah Saleh at the top of the list of beneficiaries if Saddam's plans were a success. There were suggestions that Saleh's reward would be control of the long-lost province of Asir in southwest Saudi Arabia. A division of Pakistanis was dispatched to the south to guard against any "plots" launched from across the border.

The Jordanians also were seen as part of the grand conspiracy, a view King Hussein fueled by insisting that those wishing to honor him should call him "Sharif." In Saudi eyes it was a gesture that proved that King Hussein hoped to regain the Hijaz (in western Saudi Arabia) as a reward for his support of the Iraqi invasion. In 1924, King Hussein's great-grandfather was driven from the Hijaz and forced to relocate in the dusty Arab backwater town of Amman. It was the last piece of ground won by Ibn Saud's army and put the finishing touches on what is now considered modern Saudi Arabia.

All of the contradictions and historical tensions of the Arab world were now out in the open. Saddam Hussein's invasion had freed the House of Saud from the constraints of pan-Arabism and the policies of two generations.

The American offensive plan presented General Khalid with some stark choices. The Saudi commander was convinced that the bulk of Saddam's army would not put up much of a fight. He was getting regular intelligence briefings about the mood of the Iraqi army from the flow of defectors coming across the border, and the numbers increased as the occupation continued. In January, the air bombardment prompted unprecedented numbers of Iraqi soldiers to simply walk away from their units and return home. At the same time, General Khalid also was convinced that Saddam was capable of pushing the occupation of Kuwait to the brink of war and beyond—a not altogether bad outcome since the return to the status quo was unacceptable to the Saudi prince. "I can't live with him until he's one meter under the sand," Khalid ibn Sultan said.

But the Americans had made it clear that while the air force could start the war, the army had to finish it. On the ground, that meant the Saudi army would have to fight against the Iraqi army in Kuwait, a prospect for which the Saudi armed forces were ill prepared. Despite billions of dollars spent on defense, the Saudi army lacked the experience, the organization, and the training to fight a land war. The Saudi national guard, the more organized of the forces within the kingdom, would not be crossing the border in an offensive war since its role was solely to protect the royal family and the oil fields.

Before the Iraqi invasion, Saudi Arabia's ground force numbered about 40,000 men and 250 tanks, plus 35,000 in the national guard. The two forces were organized under separate commands, a structure designed to guard against internal rather than external threats. Attempted coups within the Saudi military in the 1950s and 1960s had shown the House of Saud the danger of allowing one military force to become too powerful. But while the dual structure ensured a balance of forces inside the country, it was inadequate for the crisis at hand.

There was another problem. Much of the maintenance on military equipment was done by non-Saudis—most of it by the now suspect Yemenis. A recruiting drive was on in the kingdom, and while there were plenty of Saudi men willing to join the military, they were unprepared and untrained for a ground offensive.

The political instincts of the prince led him to the conclusion that

Saudi soldiers would have to be on the front line in any fight with the Iraqis. He said so publicly to a group of U.S. Marines in a speech at the Saudi port of Jubail. He made sure that the offensive plan would reflect his thinking. "I want Saudi blood spilled before anyone else," said Prince Khalid. He added later, "The Americans came to help us and that's the least we can do, put our blood on the front line. I was determined that my forces were going to be first. I wasn't willing to compromise on that. Some of my people tried to convince me. They said, 'We don't have the experience. Why don't we go in behind the marines.' I was determined that my forces were going to be first."

In Saudi Arabia's tribal tradition a sheikh has to provide for the security of his people to maintain their loyalty. Saudi Arabia's Western-educated commoners were raising this cultural question in a modern form: How could Saudi Arabia spent millions of dollars on defense and have so little to show for it in a time of crisis?

It was well known that weapons purchases were a prime source of corruption in the kingdom. Western military attachés long reported that the Saudis bought weapon systems that they didn't need and paid inflated prices for what they had. Saudi middlemen made millions on the contracts, yet there were warehouses filled with military trucks and vehicles that weren't maintained. It was clear that no one in the country had envisioned Saudi Arabia fighting a war. Khalid's decision to put the Saudi army on the front line would mean dramatic changes in the structure of the Saudi military.

"We had never entered a war before," said General Khalid months after the fighting. "We had a lot to learn. In the beginning I would hear people talk. They were saying our forces are terrible; our air force is terrible. They said we would never attack, or if we did then we would fumble." Khalid had quickly understood that military might had more weight than oil wealth and that Arab countries such as Syria, Egypt, and Iraq had far greater clout in the region than Saudi Arabia. The kingdom's military culture would have to change and Desert Shield provided an opportunity for the largest joint training exercise ever carried out on Saudi soil.

The U.S. military had worked with the Saudis in the past. The Vinnell Corporation of Los Angeles was the key contractor to train the national guard, hiring a number of Vietnam veterans to turn it into a modern fighting force with artillery and air defense support. The Saudi Officer Corps had many graduates from American military colleges and training courses and the Saudi fighting doctrine was right out of the training manuals of the U.S. military. But while the Saudis and the Americans spoke the same military language, there was a vast gap in experience between them.

"It's a defensive army that doesn't go to the woods very often," said Major John Peska, assigned to train the Saudi Eighth Armored Battalion. "The Saudis didn't have the equipment to go out into the desert. They had to buy the stuff on the open market when we started. They bought tents and carpets. All the equipment was brand new."

Domestic political considerations prevented the Saudi army from participating in the large-scale desert exercises known as Bright Star that were staged each year in the region. Saudi Arabia's religious leaders saw the United States as anti-Islam. In addition, the Saudi public saw America as devoted to Israel and the source of Arab suffering. Desert Shield provided General Khalid bin Sultan the opportunity to make up for lost time. At the end of October, the U.S. Air Force opened a school for Saudi military personnel at King Khalid Military City. KKMC is a sprawling complex of officers' quarters, administrative offices, and airfields in the middle of a desolate and inhospitable desert about 360 miles northeast of Riyadh near the Iraqi border. The Saudis had completed the 7-billion-dollar city, part of a ten-year military project, in 1986, with the help of the U.S. Corps of Engineers.

At street level, KKMC looked like an American college campus. The administration building is set off by a large marble plaza with a marble staircase that leads to a pool and a dazzling fountain. The Saudis were proud enough of this ultramodern military installation to invite Saddam Hussein for a tour just three months before his invasion of Kuwait.

When the American Air Force party arrived in October 1990, they were assigned to office space that had never been used. The facility was complete down to the office furniture that was dusty from years of storage. "It was as if they were waiting for us," said Lieutenant Colonel Martin Semik, chief liaison officer of the project.

The Americans had to teach the Saudis the fundamentals of close air support, a key element in the American air/land battlefield technique adopted as an official American doctrine in 1985. It was a technique that owed more to rugby than to football, incorporating a fast-moving, dynamic battlefield with high-tech artillery and air power at the service of ground force commanders.

For the Saudis and the other Arab armies in the coalition, the war with Iraq was to be the first time in their military histories that they would go into battle with "friendly" jets overhead. The Americans had four months to instruct the Saudis in the doctrine and prove an American maxim: "You fight as you train."

The first goal was to get the Arabs to accept the idea of having friendly aircraft flying overhead during a ground fight. Their own doctrines had been shaped by the Arab-Israeli wars, and the Egyptians and the Syrians had direct experience with what air power could do. Even the Israelis themselves were wary of the complicated procedures necessary for close air support. The "fog of war" could blur the battle lines between the friendly forces and the enemy.

"We had to show the Syrians what American planes looked like," said Captain Scott Purdue, the U.S. Air Force liaison officer for the Syrian army. They had never seen an American A-10 jet. This slow-flying plane, with a stubby snout, had two nicknames depending on one's perspective. The aristocracy of the air force, the F-18 pilots who flew the fast jets, called them "hogs" whereas to the ground soldiers they were "tank killers" because the planes could maneuver low over the battlefield and hunt for tanks. A titanium tub around the cockpit protected the pilot from artillery shells. Purdue called for training runs that would simulate the kind of maneuvers called for in knocking out Iraqi tanks and the Syrian ground troops got their first glimpse of an A-10 as it swooped down to 500 feet over their tanks.

"I flew the American jets over the Syrians so our pilots could see what their tanks looked like," said Purdue. The Syrians brought their Russian-built T-62 tanks, the same model that Saddam bought from Moscow.

At the end of November, Air Force Sergeant Charlie O'Riordan faced thirty-five Saudi noncommissioned officers in a makeshift class room at King Khalid Military City. His job was to teach them how to work the radios that call in the jets. O'Riordan taught them the basics of command and control, the communications system that keeps the military machine working. He taught them the basics of close air support, how to order a jet into the battlefield, and why a ground commander might need one. "I used the analogy of a boxer," said O'Riordan. "It gives one guy longer arms." He taught them about the hierarchy of the chain of command. "I told them that the hierarchy serves the people on the battlefield. Once they got that concept down, they could understand the air/land battlefield."

Seven days a week, with time off for prayer and tea breaks, O'Riordan taught them flexibility and management, concepts that were new to the Saudi Arabian army. When he was not teaching, he and a three-man air force team were running a radio network off the balcony of an apartment at the military city, so they could call in American jets for practice runs over the Arab armies in the desert. At the same time, the Saudis were honing the skills of their anti-aircraft gunners on the American planes. O'Riordan's radio call sign was "Why Me," a reflection of the difficulties of the job.

O'Riordan learned to stop the classes for Muslim prayer. He learned that tea breaks were an essential ingredient to education and he also learned the difference between "good to go," and *abshire*. Cultures can be defined by the untranslatable common sayings that are the equivalent of linguistic small change. For the American military, "good to go" was the catch phrase of Desert Storm, a greeting and a battle cry. It had a variety of meanings, but in the broadest context it meant confidence that the next act or order could be accomplished because of the expertise gained from extensive training. It defined a cultural attitude to problem solving.

The Saudis also had a variety of untranslatable phrases, but the one that best describes the character of the country is *abshir,* the "Have a nice day" of Saudi Arabia. It describes an attitude toward problems and life in general that leaves much to fate and Allah.

"I've trained with the American army, the Japanese army, and the Koreans. This was the most difficult," said O'Riordan. "If I hadn't had those experiences, I couldn't have done it. You have to accept that people don't do things the way that we do. Does it get done, yes. They just manage themselves in different ways."

At the same time that the air force opened classes and American mine-clearing experts offered workshops, special forces teams began a weekly assessment of the Saudi army that ran to forty pages. They reported on battalion staff, the ability to write clear, concise orders, the level of training, and the capabilities of the officers. "The area commanders were not used to dealing with Riyadh," said Major Peska. "The Saudi brigades were autonomous with very little guidance from the capital. When they tried to create a division there was lots of resentment because of that. This was a regional army and they didn't want to change. In the beginning, they didn't want to take orders from Riyadh; they always asked for orders in writing. By the end of our time, we had broken through some of the autonomy."

There was formidable internal opposition to Khalid's plan to reshape the Saudi army. The military mindset of the Saudi commanders was a function of the nature and history of the country. Saudis were loyal to their family, their tribe, and their region—in that order. General

Khalid saw an opportunity to mold the military in a way that would go beyond the immediate crisis.

Major John Peska had a more immediate problem. The thirty-year-old captain had orders to make sure that the Saudi Eighth Armored Brigade was trained for a chemical weapon attack. It was well known that Iraq had an enormous armory of chemical weapons with four facilities that produced the deadliest poison devised in the twentieth century. The Samarra plant, 45 miles northwest of Baghdad, manufactured nitrogen mustard gas, a World War I–vintage concoction that attacked the mucous membranes and caused blisters on the skin. Death comes from "dry-land drowning," when internal blisters explode and fill the lungs with fluid. Saddam's scientists had learned to make Tabun, a colorless, odorless, highly concentrated nerve agent that attacks the central nervous system and causes convulsions and death. Sarin, also produced at the Samarra plant, is ten times as lethal as Tabun.

Saddam used mustard gas to subdue Iranian soldiers and Kurdish civilians, and U.S. commanders were convinced he would use chemical weapons in the showdown with the U.S.-led coalition. But the Saudis had practiced a determined denial on the issue of chemical weapons. The stories of Saddam's attacks on the Kurds had not been reported in Saudi Arabia's controlled press. At the time, it would have been impolite to say such things about an Arab champion.

The Saudi army's purchase of chemical weapons equipment had been a "mishmash" in Peska's words. "We had to get them the proper equipment so we could conduct the exercise," said Peska. "They had equipment from everywhere, German, Italian." The next task was to get the Saudi soldiers to shave their beards. Survival from poison gas attack requires an airtight seal on the gas mask, but Peska found that the military mullahs, the religious men who watched over the souls of the soldiers, were against his proposal.

"The soldiers said they wouldn't shave," said Peska. "We tried to solve the problem by going to the mullah. We talked to him and tried to explain the problem. We showed him that shaving would make the masks fit better. We even used banana oil to show him that the gas could get in there. The mullah just kept saying 'Inshallah' ['If God wills']. There was nothing we could do."

The struggle in the Saudi military was a reflection of the struggle within Saudi Arabia's civilian society. The more progressive Saudi soldiers began to sport goatees to accommodate the gas masks. The militantly religious kept their full beards and Inshallah won again.

• • •

January 15, 1991, was the United Nations deadline for Saddam Hussein to leave Kuwait. The day was introduced by the sound of jet planes and the wail of air raid sirens. A bleak desert winter replaced summer's relentless sun; the optimism that war could be avoided had evaporated. Reality hit with the force of an Iraqi scud missile. Suddenly Saudis sported gas masks in shoulder bags. In Dhahran and Riyadh, parents reported that children, afraid of the claps of Patriot missiles meeting Iraqi scuds in midair, could not sleep. Flights to Jeddah, a city on the west coast out of scud range, were overbooked on the eve of the United Nations deadline and all civilian flights were canceled as the first bombers headed toward Iraqi targets. The school term had ended early and Saudi children and their parents hunkered down for their first television war. For the first time in the country's history, Saudi Arabia's television authority rebroadcast six hours of programming from Cable News Network every day. If Saudi Arabia's conservative religious establishment objected to such a secular use of the airwaves, their complaints went unheeded by the House of Saud.

Seven days after the air war began, Saudi Arabia produced its first war hero. Air Force Captain Ayedh Al-Shamrani, a thirty-year-old F-15 pilot, had shot down two Iraqi Mirage F-1 jets. On the night of his accomplishment, Al-Shamrani's fellow pilots gave him a party. They spread a cloth on the floor of the flight room for a large metal platter of chicken and rice and sat cross-legged on the floor in their green flight suits, dipping their hands into the mounds of warm food.

The squadron's chief warrant officer baked a cake decorated with an Iraqi flag torn into two by a Saudi missile. The pilots sawed off hunks of the cake and joked with Al-Shamrani in the familiar way of a men's locker room. It was the sort of gathering that would have been appropriate for a victorious party of bedouin raiders returning to their desert tents, but these raiders were riding the most modern war-fighting machines of the twentieth century.

A television crew from Saudi Arabia's English channel climbed on the leather couch to get a shot of the feast. Gray cables snaked over the room as the Saudi T.V. crew interviewed the new hero and introduced him to the Saudi public. Al-Shamrani, a short wiry man with a broad smile, was uncomfortable with the attention. In the midst of the celebration, the Saudi pilots kept one eye on a television in the corner of the room tuned to CNN. Talk stopped for every scrap of news about the day's mission. They had watched the CNN reports of American pilot successes in the first days of the war and now it was their turn to revel in glory.

The squadron commander, Prince Bandar Abdulla Saud al Kabir, a relative of the king, hunched over the back of a chair to watch the news, drawing on a cigarette and smiling at the CNN reports of Saudi kills. "No more Mr. Nice Guy," he said.

Before the crisis, Saudi Arabia's own evening news program was known as "Kissing" news, consisting of the Saudi king or other Arab dignitaries pecking each other on the cheek at airport arrival ceremonies. With the war, the kissing king was replaced by a Saudi military briefer, General al-Robiyan, dressed in the same chocolate chip—colored desert camouflage favored by his American military counterparts. The forty-year-old air force general was prepped each day by an American public relations firm hired by General Khalid bin Sultan. Not all the lessons the Saudis were learning about the management of modern warfare were on the battlefield.

F I V E

LADIES WITH AN ATTITUDE

I never thought I'd live to see
the daughter of the Peninsula of principles making light
attempting to remove the Hijab as though
she were in a nation losing its might.
—A poem appeal from a young girl to the Custodian of
the Two Holy Mosques, November 1990

"There's a lady on the other line who says there are women driving in Riyadh." Khalid al Moeena's voice had shifted to a high intensity as he finished the sentence. Moeena was a self-proclaimed Saudi liberal. He was the editor-in-chief of the *Arab News,* one of Saudi Arabia's English-language newspapers.

We had been talking on the telephone about the topic that obsessed every Saudi. Would Saddam heed the warnings from Washington and pull out of Kuwait? Another call interrupted the conversation. When Moeena came back on the line he was clearly agitated. Women driving in Riyadh? This was certainly unexpected news.

Khalid's sense of the importance of the event was correct. Demonstrations were forbidden in the kingdom. Women were forbidden to drive in Saudi Arabia. The flaunting of the two forbiddens was potentially explosive. The topic had become more sensitive since the Iraqi invasion. There are no restrictions on women drivers in Kuwait and many Kuwaiti women drove the family Land Rover over the desert to safety in Saudi Arabia while their husbands stayed behind to protect their property.

The arrival of the American troops raised the issue again. American women in the U.S. military were given special permission to drive military vehicles. The deal had been struck between General Norman Schwarzkopf and General Khalid bin Sultan, the Saudi general in charge of the coalition forces. It was one of the only concessions made to American cultural sensibilities. The American media seized on the issue with an interest sharpened by the fact that there were more than a dozen female correspondents who were directly affected by the driving ban. Congresswoman Pat Schroeder had raised the question on the floor of the House. She asked the House members if the United States should support a country that didn't let women citizens drive. It was a remarkable criterion for foreign policy considerations. Americans who knew very little about the location of Saudi Arabia were well aware of the fact that women were not allowed to drive there.

The demonstration in Riyadh was big news in Saudi Arabia. However, it was such big news that the incident never appeared in any Saudi newspaper, including the *Arab News,* or any Saudi television news program. Nevertheless, in the next twenty-four hours almost every Saudi in the kingdom would know about the driving protest in Riyadh. Almost everyone had an opinion about it.

The facts as they first emerged from Riyadh that day in November were certainly provocative by the kingdom's standards. In the parking lot of a small Riyadh supermarket on Abdul Aziz Road, forty-nine Saudi women gathered. All were dressed in black. The cloak and veil dictated by Saudi Arabia's conservative form of Islam was seen as necessary to ensure that this protest had only one message.

More than a dozen expensive BMW, Cadillac, and Toyota luxury sedans stood ready. One of the protesters chose to drive the 1983 Buick she had bought in the United States and had shipped home after getting a Ph.D. in education from the University of Michigan. The women slid into the drivers' seats while their male chauffeurs, mostly Asian men, sat on their haunches in the gravel parking lot. There were many witnesses. The story of the protest had spread by word of mouth in Riyadh and more than two hundred Saudis had turned out to watch what would happen next.

The religious establishment had forbidden women to drive by denying them the right to have drivers' licenses. They claimed their justification came from the Koran, but it was more the conservative traditions of Saudi Arabia than religion that accounted for the ban. The prohibition was a testament to the isolation of generations of Saudis from colonial masters and Western ideas. Saudi Arabia is the only Muslim country that has such a ban.

The restriction was underlined by a Fatwa. The Fatwa came from the pen of the blind cleric Sheikh Adb al al-Aziz bin Baz, a man well known for having once issued a Fatwa declaring that the earth is flat. bin Baz is the head of an organization known as the Islamic Research, Ruling, Call and Guidance. He is the chief jurisprudence in Saudi Arabia in matters of the Koran, a stern and dour man who is the enforcer of Saudi Arabia's ascetic form of Islam.

In Saudi Arabia the Koran serves as the constitution of the country. The ideology that gives the House of Saud legitimacy is its ability to promote an Islamic way of life as defined by the ruler and the *ulama,* a group of religious scholars headed by Shaikh Ibn Baz. In modern Saudi Arabia the system is simple. The king rules the state and the religious establishment rules the society. In a country as deeply religious as Saudi Arabia, the House of Saud controlled the wealth of the country, but bin Baz laid claim to its soul.

In the liberal salons of Dhahran and Jeddah, I had heard Saudi women openly express their frustrations with the driving ban. Some talked of a mass demonstration. "If three hundred women just get in their cars and drive, what can they do to us?" they would ask. A few women recommended a less confrontational approach. Perhaps one day they would simply drive their children to the doctor's office and see what happened. Other Saudi women argued that driving a car was not the major problem. There was more frustration over the lack of job opportunities for the thousands of women who were graduating from the country's universities.

With Saudi Arabia's strict separation of the sexes, jobs for women were limited to professions that would ensure segregation. It was possible to run a business from home, but it required a male manager for such tasks as getting a business license, making a deposit at the bank, and entering most government ministries.

There were many other more important restrictions on Saudi women. The only way a Saudi woman could get a passport or leave the country was with the written permission of her husband or father. Legally, a Saudi woman cannot be in the public company of a man who is not her husband or a close male relative. She cannot be in a car with any man who is not closely related to her unless he is the family chauffeur. A Saudi woman cannot work in an office with a man, travel alone, or stay in a hotel alone.

The religious police, known as the mutawaeen, were vigorous in enforcing the rules. They patrolled the cities in their signature Suburban GMC jeeps as an arm of the Committee to Promote Virtue and Prevent Vice. The agency was institutionalized by the state in the 1930s. The Arabic word *Mutawa* conveys the sense of obedience. However, in the past decade the Mutowa had become more like religious internal security police. Many Saudis complained that the Mutowa were using intimidation and coercion in a way that distorted their original role. Many of the most fervent mutoween had volunteered for the job and carried out patrols without pay. Their power over fellow citizens was seductive in a country where the only other path to power was to be born into the House of Saud.

For the wealthy women of Saudi Arabia there were benefits to the chauffeur system. For one thing, it meant never having to find a parking space. However, the economics of the driving ban were staggering. Saudi Arabia had 300,000 full-time private chauffeurs. Most of the drivers were imported workers from Asia. This was hardly a burden in a wealthy household, but for the middle class and the poor an extra employee was a financial hardship. Bedouin families simply ignored the ban. It was not unusual to see a bedouin woman behind the wheel of a pickup truck on a desolate desert road.

On the day before the protest, the organizers of the driving demonstration sent a letter to Riyadh's governor, Prince Salman bin Abd al-Aziz. In the letter, the women thanked King Fahd for his generosity in "opening the door" to Saudi women to volunteer to serve the country. They then asked him to open his "paternal heart" and look with sympathy on what they called a "humane demand" to drive in Riyadh. As quoted below, the letter laid out the arguments for lifting the prohibition on driving using logic and Islam in equal measures:

1. Employing a chauffeur will result in the presence of a foreign man in the home and create inevitable situations in which a woman is present with him alone in the car.
2. Relieving financial burdens placed on many families as a result of the need to employ a chauffeur.
3. Many immoral acts may occur within the home as the result of the presence of a chauffeur and a maid together in the house.

4. It is our belief that women can take the place of men during times of crisis such as those being witnessed by our country these days as a result of the threats of those full of hatred. Such circumstances require that men should go to the battlefield to defend the country and women should defend the internal front.
5. Such a step would give women more confidence in their ability to shoulder their responsibilities to share in building the nation and participate in all fields.

The protest organizers ended their appeal with their best argument. The Prophet Mohammad and the first four caliphs had been defenders of the rights of women, they said. The Prophet had instructed his followers to take half of their religion from his wife Aisha. Early Islamic history had examples of women who participated in the Islamic conquests. Women rode camels, the transport of the day. The evidence was there for all to see, argued the demonstrators, "such is the greatness of the teacher of humanity and the master of men in leaving lessons and examples that are as clear as the sunlight to dispel the darkness of ignorance and backwardness to remain strong and firm in the face of those seeking to spread delusion."

The protesters didn't wait for an answer. There was some reason to believe that the protest had royal backing. The issue of women driving had been an open debate in the country for more than a decade. A few years earlier, a proposal to allow women doctors to drive had been suggested as a way to ease the issue into the public consciousness, but the government had taken no action.

The American deployment and the addition of hundreds of foreign journalists in the country resulted in a score of negative reports on Saudi Arabia's political system. A few of the liberal princes suggested that the only way to push social change in the country was to seize the initiative.

In the 1960s, King Fahd, then the minister of education, had championed education for girls against stiff resistance from religious conservatives. The protesters were the first generation of Saudis who benefited directly from his stand. They had been educated in Saudi Arabian girls' schools and gone on for degrees in higher education in the West at government expense. These were the wives and daughters of some of Saudi Arabia's most prominent clans. Some were related to important government officials and members of the religious establishment. They could not have mounted their protest without the support and approval of the men in their families. The protest represented larger numbers of discontented than the forty-nine women who took part in the drive-in.

In the Riyadh parking lot, the women who were the designated drivers were nervous as they settled behind the wheel. Windshield wipers flicked off and on and electric windows rolled up and down as they fumbled with the controls in anxious energy. These women had all learned to drive in the West, but the emotional impact of driving in the Saudi capital was taking its toll. Fifteen cars glided onto the black tarmac on the Riyadh highway for an unprecedented challenge to the House of Saud from the parking lot of a grocery store.

Within twenty minutes the startled Riyadh traffic police had halted the protest. The police asked the women where they were from, sure that these were Kuwaiti women rather than Saudis. Within moments of the arrests the mutawaeen appeared on the scene. They had picked up the rumors of the day's protest and came to insist that this "crime" fell within the jurisdiction of the religious authorities. They banged on the windows of the cars. Later one mutawa would file a report on the incident. The account was widely circulated in Riyadh:

> Forty-five women in Riyadh driving and indecently dressed. The women chant "driving" and "freedom" and raise their hands. Puzzled and confused people look on. . . . Some believe what their eyes see, others do not.

The mutawaeen argued furiously with the police. This was a religious crime and the offenders must be taken to the headquarters of the religious authorities. The policemen told them that this was a matter for the traffic police and scuffled with the mutawaeen. They then formed a cordon around the women, separating them from the religious police. As the evening prayer rang out from Riyadh's mosques, a compromise was reached. The deal allowed one mutawa and one policeman to accompany the offending drivers, now passengers, to the local police station. In the front seat of each car a policeman took the driver's seat while a mutawa sat on the passengers' side and the women sat in the back.

> Arriving at the police station, they do not disembark until their leaders [sic] Hafsa Al Munif and Dr. Fatin Al Zamil do . . . the latter, a professor in medicine, gets out of the car, dragging her *hijab* and saying rudely, "I don't believe in this." . . . After being led into one of the rooms inside, the women begin dancing and clapping, pleased

that they have not been led to the Mutawes' headquarters. . . . Hafsa Al Munif says, "We don't want to speak to those with brooms," referring to the heroic Mutawes. She continues, "We only want to speak with Prince Salman . . . not to these blind scholars . . . we'll speak with open-minded people who really comprehend the challenges confronting our society." Those who feel secure of escaping punishment will misbehave. We pray to God to help us survive these bad times.

The account is written in the Arabic of the undereducated. The plain recitation of the facts with little embellishment shows the deep gap in outlook between the women and their mutawaeen witnesses. Their "crimes" are so obvious that there is no need for additional rhetoric. There was a world of difference between the mutawa reporter and the women who had mounted the protest. The report is unsigned, but he was likely a young Saudi man from a poor family. Like all mutoween, his dress would have signaled his piety. Mutawaeen do not shave and they wear ankle-length white thobes and a white loose-fitting scarf. The black-roped crown that is the usual attire for a Saudi man is considered an unnecessary luxury for these ultrareligious policemen. His worldview would have been based on his memorization of every word of the Koran.

The idea of dragging the *hijab,* the long black cloak that is the required dress for women in Saudi Arabia, was so alien to his way to thinking that he reported it with no comment. To be "open-minded and comprehend the challenges confronting Saudi society" was beyond the understanding of our anonymous Saudi mutawa.

In the first hours after the event, Prince Salman, Riyadh's governor, tried to play down the incident. The women were from important families. The House of Saud needed to retain a consensus for the American deployment at a time when the presence of American troops was under attack from the politically active religious reactionaries.

Taped cassette lectures attacking the Americans were circulating in the kingdom through an underground network. One was recorded by Safar al Hawali, the dean of Islamic studies at Umm al Qura University in Mecca. Hawali was an important figure in the camp of religious radicals in the country. While the country's mainstream religious authorities had given their public blessing to the American troops at the urging of the House of Saud, Hawali denounced the deployment. His comments were made at a sermon from the Grand Mosque in Mecca: "If

Iraq has occupied Kuwait, America has occupied Saudi Arabia," Hawali told the crowded mosque. "The real enemy is not Iraq; it is the West."

Hawali's sentiments were shared by Saudi Arabia's ultrareligious right. The Iraqi invasion of Kuwait was an illusion and a trap, he argued. Saddam's reckless land grab had been encouraged by the United States as a pretext for a foothold in Saudi Arabia. "George Bush says that the crisis is a matter of the world against Iraq. It is not. It is the West against Islam," Hawali warned his flock.

Hawali charged that those who supported the American deployment were blasphemers. In his eyes, the Americans had come to control the country and destroy the culture and religion of Saudi Arabia. "When the Mujahedeen drove the Russians from Afghanistan, you did not say, 'God helped them.' You said, 'America helped them.' Now, when we are threatened by war, you do not say, 'God will protect us.' You say, 'America will protect us.' America has become your God."

Saudi Arabia's liberals supported the American deployment. They were heartened by the American president's talk of defending human rights and democracy in the Middle East. Their usual suspicion of American intentions in the region was suspended because of domestic benefits. The crisis ushered in a virtual springtime of events that addressed the liberals' frustrations.

Compared to the days before the Iraqi invasion, Saudi newspaper coverage was open and frank. Opinion polls began appearing in the press charting public reaction to the military situation as well as social issues, such as women's rights. The king issued a decree allowing women to participate in special classes in health care, "within the context of fully preserving Islamic and social values." The plan included a provision for women to replace male health care workers who might be needed on the battlefield. Hundreds of women took advantage of the classes offered in the major cities. The atmosphere encouraged women to write editorials endorsing their contribution to Saudi society. The religious police, the Mutoween, practically disappeared in the east coast city of Dhahran, the home of the international press corps. In Jeddah, Saudi businessmen talked of easing the restrictions on foreign business partnerships. In liberal eyes it seemed that in the heat of crisis the House of Saud was reaching out to the people.

Even more significant was the king's revival of the idea of a Majlis al-Shura, or Consultative Assembly. This was a body of men who would advise the House of Saud in the running of the government. It was seen in the country as an important step toward representative government in keeping with the Koranic injunction, "In your affairs consult among yourselves."

The idea of a consultative council first surfaced almost thirty years earlier, when another external threat had challenged the House of Saud. King Faisal promised his people a say in the running of their affairs as a hedge against the secular revolutionary call from Cairo in the fiery speeches of Gamel Abdul Nasser. The proposal faded along with Nasser's appeal. Reform was overshadowed by growing domestic prosperity during the boom years of the 1970s.

The next time a Saudi king proposed the consultative council was after the bloody events in Mecca in 1979. In that year a band of home-grown religious fanatics under the leadership of Juhaiman al Utaiba preached the overthrow of the Saudi monarchy during an infamous siege of the Grand Mosque. A few years later, the government erected a splendid building for the new consultative council on a bluff over-looking the urban sprawl of Riyadh. However, the council was put on hold again as the House of Saud ordered further studies.

Now another threat rocked the House of Saud and it was not surprising that King Fahd recalled the promise again. The Iraqi invasion unleashed powerful emotions in all camps.

On one side there were the Western-educated technocrats: the liberals and modernists. They had benefited from Saudi Arabia's development policies of the 1970s. They were active in business, held important government posts, served in diplomatic missions, held seats in regional chambers of commerce, and had prominent posts in some universities. The country's bureaucracy depended on their expertise. In their most radical form they were represented by the driving protest in Riyadh. While there was no agreement on a picture for the future, they shared a sense of frustration over the constraints of the society.

On the other side were the Islamists. These included the protectors and interpreters of Wahhabism such as the officially sanctioned Abd al Aziz bin Baz and a community of establishment religious scholars and jurists. They also included a new breed of militant, potentially violent fundamentalists. They were called the "children of Juhaiman," after the leader of the unsuccessful religious rebellion in Mecca in 1979. The new militants argued forcefully that the country had been weakened by adopting Western ways. They were as political as they were religious, attacking the House of Saud for corruption and hypocrisy. Their numbers had grown in recent years as much for economic reasons as religious ones.

In the past decade, the downturn in the international oil market meant a severe beating for the Saudi economy. The discovery of non-OPEC oil, alternative energy sources, and in the early part of the 1980s a new spirit of conservation in the West, was wreaking havoc with the Saudi budget. For the first time there was unemployment in the kingdom. The generous government grants for real estate and education were shrinking.

The House of Saud's policy toward the more radical proponents of Islam was ambiguous. The modernists inside the House of Saud treated the religious radicals with caution, fearing they could become more dangerous if forced underground.

On the evening of the driving protest, Prince Salman sent his deputy, Abdullah Al Bellaihed, to the police station. The husbands of the group had assembled at the station and Bellaihed told them to take their wives home after they agreed to sign a document pledging they would not allow their wives to mount a demonstration again. Women are the responsibility of their male guardians, husbands or fathers, who are held accountable for their behavior.

The next day King Fahd tried to defuse the incident. He said that a committee of religious and legal scholars should investigate before any action was taken. Prince Salman bin Abd al Abdul Aziz called together a panel who found that there was no specific prohibition against driving in the Koran. They ruled that no laws had been broken. The panel gently recommended that the demonstration not be repeated.

But by the end of the week, the driving incident had taken on important political overtones. The change was reflected in the comments of Prince Salman when he met with the husbands of the women drivers. The prince invited the husbands to a gathering at his palace. This was not a social event. He reminded them of their privileged position in society. He chided them for allowing their wives to flout the customs of the country. "What if your wife had a flat tire while driving?" he asked the group. "Would you allow your wife to talk to a repairman on the road? What if she was in an accident and taken to jail?" It was a stern lecture in a society that counts politeness as a virtue.

Prince Salman's about-face was an indication of the struggle within the ruling family between the modernizers and the traditionalists. The pressure was building from the religious reactionaries and the House of Saud felt the hot wind of the controversy. Inside the palace, the traditionalists argued that the modernizers were moving too fast. The modernizers were not only threatening Saudi culture said the traditionalists but the monarchy itself. "This government is alive today because of Islam," the prince was emphatic in his message to his assembled male guests. "If you do anything against Islam, the government will collapse." The Saudi family could claim no historical right to govern like King Hussein of Jordan, who could trace his family roots back to the Prophet, or King Hassan of Morocco, who claimed to be a descendant of the Meccan tribe of Qurayash, the relatives of the Prophet. The House of Saud's claim rested with Abdul Azziz abd al-Aziz, the father of the current monarch, who had organized the disparate tribes of Nejd under the Islamic banner that had promised to "reassert God's will in human society."

The House of Saud's long alliance with a religious reformer named Muhammad 'Abd al-Wahhab had married religion with the sword. Abd al Wahhab had preached an ascetic form of Islam to the tribes of the Najd. Later, King Abd al Aziz ibn Saud had preached unity. Both were necessary to the survival of the House of Saud.

The driving protest prompted a social spasm that was unusual in a country that clocks social change at a glacial pace. For weeks the Iraqi invasion was forgotten as Saudi Arabia turned inward and contemplated the impact of this challenge to the established order. On the Friday following the demonstration, the preachers railed at the transgressors in the capital's mosques, charging that the female offenders had lost touch with their own society. About a thousand religious fundamentalists marched on the streets of Riyadh demanding action from the government. It was a declaration of war.

The religious radicals had warned that the American presence in Saudi Arabia would be costly and now they could say they'd been proven right. In their eyes, the most damning evidence was the fact that the protest had taken place not in Jeddah, the relatively liberal Saudi city on the west coast, but in Riyadh, the heartland of Wahhabism. The region known as Najd is the birthplace of Saudi Arabia's brand of Islam. The fact that the protest was mounted by prominent Najdi families sent alarm bells ringing in the heads of the Islamists.

Within days, another leaflet circulated in Riyadh. The document was entitled "The Names of the Fallen Women Who Call for the Spread of Vice and Corruption on Earth," and it denounced the drivers as prostitutes. The leaflet also included the names of the husbands, including a political label of "communist" or "pro-American secularist." The leaflet printed the phone numbers of the protesters and was the beginning of the threatening phone calls and harassment.

On the Sunday following the Tuesday demonstration, the women's campus of King Saud University in Riyadh became a political battleground. Women professors who had taken part in the demonstration returned to their offices to find the words *infidel* and *depraved women* scrawled on their office doors. A thirty-year-old graduate student on the campus that day recounted the opening act of a drama that would involve the Riyadh police:

> A girl barged in on one of the professors in her office. The professor had a verse from the Koran hanging on the wall that said, "God will not change unless people change what's inside them." The girl pulled the professor's hair and called her names. There were two of them who started the fight and then they ran to the campus mosque. The professor ran after them and the dean locked the gates. It was total chaos.

On campus the politically religious students were known to the others as the "mosque girls." They were part of the younger generation of Saudis who had embraced conservative and radical forms of Islam. The graduate student explained:

> I don't mix with them. I was taking a literature and arts course with a couple of the "mosque girls" and they argued with the professor that we shouldn't be studying this because it was against the Koran. They distribute leaflets that say that drinking Pepsi is bad and certain kinds of cheese and breads are forbidden. They give you cassettes about the Koran and they won't listen to anyone else's opinions.

This was a familiar story. I had talked at length about religion with a Saudi woman in Dhahran, the wife of a government official. She told me about a friend whose troubled son had joined a group of young people who believed in living life as they believed it had been in the Prophet's time. The son tried to force his more liberal sisters and mother to adopt the face veil when they left the house. He lived mostly on a diet of dates and camel's milk, refusing to touch food that wasn't around in the time of the Prophet. Pepsi, potato chips, and Rice Crispies were banned from the house. He banged on the bedroom doors in the gray hours before dawn to make sure his family gathered for morning prayers.

It was a story not unlike the experience of an American family whose teenage son had joined a religious cult. The difference, of course, was that this was no cult. It was the country's mainstream religion taken to the extreme. In a country that has no political culture, often the only avenue to rebel against the government, parents, or peers is religion.

For the next few hours the women's university was in turmoil as the showdown at the mosque continued. Nuhar, a Saudi graduate student, found herself embroiled in a demonstration within the gates of the university:

> The students were divided into two, the "mosque girls" who thought it was wrong and those who thought the professors had done the right thing. But we started to argue among ourselves. We supported what they did, but maybe this wasn't the right time. Some said this is not one of our most important issues. They should have protested against the mutawaeen who harass us at the gates of the university.

By the next day, the university bowed to the religious backlash. The women professors were suspended from their jobs. In time, the other women of the protest were suspended. Their passports were withdrawn and their husbands suffered as well. Their passports were also withdrawn. In the end, the protesters and their husbands ended up under virtual house arrest. Momentum swung to the side of the conservatives until the greater war effort took center stage.

One of the dilemmas in the country was the accelerated pace of development and an educational system that created frustrations in the country. Saudi boys and girls were encouraged to study science, architecture, computers, and engineering, the idea being to end the dependence on foreign workers as the country scrambled into the twentieth century. By the late 1980s, an estimated 60,000 Saudis had attended U.S. universities.

However, the younger generation of Saudis was more conservative than the generation of the 1960s. Many of them had been educated in Saudi universities, not American ones, due partly to a Saudi policy to build and staff national universities. Many young, educated Saudis have been molded by Arab, rather than Western, professors with a strong dose of Koranic teaching. Another significant factor in the conservatism of youth was the decrease in scholarships abroad for women.

It was no accident that the women who participated in the driving incident were all over thirty. This was no youthful protest. These women were chaffing under the intense restrictions imposed on Saudis in general and women in particular. What was surprising for a Westerner was that most Saudis did accept the restrictions. There was a strong pride in Saudi Arabia's distinctive heritage. Saudis saw themselves as pure-blooded Arabs untainted by intermarriage with the non-Arab tribes of the Middle East.

The country was the birthplace of Islam and Saudis could trace their ancestry to the noble tribal families who first believed. Perhaps most important, there was a widespread understanding that it was the strong embrace of Saudi culture that was the hedge against the enormous social disruptions of unimaginable wealth. It had served them well. The country had gone from mud huts to mansions in two generations and remained one of the most stable societies in the Middle East.

The young woman at the Medical College in Jeddah couldn't have been more than twenty years old. She was wearing a loose-fitting white smock and pants. A white scarf hid her hair and even in this all-female domain she wore another piece of white silk tied in a way that only revealed her dark eyes. She led the way to an empty examining room. The hallway echoed with the soft footfalls of the Filipino nurses on staff. In this private room, Linjawi felt comfortable enough to drop her face veil so we could talk.

Amal Linjawi had not wanted to be in the first class of female dental students in Jeddah. She was here because her high school academic record was excellent. School officials had convinced her father that she was a good candidate for the program. Jeddah needed more female dentists to accommodate Saudi Arabia's strict separation of the sexes. Would she treat male patients? Linjawi closed her eyes and thought about the question.

"Women like to be treated by women dentists," she said, and then paused to think some more. Her answer was slow and tentative. "I would like to say no to treating any men." Her voice was high and timorous, like that of a child.

"From any point of view, from our religion, we're not comfortable with men. It's better for men to be treated by men because some males . . . the way they look at a woman . . . ." She looked up to see if I understood.

"Even if she's a professional woman?"

"Yes, because a man is a man and a woman is a woman. It's something inside them which they can't hold back."

Linjawi's childlike voice was now the voice of a woman. One product of Saudi Arabia's strict policy of separating men and women was an obsession with sex. It was the major taboo in the society and a major fascination. The mutawa spent much of their time preventing any congress between unrelated and unmarried men and women. Restaurants had a family section to keep the women out of sight of men. The Riyadh zoo had segregated visiting hours. Even in so-called liberal Saudi homes, an invitation to dinner usually meant an evening of conversation with the women of the family while the men ate and chatted in another room.

Sex was at the heart of the reaction to the driving protest. A woman driving raised all kinds of possibilities. The face veil would have to go as an impediment to the driver's vision. A flat tire meant a conversation with a mechanic, which many Saudis saw as an invitation to a sexual encounter.

Even the driving protesters were cautious in their call for a change in the system. One of the leaders of the protest, Aisha Al Mana, joined with a group of rich Saudi women to open an institute to promote job opportunities for women. The institute was the first of its kind, buying computers and offering special courses for the girls' schools of Riyadh. Al Mana had convinced the religious authorities, who control girls' education, that the computer classes were in keeping with the Koran. In addition, the institute made a few studies of Saudi factories and made recommendations to the Saudi businessmen on how they could place women in the workplace. But even Al Mana's studies were based on the concept of a segregated workplace. Her vision for the working Saudi woman was an all-female accounting office pecking out the company's business on a bank of computers.

Amal Linjawi had heard of the demonstrations in Riyadh. "It depends on the kinds of freedom they want. If they return back to our religion they'll find all the freedom they want. I don't know what they really want. And anyway, who are these women? Maybe they are very far from our religion even if they say they are Muslims." For the first time, Linjawi's voice was defiant. She was sure of her answers.

Riyadh's miracle mile of marbled shopping malls was often a place to get a bearing on this confusing culture. The mall was a contradiction in itself. These gleaming marble palaces of consumerism had replaced the old dark winding streets of the souk, the Middle East's traditional market. The souk had been the predominant domain of men. These shops filled with perfumes and bolts of cloth invited women customers. The only way to get here was in a car.

The Al Akareyah Mall in Riyadh was the haunt of the new generation of Saudis. The mall was always crowded with young families perusing the windows of this consumer paradise. The mutawaeen patrolled the arcade in their signature ankle-length white thobes, but my press card,

worn prominently on a chain around my neck, warded off their harassing attacks. The mall was the only place for chance encounters with
average Saudis. It was a place to check my Western perceptions against
the notions of this society.

It was autumn in Riyadh; the afternoon temperature still registered
above the 90-degree mark. The cool and quiet marble interior of Al
Akareyah, with rushing water fountains, was a modern oasis for the
Saudi shopper. Behind the cash register of the largest men's clothing
shop in the mall, Fawaz Abu Khair sat drinking coffee. He was the
owner and manager of a store that sold Western-style suits and pants,
but Abu Khair presided over the sales dressed in the traditional white
thobe and black-crowned headdress. His two Lebanese employees ran
up the totals for a line of customers.

At twenty-seven, Abu Khair had followed his father into the world
of business after a stint at a British university. He had loved his time
in England, but was glad to be back home. Abu Khair ordered two
more small glasses of Arabic coffee. "I've lived outside Saudi for seven
years. So when I came back, I saw great changes in the people themselves." He paused to check my reactions.

"Yeah, because I remember before I left, I had a girlfriend here. It
was almost top secret. Now, it's not like that. You can go up and chat
up a girl to be quite honest." His English had the cadence of a Lon-
doner.

"It's the fashion now . . . not many girls will get married anymore
unless they're in love. Not like before . . . when they never saw their
husband until the wedding day."

Relations between men and women were the bellwether of change
in this society. The invisibility of women was the measure of the kingdom's piety according to the religious authorities. It was the social issue
that measured the strength of the religious institutions that had fought
against the introduction of radio, television, the education of women,
and village health care. For Abu Khair, the pace of change in Saudi
Arabia was not the glacier of my understanding but the speed of a
freight train. He had discussed the driving protest with his family.
There had been an informal poll of sisters, mother, and fiancée. They
all agreed they did not want to drive. Why should they when a chauffeur
was available. According to Abu Khair, the family saw the protesters
in Riyadh as liberal radicals pushing the country faster than it could
go. The family poll was enough to convince him that the government's
decision had been correct.

Abu Khair had tasted the best of English culture. Like many Saudi men, he had sown his wild oats in the West and came home to claim his place in this unnervingly predictable society. "When in Rome, do what the Romans do," was his answer to the question of whether it was right for the religious police to scale the walls of a Westerner's house and arrest those inside who had been drinking.

However, Abu Khair was no religious radical. He was a practical Saudi businessman. His disdain for the mutawa came from their behavior in the mall. The mutawa harassed the women customers by barking orders to "cover up" to those women who didn't cover their entire face. They rounded up Saudi youth they suspected of ogling girls. The music shops at the mall sported signs that declared "No Women Allowed." For the mutowa, Western rock and roll was dangerously provocative. In Dhahran, the mutowa had once gone on a rampage, storming into houseware shops and smashing crystal wine glasses under the assumption that the vessel was as sinful as the act.

"Yes, the mutowa are against many things. Some extremists are even against television, but they are just hopeless," said Abu Khair in a voice filled with disgust. "These are the small mutowa. They don't know what they're talking about. Most of them have a beard, but inside . . . they don't know anything. Some of them don't believe, maybe. It's a cover, if you like, and these are the people who make trouble."

A Western diplomat had once compared Saudi Arabian society to the American television program "The Brady Bunch." He was describing a country of enormous homogeneity. The conservative religious establishment reflected the temperament of the people and the consensus of the country. Consensus—*ijama* in Arabic—is a hallowed concept in Muslim societies.

The country's system of Islamic law also reinforced the conservative outlook of the people. Saudi Arabian jurisprudence was based on the Hanbali school, one of four legal schools of thought in the Sunni Muslim tradition. Hanbali was a code that had grown and flourished during the ninth century and was the most moralistic of the Islamic legal schools. It was designed to recapture the simplicity and purity of the first community of Muslims in Medina.

It was the radicals, both the liberals and the religious, who were strange in the context of Saudi society. They were outside of the consensus of the country.

In the weeks following the driving protest, Saudis again turned their attention to the Gulf War, but the process of social change was quickening. The iceberg was not only moving but it was starting to boil.

One of the men who would stir the pot was Saudi Arabia's ambassador to Bahrain. Ten days after the driving protest, Ghazi Al Gosaibi would write an article in a London-based, Saudi-financed newspaper, *Al-Sharq Al-Awsat*. His writings became a lightning rod for the Islamic radicals. In their eyes, Gosaibi's articles were provocative, but the fact that Saudi Arabia's government-controlled news program broadcast the content of the article was proof that their message had failed to convince the House of Saud that the radicals meant business.

At the same time that Saudi television was broadcasting a children's show with little girls singing a song that expressed contempt for driving, Gosaibi was appealing to other common experiences of his countrymen. Gosaibi's article was a simple appeal to common sense. He argued that Saudi Arabia had changed dramatically in the past twenty-five years. There was a time when there were no schools for girls in the kingdom and now there are nearly one million female students in Saudi Arabia. In the not-so-distant past, wrote Gosaibi, Saudi Arabia was isolated from the rest of the world, but now "even the smallest village has direct contact with every spot in the world." The number of foreigners in the country can now be "counted in the millions," and while there was a time when it was rare to find a citizen with a car, "today, it is rare to find a citizen who is contented to have only one car."

Gosaibi wrote that during these times of momentous change Saudi Arabia had changed as well. While the religious establishment opposed the introduction of radio and television, and opposed the education of women and the entrance of women in the workplace, the change had come. The religious establishment revised their religious rulings—Fatwas—to reflect the change.

Gosaibi's point was clear: The country's history showed that religious opinions were subject to revision. "We would do well to differentiate between matters forbidden by Islamic law which cannot be argued and matters frowned upon by customs and mores," he wrote.

Gosaibi was an ardent supporter of the American deployment in Saudi Arabia. He had written long and articulate articles against the Iraqi regime from his post in Bahrain. He reminded his audience that this was no time to argue about "minor issues in the presence of a neighboring sisterly country which has usurped another, while five and a half thousand tanks and a half a million men are massed on our borders, while one thousand missiles are aimed at our cities, while one thousand planes are posed to swoop down on us. There is no scope for having dialogue on certain issues which some may see as major, but which become minor when they are compared with the issue to be or not to be."

Perhaps if some other Saudi had written an article in *Al-Sharq Al-Awsat* the matter might have been put to rest. Perhaps if the government-controlled television news program had not repeated his remarks the emotions stirred by the driving protest would have cooled in time. But Ghazi Al Gosaibi was a remarkable figure in Saudi Arabia's political culture. His position in the unremarkable job of ambassador to Bahrain belied his importance in the domestic history of the country.

Ghazi Al Gosaibi was a leading intellectual, social commentator, and accomplished poet. He was a symbol of the aspirations of the class of Western-educated technocrats who were asking for a larger say in the affairs of the country. His education was from prestigious American universities. His climb through the ranks of the Saudi bureaucracy was guided by King Fahd himself.

Fahd sheltered him early in his career when Gosaibi's poetry was under attack from religious radicals who found his verses did not meet their standards of reverence. In 1978, Gosaibi was at the center of controversy again over an interview published in *Newsweek*. The article explained that there were seven thousand young Saudis studying in the United States and that many of them would return home with secular ideas. A letter sent to Gosaibi by a man named Abdullah Bin Mohammad Bin Hameed and widely circulated in the kingdom was a reflection of an attack by the religious right:

> I do not think that you need an explanation of the advantages of Islam and the differences between the happy secure safe comfortable life of the Muslims and the life of the Westerns, which is full of debauchery and theft.
>
> You have perhaps realized the backwardness and disintegration that have recently brought defeats, dispossession and catastrophes upon the Muslims have been caused by their deviation from their religion and receiving their educations from the nations of nonbelievers by sending their sons to the enemies, who have taught them loose behavior . . . and returned to their country empty of any belief and alienated from Islam and worked to implement what they have learned abroad. Brother Ghazi, if that disgraceful statement was really made by you, it is a great sin and you must retract it by repenting to God Almighty, making your repentance public so that people's minds and consciences may rest assured that those who are in charge of their affairs return to righteousness hastily.

In the relatively liberal atmosphere of the 1970s, Gosaibi survived the religious attack unscathed. His reputation as an uncorruptible government official was in his favor and perhaps it was the reason that King Fahd appointed him to the Ministry of Health. It was a move that would result in his political exile.

In his new position, Gosaibi had tried to streamline a bloated health care system. He chose as his target hospitals that were under the control of powerful members of the House of Saud. His work earned him an enemy list that included senior members of the royal family. It was a poem printed in Riyadh's *Al-Jarzirah* newspaper that proved to be Gosaibi's ultimate undoing. The poem was not addressed directly to King Fahd, but the verses left little doubt about the subject:

Why should I go on singing while there are a thousand slanderers and backbiters going between you and me?

They deluded you and you liked their deceitfulness, but you used to abhor the artificial perfume.

Tell the slanderers that I am coming with white banner held high so that they may walk and run in my earth.

Gosaibi was fired within days of the publication of the poem. The announcement of his fall from grace was printed in the same paper that had printed his poem.

For six years, Ghazi Al Gosaibi kept a relatively low profile in the Saudi Arabian Embassy in Bahrain. He unsheathed his weapon of words again as the Iraqi tanks rolled over the border of Kuwait. He was primed and ready to go when the forty-nine Saudi women embarked on their protest.

The leaflet and cassette war of domestic politics in Saudi Arabia continued to build. Saudis collected the writings of Gosaibi and the responses from his opposition. Saudis kept their well-read copies in the bottom of desk drawers and in secret places at home. The pile of papers swelled with the addition of poems attacking the women drivers and others praising their courage. The revolution in foreign policy now had a domestic component. "No more Mr. Nice Guy" was the rallying cry for the liberals and the reactionaries. This was a new phase in the country's political culture. The debate carried out on paper and poetry, in the mosques, and in the homes of the Saudi elite was a national secret that everybody knew.

Political organization was forbidden in the kingdom, so the religious right had a natural advantage. They had the mosques. A liberal university professor once complained to me that it was an unfair advantage. "The religious have cell meetings five times a day," he said with a touch of humor, referring to the prayer times in the country. The Friday sermons in the capital could be turned into a political rally by a clever speaker. One such man was Naser Al Omar. He was a particularly adept soldier in the battles with Gosaibi. Naser Al Omar was a dean of one of the colleges at the University of Imam Mohammad ibn Saud in Riyadh. His sermons were taped and became part of the collection for Saudis who were interested in the progress of the domestic war. Al Omar's speeches warned against secularist plots:

> The tragedy and problem, brethren, is that the secularists live amongst us, speak our language, wear our clothes, eat and drink with us, and some of them even pray in our mosques, and this is very dangerous. Some good people may get taken in by the plots and tricks of those evil persons. So beware of being lured. Be alert, careful, perceptive, and rational. . . . Provocation is for a Muslim to behave without wisdom, which is what they want, and I warn of this.

Al Omar warned his flock of the danger of the leaflets that were circulating in the kingdom. He advised them to bring these offensive papers to religious scholars for their comments. He called for documentation on the sins of the "secularists," but advised his followers of the consequences if they resorted to violence.

"I have heard that there are those who call for what is called violence and I have heard this verse of poetry:

Brother, the Plague has spread beyond the limit,
It's time for Jihad, it's time for sacrifice.

"Yes, the plague has spread beyond the limit, but repeating this verse of poetry or similar ones could lead to things which will have undesirable consequences. . . . If those who call for violence are to be punished, then the secularists who cause them to do so must also be punished before them. . . . We must punish those who spread sin in the country and among the people."

In the recording, Naser Al Omar's voice reverberated off the stone walls of the Riyadh mosque. He raged against the Saudi state's blindness on the issues of interest in banks and insurance, both practices forbidden by the Koran. But he saved his energy for his last point, a call to action against what he called the "incident." It was the women driving in Riyadh that prompted this speech and he gave his prescription for action:

With regard to the incident, we must do the following: (1) demand that those women be turned over to the religious system, to the religious courts; (2) reveal who is behind them and hit them with a fist of iron; (3) demand that the university for girls be established.

The next shot in the war of words was fired by Gosaibi in a series of five articles titled "Lest There Be Sedition." In effect, Gosaibi was calling on the head of the religious establishment, Sheikh Abdul Azziz Bin Baz, to declare a cease-fire between the warring groups. But Gosaibi did not go quietly. He charged that his attackers were political opportunists. Their aim, said Gosaibi, was to overthrow the House of Saud. Their method was religion in the service of politics. In his most ideologically charged article, he compared the statements of Naser Al Omar to Iran's Ayatollah, and said he had ambitions to become "the coming Khomeini of the kingdom."

S I X

THE ROAD
TO DAMASCUS

"The foreigners who came to the region were not responsible for
the event that brought them to the region. If we want these foreigners to be out as soon as possible, we have to find a solution
to this event so we might not leave a pretext . . . for them to remain
as unwanted guests."
—Damascus radio, August 20

Hafez al Asad had kept his promise. The joint honor guard on November 4 at the Yanbu port was a testament to that pledge. The green
flag of Saudi Arabia fluttered alongside the gray and blue silk banner
of a stag's head, the flag of Syria's Ninth Armored Division. The Syrian
president gave his word to the Saudi king that Syrian troops would
join the coalition and Asad was a man who kept his word. He was also
the shrewdest political operator in the Middle East. An American
president had called him brilliant. A U.S. secretary of state had written
that Asad was a "proud, tough, shrewd" negotiator who "plays out the
string to absolutely the last possible millimeter." Even Asad's enemies
had a grudging respect. The Gulf crisis would test Hafez al Asad's
reputation as a brilliant tactician and a formidable negotiator.

These Syrian troops boarded the Saudi cargo ship *Qassim* at the
Syrian port of Tartus more than a week earlier. The Saudis had to
provide transportation after an arrangement with a Soviet sealift had

fallen through. The Italian crew on the Saudi ship looked after the Syrians and their tanks on the cruise down the Mediterranean and the Red Sea even as the Syrian government launched a vitriolic press campaign against the United States.

The attack was triggered by a series of announcements in Washington. The U.S. Congress approved an arms package worth billions to Saudi Arabia. The deal included F-15 jets, Patriot antimissile missile batteries, and M1A-2 Abrams tanks. The sale raised eyebrows and voices in Israel about the price of America's new alliance in the Arab world.

In October, just as the Syrian soldiers were boarding the *Qassim* for the Saudi coast, the Bush administration announced another arms package, this time to Israel. The U.S. president promised to dispatch two advanced PAC-2 Patriot missile batteries to Israel. Israeli crews were going to Texas to train on this new piece of equipment.

This was part of the military equation when Hafez al Asad first agreed to send troops to Saudi Arabia. A surprise statement released in Damascus on October 25 attributed to an unnamed government official had urged "all Arabs to reconsider their support of American intervention in the Gulf." The report contained tough talk against the American arms shipments of Patriot missiles, F-15 fighter jets, and helicopters to the Jewish state. The press offensive was vintage Syrian tactics and it appeared designed to unsettle the Arab coalition so carefully built by the Saudis and the Americans.

The Syrian Arab News Agency (SANA) report said, "The Syrian government had woken up to the fact that the United States and Israel were implementing a region-wide plot against the Arabs by diverting their attention with the Gulf crisis as Israel prepared to deliver the fatal blow to Arab resistance."

Lebanese newspapers reported renewed contacts between the Syrians and the Jordanians. King Hussein was Saddam Hussein's chief ally in the region, performing like a lawyer for the Iraqi leader, arguing his client's merits in Washington and in Arab capitals. The Syrian announcement in SANA had addressed Jordan's greatest fears:

Syria hoped that Washington's position in the Gulf was motivated by the defense of international law and that Washington would work with more credibility toward a just, comprehensive settlement of the Middle East issue, but all the evidence indicates that the American-Israeli goal is to strike the Arabs, weaken them, expand at the expense of their territories, and liquidate the Palestinian issue by implementing the plan to "transfer" the Palestinians east into Jordan.

These were not the pronouncements of an ally. While American and Saudi officials kept quiet about their concerns, the *Wall Street Journal* gave voice to their thinking by claiming "the international pariah and source of treachery" would not dispatch its armor to join the coalition. On November 4, Hafez al Asad had proved them wrong.

The Syrian president had much to gain by his membership in this American-dominated club against Iraq. Already there were large sums of aid money on the way from Riyadh and Kuwait. More important for Asad, he had eliminated a pesky enemy in Lebanon with what appeared to be the tacit approval of his Gulf crisis allies. On October 13, the vain and noisy Lebanese General Michael Aoun fled his concrete bunker beneath the shell-shattered presidential palace in East Beirut to take refuge in the French Embassy. Syrian tanks and heavy artillery put an end to Aoun's military morality play for Lebanese sovereignty.

Hafez al Asad set his own goals for the crisis. Lebanon was the glittering prize. Before the invasion of Kuwait, Aoun had been not so secretly armed by Iraq. The United Nations' boycott had a side benefit for the Syrian leader. The arms shipments stopped. The time was right; the last challenge to a pax Syriana in Lebanon was out of the way.

American arms to Israel was a troublesome development for a man who was deeply in debt to the Soviet Union for a policy of building strategic parity with his southern neighbor. Asad had seized power in a bloodless coup in 1970 during the second great surge of Soviet aid to Syria. He had almost reached his goal of military parity with Israel when the Soviet Union collapsed.

If Iraq was defeated, and Asad must have calculated that this was a strong possibility, there would be a power vacuum in the Middle East. Iraq was Syria's strategic reserve, the bench team for any future wars with the Israelis. It was hard enough to justify joining the Americans. How could he explain his position to a country fed on anti-Israeli rhetoric if Israel got involved in this fight? Asad was not shy about his displeasure over the arms delivery.

The Saudis were relieved enough when the *Qassim* finally docked at Yanbu. Government officials had chartered a plane for the reporters and photographers and catered the two-hour flight from Dhahran on the east coast to Yanbu on the west. Saudi newspapers had reproduced selective articles from the Syrian press that called for a military solution in Kuwait. There was no mention of the aid money or the Patriots for Israel on this day. Reporters swarmed over Saudi General Khalid ibn Sultan as he emerged from his powder-blue Cadillac.

The Syrians are "here to fight if necessary," Khalid said and beamed for the photographers. If Khalid was surprised that Asad had sent 145 of his older-model T-62 tanks rather than the top-of-the-line Soviet-made T-72s, he didn't say so. The Saudis paid 500 million dollars to Damascus with a promise of another 500 million in economic aid. The money apparently didn't buy the best of the Syrian arsenal, but Syria's participation in the coalition was important enough that Khalid might have smiled just as broadly if the Syrians had embarked from the *Qassim* on roller skates.

In military terms the Ninth Armored Division was more useful to the coalition at home. Syria shared a long border with western Iraq. Syrian troops deployed along that border would have split Saddam's troop deployment. However, in political terms Syria was an invaluable addition to the coalition. Syria had impeccable credentials as the vanguard of Arab nationalism. It was a banner that the Saudis and the Egyptians lacked. It was important for the politics of the coalition for Syrian troops to play a prominent role in the front line in Saudi Arabia.

This was the vanguard of the 20,000 Syrian troops that Asad had pledged to the coalition. There were 3000 Syrians on board the *Qassim*. The remainder of the Ninth Armored Division was expected to arrive in a few weeks. Another 1000 Syrian soldiers were being dispatched to the United Arab Emirates.

The Ninth Division had been chosen carefully. They were normally deployed near the Golan Heights on the disputed border with Israel. The Ninth was a crack division, but there was another characteristic that had made them the right choice for this job: These men were from Asad's own minority Alawite Muslim sect. Considering the sensitivity of this endeavor, their loyalty was important.

According to reports from Paris, the Syrian Ninth Armored Division was to replace French troops near the Kuwaiti border. According to those same reports, the Saudis were said to believe that the "Arab forces on the front line would make the situation politically more palatable to the Arab world."

Major General Ali Habib, commander of the Syrian troops, strode down the iron gang plank to the quay side. He was a stocky man with a paunch that stretched his crisp army uniform. A carefully groomed black mustache graced his upper lip. It was the only part of his face that moved as he eyed the squall of reporters waiting for him. Habib's army boots crumped down the metal ramp to the black tarmac of the Yanbu port as the Syrian tank drivers on board the *Qassim* prepared their T-62 tanks, newly painted with desert camouflage, for the first ride on Saudi soil.

Habib ignored the shouted questions of the media until a reporter asked if he was happy to be fighting alongside the Americans. Habib smiled broadly, then chuckled, and shook his head. "No." It was the only official pronouncement from the Syrian military that day.

The honor guard was already in place for the official welcoming ceremony. A dozen Syrian T-62 tanks and four brand new ZSU tracked radar-guided anti-aircraft guns had been unloaded earlier to serve as a backdrop for this political theater. The Saudi general and the Syrian commander embraced. The welcome speech was full of praise for the Syrians. There was much talk about the Syrians and the Saudis fighting in the same trenches. The Syrians would be under Saudi command, said Khalid bin Sultan, but "they always have a direct line with President Asad." He hardly needed to remind these Syrian soldiers. Each Syrian tank had the face of the Syrian leader stenciled in black near the gun turret.

Asad's public pronouncements for sending a Syrian contingent hadn't changed from his first statements in August to the second deployment in November. Asad promised these troops to King Fahd. Asad said the Syrian troops were in Saudi Arabia to protect the holy places in Mecca and Medina. Asad also said he believed that the Arab soldiers would eventually replace the Western forces. On November 8, an editorial in the official newspaper of Syria's Ba'th party spelled out the terms once again. The Syrian troops sent to Saudi Arabia were there to defend Saudi Arabia, not to attack Iraq.

Asad's public position was no different from that of every other national leader who had assigned troops to the coalition. President George Bush told the American people that the American military was in Saudi Arabia for defensive purposes. However, in private, the Americans were already polling the Arab commanders to find out who was on board for an offensive operation against Iraq. Syria had justified its presence in the Gulf by saying they were there to prevent war, not to wage it. Syria's Ba'thist ideology of "one Arab nation" made their participation in a move over the Kuwaiti border unlikely.

• • •

Hafez al Asad had decided to join the American-led coalition even before his meeting with John Kelly, the U.S. under secretary of state. A few days before the Arab summit in Cairo, the Syrian press issued a statement declaring Syria's intention to place Syrian troops "between the two potentially belligerent forces" in the Gulf, namely, Iraq and the United States.

It was Saudi Foreign Minster Saud al Faisal who urged the Americans to send a delegation to Damascus. Saud argued that the Syrians had been "helpful" at the Arab summit in Cairo and a high-level visit by the Americans would be "wise." Kelly met with the Saudi foreign minister in Riyadh and he added a Damascus stop to his Middle East tour.

According to an American official on the trip, Asad was briefed on the general disposition of American troops. The American delegation told the Syrian president that the United States would "look favorably" on Syria's participation. "We both have a common interest," John Kelly told the Syrian president according to an American official present at the time. Kelly explained what kind of force the Americans were putting in the desert. The meeting was three hours long. There was nothing dramatic about the encounter, considering that Asad, a man who had made a career and a religion of Arab nationalism, was making a dramatic turn toward the West.

Perhaps more than any other Arab leader, Asad understood the implications of the changing relationship of the superpowers. He had cautiously tacked West in the new political wind. The turn could be dated to the change in the Soviet Union under the leadership of Mikhail Gorbachev. In 1987, Asad was invited to Moscow for the first face-to-face meeting with the new Soviet leader. Gorbachev said publicly what the Syrians had been hearing privately for some time. The Soviet Union would no longer underwrite Asad's dream of strategic parity with the Jewish state. He told Asad it was unnatural for the Soviet Union not to have relations with Israel. Soviet Foreign Minister Edvard Shevardnadze made it clear that while the Soviet Union would maintain Syria's defensive needs, the days of supplying offensive weapons were over. A new ambassador, known to support Moscow's new thinking, was posted to Damascus.

By 1987, Soviet arms sales to Damascus were already shrinking. In 1989, at a chemical weapons conference in Paris, the Soviets opposed an Arab plan to link chemical weapons production with nuclear proliferation, a signal understood by Israel, the only country in the region to have nuclear weapons. The era of military confrontation was coming to an end. Syria's policy of strategic parity would have to yield to one of diplomatic parity. The region's master tactician would have to find a way to make a virtue out of necessity.

The new tack in Damascus was clear even before the Iraqi invasion. The Western hostage crisis in Lebanon had prompted a working relationship between Washington and Damascus. In 1988, the Lebanese elections opened discreet cooperation between George Shultz's state department and the Syrians as they both worked behind the scenes to back a presidential candidate.

In the Arab arena, Asad started his slow and cautious course in 1987 at an Islamic Conference Organization meeting in Kuwait. The conferees were focused on the Iran-Iraq War, but Asad used the occasion for an unusual meeting with Egyptian President Hosni Mubarek. Two years later, on December 27, 1989, Asad ended more than a decade of estrangement with Cairo and opened relations. (They had been broken off after the Camp David peace agreement.)

Asad had to change directions. Syria's economy was in pitiful shape. Damascus was a drab place, a little like an eastern European capital. Daily electricity cuts in the capital as well as chronic shortages of hard currency were the norm. Privilege was measured by access to toilet paper and boxes of tissues, commodities available on the black market that regularly disappeared from Syrian shops for months at a time. Syria's debt to the Soviet Union was enormous. While some of the money was paid off in barter deals with the new entrepreneurs from the republics, only trade with Europe and the United States would bring hard cash into the government coffers.

Syria had already paid dearly for her lonely alignment with Tehran during the Gulf War. Iraq's victory in the contest had left Asad politically isolated and vulnerable to Iraqi meddling in Lebanon.

The rapprochement with Egypt at the end of 1989 was a signal to the Americans. At the time, Washington and Cairo were promoting a dialogue between the Israelis and the Palestinians. While Asad was not interested in taking part in the talks, he was not going to stand in the way either. The Americans were well aware of the Middle East formula first expressed by Jordan's king years ago: You can't make war in the Middle East without Egypt and you can't make peace without Syria.

The ideological leaps required to make friends with the one Arab country that had made peace with Israel were never mentioned. In the Arab world they rarely are, and besides, Mubarek and Asad had old school ties. Both had been trained as pilots in the Soviet Union. By

August 2, 1990, the direction of Syrian politics was clear. The only question was the speed of the moves. The Gulf crisis provided a short-cut.

Syria would have to prove good intentions to get serious attention from Washington. A commitment of troops to the coalition was a satisfactory beginning. Some of the results were seen in a meeting in the third week of August with a high-ranking American official. Kelly and Asad discussed the recent vote in the United Nations. Just a few days earlier, the United Nations Security Council had passed Resolution 661, a vote that would mean a virtual siege of Iraq.

"What took you so long?" asked the Syrian president. "I declared an economic boycott against Iraq in 1982."

Syria had closed Baghdad's oil pipeline that stretched from the Iraq oil fields to the Syrian port of Biwas. The Arab world's two Ba'thist regimes had a long history of enmity by 1982. However, Asad's decision would cost him. Kuwait suspended all financial aid to Damascus in retaliation for Syria's lonely support of Tehran.

Five days after the Iraqi invasion of Kuwait, Iraq's oil minister, Issam abd al Rahim al Chalabi, arrived in Damascus on a trip arranged through the mediation of the Jordanians. Al Chalabi had a simple but important deal to offer. In the name of Arab solidarity, al Chalabi asked that the Syrians reverse an eight-year policy and reopen the Iraqi oil pipeline. Al Chalabi offered to share Baghdad's oil revenues.

There was quiet support in the middle-class salons of Damascus for Saddam's bold move into Kuwait. The Syrians had their own gripes against the Kuwaitis; many saw them as rich, spoiled Arabs who deserved the come-uppance. There was a popular feeling among the Syrians that the Gulf states controlled a disproportionate share of the oil wealth and had squandered the oil power. The official talks with the Iraqi oil minister continued for two days and al Chalabi was given a grand tour of Syria's Banyas Oil Terminal.

It is likely that Hafez al Asad appreciated the irony of the gesture. Perhaps it is why the visit lasted as long as it did. For Saddam, it was the equivalent of a riverboat gambler's bet. It was an offer of all or nothing to Saddam's Ba'thist rival.

Many Middle East commentators had compared Hafez al Asad and Saddam Hussein and found similarities. These were the two men who represented the face of Ba'thism in the Arab world. Asad and Saddam came from humble beginnings and both knew humiliating poverty as young men. Asad was the ninth child of eleven from a poor farming district in northern Syria. Both men belonged to minority communities in their respective countries. They had both embraced the ideology of Ba'thism (revival or renaissance) in their youth. They shared a commitment to Arab unity and the almost mystical belief in "one Arab nation" that carried the hope of restoring Arab dignity and destiny.

Both men ran regimes with an iron hand with the help of an extensive network of security police and intelligence operatives. They both had used terrorism as an arm of foreign policy, although Asad's hired thugs were more often turned on Syrian and Palestinian foes. Both men surrounded themselves with loyalists. For Saddam it was his relatives from his home village of Takrit. For Asad it was members of the Alawite Muslim sect. Saddam had ordered the gassing of his own citizens in the Kurdish villages of the north. Asad's brother, Rifaat, led the charge against Muslim fundamentalists in the Syrian city of Hama that left more than 15,000 dead.

There was no argument that Hafez al Asad ran a regime that was almost as unattractive as Saddam's. There the similarities ended. Discounting Lebanon, Asad avoided the foreign adventures of his rival in Baghdad. His air force experience and training as a fighter pilot in the Soviet Union had added a level of sophistication that his Baghdad colleague lacked. Asad was a nondrinking vegetarian who led an ascetic life. He was a man who read extensively and understood the lessons of history. Asad had a sense of humor. He had transformed a small country of 12 million people into a political center of gravity in the Middle East. He had done it without the revenues of oil that paid for Saddam's pointless warfare. Asad played the game of Middle East politics well. In the past few years, he rebuilt the coalition of Cairo, Riyadh, and Damascus. He was the master of brinksmanship, but he knew the limits of his actions. It gave him the flexibility to choose his next move carefully.

Syria delivered the answer to the Iraqi oil minister at the end of the two-day meeting. The Syrian reply was just as simple as the Iraqi request, although disingenuous in light of the stakes. Damascus turned down the Iraqi proposal, claiming that such an important step could only be taken within the framework of complete normalization of relations. It was diplomatic language for "take a hike."

Syria made no mention of the fact that another Arab visitor had doubled the Iraqi offer. Saudi Arabian Prince Abdullah was in Damascus at the same time. Abdullah was known as the Arab nationalist in the Saudi ruling family. He had close connections with the Syrian president. The Saudi's wife was Syrian-born and Abdullah had a close relationship with Asad's brother Rifaat.

One day later at the Cairo summit Syria voted with twelve other Arab governments to support the presence of American troops in Saudi Arabia. On August 15, the first contingent of Syrian soldiers arrived in Saudi Arabia. The first installment on Hafez al Asad's promise was about a thousand men from a Syrian commando unit.

There had been much international wheeling and dealing in the months between the first arrival of the Syrian commando unit and the second deployment of the Ninth Syrian Armored Division. The costs and benefits of joining the coalition against Iraq were more clear.

The United States had announced a plan to forgive Egypt's massive 7.1-billion-dollar debt. Egypt had already received 2 billion dollars from the Saudis and the United Arab Emirates. The Gulf Cooperation Council was preparing an annual Egyptian aid program that would range between 1 billion and two billion dollars, in addition to the announced intention to sink 2 to 3 billion dollars in investments. Turkey had announced that Saudi Arabia and the UAE were to supply the country with oil to replace the deliveries from Iraq.

Syria saw its benefits as small by comparison. America's allies in Europe had lifted sanctions imposed on Iran but kept their anti-Syrian sanctions in place. The French government was particularly critical of Asad's actions in Beirut and the Paris press was calling for a Syrian withdrawal. The United States had yet to remove Syria from the State Department list of countries who supported terrorism, a key to gaining favorable trade relations with Washington. Damascus was annoyed by the American press campaign of anti-Syrian articles. The Syrian leader was performing some valuable work for the anti-Saddam coalition.

At the end of August, Asad made a rare foreign visit to Tehran. The Gulf crisis had reactivated their alliance that had grown cold since the end of the Iran-Iraq War. Following two days of meetings, Iranian President Hashemi Ali Akbar Rafsanjani said his country did not object to the presence of foreign troops in the Gulf to contain Iraqi aggression. More important was the discussion about the United Nations sanctions against the Baghdad regime. Both Iran and Syria had long borders with Iraq, and the Syrians agreed to play a role in enforcing the sanctions.

In October, Syrian Foreign Minister Farouq al Shar'a delivered a blistering attack on Baghdad at the United Nations. He accused Saddam of diverting attention from the Palestinian issue. Syria rejected Baghdad's link of Israel's occupation of Arab lands with Iraq's occupation of Kuwait.

By late October, the Syrian press began to reflect a more ambiguous attitude in Damascus. At the same time that the government-controlled newspaper *Tishrin* was chanting the anti-American line, another Syrian daily, *al-Thawra,* warned that the international community was running out of patience with Iraq's intransigence. The newspaper predicted that a highly destructive war was just around the corner. While *al Thawra* commended the Arab leaders who were trying to find a peaceful solution to the problem, the newspaper *Tishrin* rebuked those who harped on an "Arab solution."

The Syrian press was more comfortable with its old role of driving home the theme of Syria's special mission to block Zionist expansionism and uphold Arab honor and help the Palestinians regain their "usurped" homeland. The Gulf crisis presented uncharted rhetorical waters. It also reflected the caution of the Syrian leader.

Hafez al Asad had been shaped as much by his membership in a minority Muslim sect that had once supplied bourgeois Damascus with its cleaning ladies as by his nation's history. His identification with the Alawite sect left him open to charges that he was pursuing what was best for his own kind. His nationalist credentials had to be beyond reproach. He was a man who understood the price of power as well as the cost of war. He would be judged on his ability to get the best deal for all of Syria.

A second American delegation arrived in the Syrian capital three days after the Syrian Ninth Division docked at Yanbu. On November 7, John Kelly was back in Damascus again. This time the meetings were with Foreign Minister Farouq al Shar'a. This time the mood in Damascus had changed in subtle ways. The Syrian minister was cool to his American visitors. There was a hint of apprehension in Shara's tone. "They thought we were going to use them, and at the same time they thought that we were going to take them off the terrorist list, which we haven't to this day," said an American official who participated in the talks. Al Shar'a made it clear that the Syrian troops were in Saudi Arabia to cooperate with the Saudis. They were not to come under American control.

The Americans had an agenda of their own. In every meeting with the Syrians the State Department representatives had instructions to bring up the following topics: human rights, hostages in Lebanon, treatment of Syrian Jews, and terrorism. Ahmed Jabril, the ex-Syrian army officer who headed a renegade faction within the Palestinian movement, had his headquarters in Damascus. The Popular Front for the Liberation of Palestine—General Command had been targeted in the Western press as responsible for the terrorist attack on a Pan

American flight that had exploded over Lockerbie, Scotland, in 1989. The initial international investigations had laid the blame for the attack on Jabril's operatives.

The issue had been raised with the Syrian president in the August meeting with Kelly. "Give me the evidence that he participated," said the Syrian president. The Lockerbie case remained under investigation and there was no hard proof.

Kelly had raised the subject again in his meeting with Farouq al Shar'a. This time the Syrians were impatient with the American agenda. Syria's place on the terrorist list could be attributed in part to the peculiarities of American policy. The Americans had struck Iraq from the list in 1982 when it had been convenient to do so. Terrorism was a sensitive issue in the Middle East because the definition was subjective.

Syrian officials said the Americans were ungrateful for Syria's help. They accused Washington of insensitivity to Syrian public opinion. Terrorism was an inappropriate subject, said Syrian officials, at a time of crisis.

According to Arab sources in contact with the U.S. Central Intelligence Agency, Syria was supplying information to help shut down terrorist cells in Europe and the Middle East. Saddam Hussein had planned to activate the terrorist card. By late September, two Palestinian leaders had issued warnings that they would strike. George Habash, head of the Popular Front for the Liberation of Palestine, had threatened military action if the United States attacked Iraq. Abu Abbas, the leader of the Palestine Liberation Front, warned of retaliation against U.S. targets if any Iraqi aircraft were harmed by the enforcement of the United Nations blockade. There is no evidence that Syrian information prevented terrorist attacks, but the fact is that there were no serious incidents for the duration of the crisis. The Palestinian groups based in Damascus were allowed to say what they liked, but the Syrian security kept a close watch on their movements.

In this early November meeting another issue was of vital importance for the Americans. "We talked to the Syrians about whether it would be useful to have another United Nations resolution, the one that talked about 'all necessary means,' " said an American official in the delegation to Damascus. "All necessary means" was diplomatic language for an offensive operation against the Iraqi army in Kuwait. The Americans and the British had argued that Article 51 of the United Nations Charter gave the necessary authority. There was concern in Washington and in London that a vote on another united resolution with such explicit language was politically dangerous. There would be opposition from the third world delegations in New York. A defeat at the United Nations would be a political disaster.

It was reasonable to think that at this point in the crisis there would be no war. There appeared to be much room for compromise. The Soviet envoy, Yevgeny Primakov, had been shuttling in and out of the Iraqi capital. His credentials were well known in Damascus where he had been based as a Pravda correspondent in the 1950s. European diplomats, ex-politicians, and other assorted political wannabees had been pictured sitting stiffly next to Saddam Hussein in hostage negotiations. Saudi Defense Minister Prince Sultan bin abd al-aziz said on October 21 that Saudi Arabia "sees no harm in any Arab country giving its Arab sister land, a site, or a position on the sea." While Prince Sultan said his comments were misinterpreted, his remarks were seized upon in Europe as a bid for Kuwait to give over the islands of Bubiyan and Warba as an incentive for Iraqi withdrawal.

The bids for compromise had reverberations in the streets of Damascus. Syrian officials complained to their American counterparts that they were having trouble with public opinion. Syria's clandestine Muslim brothers had given their support to Saddam. There were reports in the Western press of violent pro-Saddam demonstrations in the Syrian towns that straddled the Iraq border. No Western journalist had actually seen the demonstrations and the Syrians maintained that the reports were the fantasies of Jordanian intelligence. However, Asad had taken the unusual step of organizing a series of briefings for Ba'th party regulars and military officers to explain his policy. An explicit United Nations resolution might help to quiet the unease. The Syrians told the Americans that a United Nations resolution was necessary.

The Saudis gave the same answer to U.S. Secretary of State James Baker. The Saudi argument raised another troubling point. A war with Iraq pitted Arabs against Arabs and the Saudis argued that if Arabs had to fight Arabs they would require an international cover. The message was clear. The Americans would have to wage a political war in New York before the real war in Kuwait.

"The Syrians said they thought Article 51 was sufficient, but another resolution would help with their public opinion," said an American official involved with the talks. "There was a real debate on the issue. The Syrians advised us not to go after the resolution unless we were sure we could get it. They told us that if we failed it would be a propaganda coup for Saddam."

Within a few weeks, Asad's great gamble began to pay off. A senior official from Britain's foreign office, David Gore Booth, arrived in Damascus for talks aimed at restoring relations. The British had cut ties in 1986 when Nazar Hindawi, a Jordanian-Palestinian with a Syrian passport, was convicted of trying to blow up an El-Al airliner leaving Heathrow Airport in London. New aid money from Europe was earmarked for Syria. The Syrian foreign minister was given the red carpet treatment on a trip to Rome.

On November 23, Asad received the ultimate seal of approval. In a hastily arranged meeting in Geneva, President George Bush shook hands with the Syrian leader to the consternation of the Israelis. It was a remarkable political symbol. It had been thirteen years since an American president had offered a hand to the Syrian leader. It had been more than a decade since the Syrian leader had felt he'd gotten a fair hearing from an American president.

President Jimmy Carter had offered friendship to Syria in the same European city in 1977. The two men had met at a summit arranged to bring peace to the Middle East following the 1973 Arab-Israeli War. It was a high point in Syrian-American relations that would soon sour as events in the Middle East took an unexpected turn. The Western tilt in Damascus collapsed as Jimmy Carter negotiated the Camp David agreements. In Syrian eyes it was a separate and unacceptable peace. More than a decade of distrust had colored relations between Damascus and Washington.

The Geneva meeting in November brought the relationship full circle. However, Asad would need more to close the gap between the contradictions of his policy and the popular sentiments at home. A meeting in Geneva with the president of the United States was the first installment of relations that could open the door to trade and respect in the West. President Bush raised the issue of Ahmed Jabril once again. Asad's answer became the talk of the diplomatic circuit in Damascus for months to come. "If I hand over Jabril," said the Syrian president, "then he will hire a smart American lawyer to get him out of jail. Once he's out, he'll get a green card [a document that allows a foreigner to work in the United States]. That would be a big problem for you. It is better that I take care of Ahmed Jabril."

Like all of the Arab contingents, the Syrians made their camp in the vast desert plains of northern Saudi Arabia. They signed on for the Schwarzkopf enterprise and were accorded all of the privileges of every other Arab battalion in the theater including an American special forces and air force liaison team.

U.S. Air Force Captain Scott Purdue was one of the first Americans to be assigned to the Syrian forces. He had come to Saudi Arabia from the Fifth Corp in Frankfurt, Germany. Purdue was a thirty-three-year-old soft-spoken Southerner whose only knowledge of the Arabs came from reading Leon Uris' novel *The Haj*. With this fairly racist portrayal of Arabs in his head, Purdue was hardly prepared for the Syrians.

"Most of the time they were nice," said Purdue. "They really didn't trust us, and they didn't think a war was going to happen, and if a war wasn't going to happen, they didn't want to work with the Americans."

In the early days of the deployment, the Saudis organized a media trip every Tuesday to Hafr al-Batin, an outpost town in the Saudi desert 50 miles from the Kuwaiti border. Hafr al-Batin was the hub of the Arab coalition forces and the Saudis had caught on fast to the value of publicity for the Arab armies that had joined the coalition. Weekly at 6 A.M. sharp the Saudi Royal Air Force C-130 transport rumbled down the tarmac runway at the Dhahran Military Air Base for the ninety-minute flight north to Hafr al-Batin.

When the plane door opened, the heat of the engines combined with the hot air of a desert day. The landing swept up the scorched sand and blew it in gusts that scraped the skin and eyes. There was nothing pretty about Hafr al-Batin. It was not a quaint town. The two-lane highway past the concrete houses and shops was strewn with abandoned cars, the debris of a careless consumer society. The small gas stations that dotted the road to the desert were well-stocked mini supermarkets. Even in the most remote stop, the shelves were full of Pringles potato chips and Twinkies. The populace in this part of the desert had apparently developed a taste for Diet Pepsi, the red and silver cans stacked and sweating in the stand-up coolers at the back of the stores. As the weeks wore on, the trips to Hafr al-Batin became a hunt for the illusive Syrians.

Saudi Air Force Officer Colonel Ibrahim Sharif was the expedition leader for all trips to Hafr al-Batin. He was an unusually efficient and open man with a wry sense of humor who ended most of his sentences with the phrase "bloody hell." Colonel Sharif was from a Najdi family in Riyadh, but he didn't have much tolerance for the dour atmosphere of the Saudi capital. He had taken to his job as media liaison for the international press in the eastern province with some gusto. He had gone out of his way to facilitate even the most difficult requests such as arranging for a bus to make the six-hour drive to the border town of Khafji at 3 A.M. Journalists had gotten word about a new flood of Kuwaiti refugees and pressed Sharif to arrange a bus on two hours notice. He caught hell in the morning from a Saudi prince for not asking permission. "We had to take them up there," said Sharif, shaking his head over breakfast. "Bloody hell!"

The Syrians were trying the patience of Colonel Sharif. For weeks he promised to produce the Syrians for a press corps that had grown tired of the long plane and bus rides to interview more Egyptians and Saudis. Even the spectacle of Egyptian rangers eating live snakes and rabbits to show off their ability at desert survival did not quell the news lust for the Syrians. The addition of Syrian commando units to the Arab coalition was news, but the Syrians remained phantoms in the desert.

American military personnel weren't having much better luck. Captain James Korentz and Lieutenant Colonel Bill Davis of the Fifth Special Forces had been assigned to the Syrian commando unit. They were there as advisors or trainers or whatever else it took to level the disparities of military doctrine, tactical concepts, culture, and language. The Syrian commander agreed to host the American teams, providing them with food and water. On October 31, Korentz and Davis drove into the desert to arrange their living quarters. The Syrian commander ordered their tent to be place 2.2 kilometers away from the Syrian camp.

"It was so different with the other ones," said Korentz. "We met the Egyptian rangers and we couldn't get away. We ended up spending ten hours with the Egyptians partying and drinking tea."

In these early months of the deployment in the desert the politics and mutual suspicions between Damascus and Washington reached a long hand into this inhospitable terrain. It was all a political game in the beginning understood in Riyadh as a matter of patience. The American Special Forces commander had sent a request to Riyadh to "disengage" from the Syrians. The message back said, "No, wait it out." They would have to redouble their efforts.

"There was somebody holding the button back in Damascus," said Korentz. "We approached them four or five times. They'd come over to our camp until some of the higher-ups found out and then they wouldn't allow it. The friendship was there but somebody was constraining it."

"It didn't take a rocket scientist to figure out the problem with the Special Forces," said Air Force Master Sergeant James Black. "American Special Forces units were up against the Syrians in the Bekáa Valley in Lebanon in the early 1980s." Who could be sure that they wouldn't face each other again?

Fighting together, or dying together, the dark images of survival that make military men bond on the battlefield were missing in the hot summer months. The Syrian commanders would eventually embrace their American counterparts, but that was far in the future. In October and November, the oppression of heat seemed to add to the irritability. The training schedules so carefully prepared by the American special forces team were shoved in a drawer when delivered to the Syrian commander. There were no explicit instructions yet from Damascus. A volleyball game initiated by the Americans was halted when a Syrian officer grabbed the ball out of the air and stalked back to his tent. There had been no permission for this kind of activity from Syria.

And yet there were moments when the brotherhood of soldiering overcame the cynical politics of Washington and Damascus. There was a recognition by the Americans on the ground that the Syrians were professionals. They had the smell of past combat. It was an odor that tickled the olfactories of the American military. The Americans saw the Syrians as "real" soldiers like themselves.

In addition, the Syrians did not have to check with the Koran to guide their behavior. They missed a cold beer just as much as the Americans. These were secular, urban, educated officers. When they did talk to the Americans, there were spirited discussions about the politics of the Middle East. They offered insights into Soviet fighting doctrine. In an earlier political era, they trained with the Iraqis and had detailed knowledge of Iraqi military capabilities. Any contact with the Syrians was interesting and valued among the Americans who served as their liaison team in the desert. Master Sergeant James Black had his first run-in with the Syrian commandos when he went in search of their camp to check on Air Force Captain Scott Purdue.

"This first time I went out there I got captured by the Syrians," said Black, and chuckled. He was a tall dark-haired man whose humor ran to the absurdity of war. "A lot of times if you didn't know where a unit was you just drove around in the desert until you saw something you could recognize."

Black stumbled into the Syrian camp at night and was confronted with two Syrian guards who didn't speak English. He was ordered out of his HumVee at gunpoint while one of the guards went off to find the commanding officer.

"I had my airborne wings on my uniform. It gave me a topic of conversation. I noticed the wings on the Syrian. That's when we started a conversation trying to do it in broken English. We tried to work out that we were here to check up on our guys. Then he noticed that I had jump wings. I found out that they were all free-fall guys." It was the shared experience of falling out of an airplane that had bridged the gaps of culture, language, and politics. Black shared his first cup of sweet scalding green tea in the Syrian command tent.

The arrival of the Syrian Ninth Armored Division in November changed the atmosphere somewhat. General Ali Habib was more receptive to the Americans, and when they told him about the attitude of the Syrian commandos he replied, "Who would want to deal with those cutthroats?" Air Force Captain Scott Purdue spent some nights with the Syrian armored commanders playing a French card game. It might as well have been a scene out of a Damascus coffee house. The dim light threw shadows over the cards while cigarette smoke curled up the tent flaps. The stiff brew of black Syrian coffee loaded with sugar could ruin a night's sleep. The Syrians' packages from home were a special treat for the Americans: sugared apricots stuffed with nuts.

The Syrians had been designated a reserve force in the battle lineup and said they would not need the protection of American jets on the battlefield. The air force and special forces guys had been sent out from Riyadh to coordinate close air support. Since the Syrians said they didn't need the help, the Americans had to find other ways to pass the time.

In the daytime, Purdue organized practice flights for the air force pilots who would have to fly close air for other Arab units. The Syrian commander agreed to shut down his division's air defense and the American pilots would swoop down over the Syrian tanks.

Lieutenant Colonel Daniel Brownlee had a special assignment in the months of training and waiting. As the intelligence officer of the Fifth Special Forces group, his job was to find out whether the Syrians intended to fight. He asked the question each week. During September, October, and November, the answers from the Syrian commanders were opaque. By December, Brownlee had to ask the question straight out. "Are you guys going to participate or not?"

"Frankly, in terms of the Syrians, I don't think they knew. The commander of the Syrian Ninth said, 'We'll have to wait for the sun to shine in Damascus,' " said Brownlee.

It seemed a sad but safe bet in the second week of January that the war was uncomfortably near. People began taping the windows that let light but no air into the tiny rooms at the Dhahran International Hotel. There was a rush to sign up for chemical weapons protection classes and there were serious discussions about the merits of the

British chemical protection suit over the American version. A pamphlet that was circulating in the community of Asian workers advised that the best way to survive a chemical weapons attack was to get in the bathtub and cover up with wet towels. After a few courses in the protection offered by the bulky charcoal-lined suits, the advice to stay in the bathtub seemed reasonable. The private fears of combat gave the New Year's eve celebration at the hotel a manic air. The Associated Press office on the top floor of the hotel had been decorated with party tinsel. Eddie Lederer, the AP bureau chief in Dhahran, ordered Saudi champagne, a misnomer that described an overly sweet combination of sparkling water and apple juice. Larry Jolidan, the *U.S.A. Today* correspondent, a jolly man from Arkansas, brought a blow-up doll sent from his colleagues in Washington. Jolidan had been in Saudi Arabia longer than any other correspondent. He had solemnly named this pink plastic balloon "Deseré Storm." We marveled at the fact that "Deseré" had made it through the mail. It said something about the imagination of the dour Saudi men whose job it was to paw through the mail and remove bibles and pictures of females not fully covered. The party featured a long pork sausage that I had snuck into the country in my luggage. There was a childish delight in breaking the Saudi prohibition against pork in the kingdom. None of us had managed to break the prohibition against alcohol and it was a dry New Year's eve.

United Nations Resolution 678 started the clock ticking more than four weeks earlier. The vote in New York was a close call. It had taken a lot of American cajoling and outright bribery to produce results. In the end, China abstained, Cuba and Yemen voted no on the ultimatum, but there was enough support to deny Saddam the "propaganda coup" the Syrians had feared.

The carefully worded resolution did offer some hope. The language contained a demand for Iraqi withdrawal from Kuwait, but allowed "one final opportunity, as a pause of goodwill, to do so." The goodwill would end on January 15.

President Bush followed his victory at the United Nations with an announcement that unnerved his Arab partners. Bush proposed one last face-to-face meeting between U.S. Secretary of State James Baker and Iraqi Foreign Minister Tariq Azziz. Bush's "pause for peace" raised more hope in the West than it did among the partners of the Arab coalition.

To the Arabs of the coalition it seemed that George Bush had seriously compromised his bargaining position. The president pledged that he would never talk to the Iraqis until they withdrew from Kuwait.

As far as the Arabs were concerned, the American president had blinked. Saddam interpreted the Bush offer just as the Arabs predicted. He would not yield.

The Saudis were shocked by the American overture. Neither King Fahd nor the usually well-wired Saudi ambassador to Washington, Prince Bandar, had been told of the plan. When CNN broadcast Bush's intentions, Adel al-Jubeir, the young Saudi diplomat who had always been available for comment, was gravely silent. Later, he tried to put the best face on the fact that Saudi Arabia's ally had failed to share a crucial bit of strategy in so delicate a matter. "It's one of the prices for getting into bed with an elephant," he said with evident dismay.

On January 9, at the Intercontinental Hotel in Geneva, the last hope for peace disappeared in the first moments of a news conference with James Baker. "Regrettably, ladies and gentlemen, in over six hours I heard nothing that suggested to me any Iraqi flexibility whatsoever on complying with United Nations Security Council resolutions."

On January 12, just three days before the United Nations deadline and five days before the first cruise missile would be unleashed from the deck of the *U.S.S. Wisconsin,* Syrian President Hafez al Asad made a remarkable radio appeal to Saddam Hussein:

> I have decided to address this message to you despite several years of differences in views and less than cordial relations, hoping that these views and relations will develop into what is good and more useful for our two countries and our nations.
>
> What we are facing makes it incumbent that we be frank and exchange views. Any harm that befalls Iraq will in the end harm Syria and the Arab nation in one way or another.

Syria was offering to protect Iraqi troops from attack if Saddam decided at this late date to withdraw. Asad had made very few public pronouncements since the beginning of the crisis. On the eve of Iraq's destruction, he was tying up loose ends, reiterating his credentials as an Arab nationalist. Asad offered a way out.

The Syrian media had not joined in the chorus of heated anti-Iraq vitriol that was the daily fare from Saudi Arabia and Egypt. Asad was playing his hand as an Arab statesman to the people of Iraq. He was also mindful of the fact that Syria was within scud range of Iraqi missiles. If Saddam could target Tel Aviv, he could target Damascus and there would be no American Patriot antimissile batteries on Syrian territory to absorb the impact.

Asad's prewar radio talk was a gentle and quiet address. In a way, it was a farewell to the Arab world's old order and to Saddam Hussein. The next weeks would bring incalculable changes to the region. It was a conflict that Asad had hoped could be avoided.

In the last moments before the war that would usher in a host of unknowns, Hafez al Asad had "played out the string to absolutely the last possible millimeter." His foreign minister publicly complained about American military aid to Israel. Farouq al Shar'a promised Syrian retaliation if Israel used Jordan to launch attacks against Iraq. Asad himself assured the Iraqi army that his troops would protect them if their leader chose to save them and withdraw from Kuwait. He allowed his critics to vent the frustrations of Syrians unsure of the course he had taken.

At the same time, he assured his allies that Syria was in the fight whether Israel joined the war or stayed out. His address to the Iraqi leader had angered the Saudis, but it seemed that Asad wanted to show that he had done his best before putting his weight behind the American-led coalition.

Saudi Arabia spent a restless night and woke on January 15 to the new reality of the crisis. The streets of Dhahran and Dammam in the eastern province were almost empty. Saudis had headed out to the countryside or had fought their way through the chaos at the airport for seats on the last flights to Jeddah, out of missile range. Those who stayed, ventured out to the tents erected in empty city lots by the government's civil defense department to buy gas masks at cut-rate prices. It had only been in the past few days that Saudis began to grasp the enormity of what was about to happen.

In two days of cold hard rain the summer dust turned into brown pools of water. More than half of Saudi Arabia's annual rainfall poured out of the dark sky, adding to the sense of gloom. The rain poured down on the soldiers of the coalition. The Americans, the French, the British, and the Arab soldiers huddled under plastic sheets. The soldiers who were moving north toward the front lines scrambled to dig trenches to protect electric lines from the deluge.

The air force public affairs officers at the Dhahran International arranged a media bus for reporters who wanted to interview the pilots of the First Tactical Fighter wing. The First Tact was housed at a Saudi air base across the six-lane highway from the Dhahran International. The trip was a five-minute drive. The pilots and their commander, Colonel John McBroom, got an inordinate amount of coverage became of their proximity to the media. I had met some of these pilots more than once in stories that centered around Thanksgiving and Christmas.

It was a pretty safe bet that these pilots from Langley AFB, Virginia, would make the first sorties when the war started. It would be their first time in combat and they were highly trained for the job. They flew the F-15C fighter jet, a powerful machine built to shoot down enemy jets and this squadron would fly "shotgun" for the fighter-bombers. On the day of the United Nations deadline, they were as confident as high school football players before a home game. One lieutenant colonel wanted to explain that this was more than bravado: "Hey, we've been scrambling against Iraqi jets all week. They know that we are locking our weapons on them before they even get off the runway. What's going to happen up there is going to be like a Volkswagen going up against a Porsche."

In the first weeks of the air war, Syrian television broadcast the pictures of Iraq's destruction. This was a new kind of war in the Middle East. The gap between Saddam Hussein's rhetoric and reality was slammed shut by the first cruise missile in the heart of the defending capital. The deadly light show over Baghdad's changing skyline was a nightly feature of Damascus television news, thanks to CNN. It was a policy that the Syrian minister of information would come to regret.

There was an undisguised euphoria in the first reactions from Washington and from the air bases of Saudi Arabia. Even George Bush recognized the danger of overconfidence and cautioned that there would be sacrifices ahead. The air war looked easy. Too easy. The exhilaration disappeared on the second day of the war when eight scud missiles arched out of the night sky from launchers in western Iraq.

Saddam had kept his promise. In Tel Aviv and further north in Haifa the 350-pound conventional warheads wobbled out of the black night over the Israeli skyline like avenging meteors from the eastern gates of the Arab world. The CNN cameras caught the white hot lights of Saddam's missiles in the last seconds of the six-minute flight. The Tel Aviv air raid sirens wailed over the live CNN television pictures. Frightened Israelis struggled with gas masks and headed for cover. The cameras showed the empty streets of Tel Aviv.

Israeli intelligence estimated Saddam had at least sixty-five fixed and mobile scud launchers. In Riyadh, the first day's assessment showed that most of the launchers had been destroyed. American intelligence reports indicated that Saddam's scud missile batteries could be knocked out on the first day of the war. The assessments were wrong. The

Americans and the Israelis had vastly underestimated the number of missiles and had not guessed that the Iraqi military had converted a fleet of flatbed trucks into mobile missile launchers. One of the few men outside of the Iraqi military who knew the details of Saddam's scud program refused to provide information to U.S. intelligence.

Brigadier General Hugo Piva had retired from the Brazilian Air Force six months before the Iraqi invasion of Kuwait. He was in Baghdad on August 2 and served as an advisor until September. The Brazilian military had been a major supplier of technology for the Iraqi missile program and provided extensive information for the Iraqis' nuclear program. The relationship had been quietly encouraged by the United States in the days when Washington was supporting the Iraqi regime. Washington changed the rules abruptly on August 2, 1990. While American officials pressured the Brazilian government to order Piva home, the situation was complicated by the fact that Saddam was holding more than three hundred Brazilian engineers and construction workers hostage along with other Westerners. The Brazilian government assured Washington that Piva would be out of Baghdad in January, but the American-led coalition went to war without the invaluable information that Piva could have provided.

The first reports of Israeli casualties were light, but Saddam scored an important political success. He understood the psychological impact of the scud missiles better than the American generals had in Riyadh. Saddam had used the scuds before. He had broken the will of the Tehran civilian population in his "War of the Cities." Saddam understood the power of these crude missiles.

A scud is an imprecise weapon of little military value. The writer and journalist P. J. O'Rourke had told the ABC radio audience that launching a scud was like trying to hit a hamster in a baseball stadium with a golf ball from the cheap seats. It was cold comfort if you were the hamster. Every once in a while the hamster got hit. Scuds terrorize by their unpredictability.

This time Saddam had an additional motive. His goal was to goad Israel into retaliation. It was a cynical calculation designed to underline the contradictions of the Arab coalition and drive Syria and Egypt out of the alliance. It didn't work. One by one the Arab governments of the coalition declared that they were in the fight.

However, the pictures of Israel's vulnerability would not soon be forgotten. It was an important moment in the psychological history of the Arab-Israeli conflict. This was not the same country whose invincibility had played on the minds of Arabs for a generation. Saudis admitted that they felt sympathy for the Israelis as they experienced their own scud attacks. The Saudis were relieved and felt a genuine sense of gratitude that Israel had decided to stay out of the war. On the streets of Damascus, there was a quiet admiration for Saddam's audacity.

Ten days after the start of the war, Syrian television abandoned CNN coverage. Syrians would be forced to turn to Jordanian T.V. and the Arabic service on Israeli radio to find out what their government did not want them to see. The Syrian minister of information appeared on television to announce Syria's concern for the Iraqi people.

A few days earlier, forty-three prominent Syrian writers, poets, and artists had published an open letter in Cyprus and Beirut. It was an unusual document in a regime where freedom of expression is practically nonexistent. Even critical graffiti was an invitation for a security police sweep. And yet, there was no retaliation for the letter writers. Syrian officials explained to their American counterparts in later meetings that this was the beginning of an opening in Syrian domestic politics.

"This criminal war affects not only Iraq but the whole Arab future," said the forty-three letter writers in their statement. The document carefully avoided direct criticism of the Damascus regime. "That is why every Arab man, wherever he is and no matter what his capabilities, should confront the U.S. criminality."

In late January, a rumor circulated in Damascus that an American pilot had been shot down over western Iraq and had parachuted to safety inside Syria. The story went on to recount that the American pilot had been captured by Syrians living in the border city with Iraq and turned over to the Iraqis. The American ambassador in Damascus, Edward Djerijian, vehemently denied the story. He denied the rumor because the story was untrue.

According to an American official in Washington, an American pilot had been shot down in Iraq near the Syrian border. The Syrian government had given permission for an American rescue operation from Turkey over Syrian airspace. American pilots based in Saudi Arabia were too far away. It was the only time during the air war that Syria opened its airspace for American pilots. Despite the efforts, the American pilot was captured by the Iraqis.

In the weeks of planning before the war, Syria turned down all requests for American access to airspace. The discussions centered on a narrow airstrip that would have reduced the flying time from Intcerlik

Air Base in Turkey to targets in Iraq. The Syrians argued that it was not necessary. "They said they preferred that we didn't, and since there were still some impediments to the relationship, they said it was better that way," said an American official involved in the talks. The joint chiefs of staff were consulted and agreed that the bulk of the air campaign would be conducted from Saudi Arabia. They could manage without the use of Syrian airspace.

Captain Scott Purdue noticed the change in Syrian attitudes as soon as the first U.S. cruise missile slammed into Baghdad. The Ninth Armored Division was now fully engaged. General Ali Habib had taken to slapping his American liaison officers on the back in the spirit of comraderie that infects military men in wartime. Syrian officers suddenly spoke English. Captain Purdue expressed relief at the transformation: "It changed when the war started. There had been some high-level discussions between Asad and Baker. You could feel some of that stuff. I can't say what they talked about. But we didn't work with them [Syrians] until the air war started; then I met with the division commander and the vice commander. We had a great relationship."

Across the 138 miles of the Saudi-Kuwait border Saddam's frontline troops hunkered down behind the mine fields, barbed wire, and oil-filled trenches. In the deathly quiet of the desert nights, Syrian reconnaissance teams patrolled their sector. The war would come to them in time.

The news of the Iraqi scuds fired at Israel reached all the way to the Syrian outpost. The Americans and the Syrian commander talked frankly about the implications over hot cups of tea. Israel was a sensitive subject for these Syrian officers. Captain Adrian Erckenbrack, a special forces officer, joined the American-Syrian team in the first weeks of January:

It was delicate. We tried to sidestep any religious discussions. There was a holy land, and we saw Jerusalem as holy. They tried to make it very clear; they wanted us to understand they didn't want us to consider them terrorists. They always kept saying, "If somebody attacks your land what would you do?" We all had ideas about whether it was right or wrong.

These were lopsided discussions. The American knowledge of the intricacies of Middle East history and hatred was gleaned from the few books they had packed for their down time in the desert. The Syrians could site chapter and verse of the time when Greater Syria included Lebanon and Palestine. In their minds it still did.

The first weeks of the air campaign made little difference in the routine in this part of the desert. There was the additional racket of jet fighters and bombers headed for targets far to the north. The time was spent talking over plans for the ground campaign. The Syrian role was determined by the politics of Damascus. The Syrian Ninth Armored Division had been designated a reserve force. Syrian tanks would remain on the Saudi side of the border as Egyptian, Saudi, and Kuwaiti tanks drove up the heart of Saddam's fortification. The Syrian soldiers chafed at their assignment. The opening hours of the air war changed their attitudes about the fight.

In the dark hours before dawn on January 30, a dozen Iraqi tanks drove over the Saudi border and headed for the Saudi town of Khafji. They approached the abandoned town with turrets faced in the direction of surrender. It was a cynical trick and it had surprised the Saudis and annoyed the marines who were assigned to help them defend the town. More than 1500 Iraqi soldiers with tanks and armored personnel carriers entered Khafji. The fight to get them out took four days and cost the Saudis a score of dead. Eleven U.S. marines died in "friendly fire" accidents.

An Iraqi military communiqué claimed that its troops had launched a lightening attack and "dealt blows to the advancing enemy armies who fled." General Schwarzkopf rightly dismissed the Iraqi probe as insignificant. However, the battle for Khafji showed that the Iraqis had more fight left than anyone expected. Lieutenant Colonel Daniel Brownlee said:

The whole complexion changed with the Syrians after the battle of Khafji. It was in the little things. We'd been trying to get all of the Arabs to follow the same procedures. We wanted every one of them to put these bright orange panels on all of their trucks and vehicles for identification from the air. The Syrians wouldn't get with the program. They said it wasn't necessary. At the battle in Khafji, a Saudi was killed in a friendly fire incident and there were other problems like that. The Syrians changed their tune. They ordered 10,000 VS-17s, these 4-foot by 2-foot purple and orange panels. Then the Syrians demanded it. It all came out in the open.

A few days later there was another surprise from the Iraqis. A company of Iraqi soldiers on a probing mission fired at a Syrian patrol. It was the first time that the Americans and the Syrians would work together.

"The Iraqi probing force did fire. The reconnaissance fired back," said Lieutenant Colonel Davis. "One guy was wounded, but that was it. There had always been a question with the Syrians—you'd better watch your back. They did fight with the Iraqis when it came down to it. It was an important turning point that night."

On February 24, 1990, the Syrian Ninth Division fired a twenty-minute artillery barrage over the rumble of tank engines. The Egyptians, Saudis, and Kuwaitis were ready to go war. Asad has said his troops were in the Saudi desert to defend Saudi Arabia, not to fight Iraq. The Syrians would not be crossing the border into Kuwait. They would spend the first three days of the ground war processing the thousands of Iraqi prisoners of war. The Syrians sent a few of their mine-clearing specialists to work with the Saudi Twentieth Division. When the cease-fire was announced, the Syrian commander ordered his troops to cross the border into Kuwait.

"The Syrians were not our friends before the war," said Captain Scott Purdue, "but as we parted after the war, they were our friends."

SEVEN

THE NEW WORLD ORDER

"We fought for good versus evil. It was clear to me: Right versus wrong. Dignity against oppression."
—George Bush, January 1992

The flight from Dubai Airport to Kuwait City took less than an hour. The old airline routes to Kuwait were open again. In the airport's waiting lounge a covey of small dark-haired women from Sri Lanka seemed as tiny as birds in their oversized blue smocks with the words "Building a New Kuwait" embroidered in large white letters on the back. I was on my way to the new Kuwait a few days less than a year since Iraqi tanks had hurtled down the six-lane highway to Kuwait City like a great Shamal wind from the north.

The waiting lounge was filled with the familiar mix of passengers for the 6 A.M. flight. There were Kuwaitis in jeans and the traditional couples in black abayas and white dishdashas. Western businessmen, their faces charred with stubble, downed their last beers before the flight. Kuwait was dry again. The beer and booze that had flowed freely in the days of the occupation were gone. As far as I could tell, the only direct benefit of the Iraqi occupation in the so-called nineteenth province was to drive down the price of whiskey in Kuwait City. For the first time in Kuwait's history, alcohol had been sold openly on the streets.

Before the invasion, Kuwaitis had driven over the Iraqi border to the port city of Basra to beat the black market price at home. Hotels such as the five-star Sheraton on the Shatt al Arab were built to attract Kuwaiti customers for weekends of pleasure and drink. It was one of the places where Iraqis had come to resent the haughtiness of their southern neighbors. It was in this climate that the fantasy of Iraq's version of history had been nurtured.

Now the stocks of whiskey had been stored away with the dreams of a quick transition to democracy. The al Sabahs had come home like parents to say that democracy would have to wait. Rebuilding was the first priority. The great influx of Kuwaitis caught out during the Iraqi occupation had been completed over the summer.

I had left Kuwait on March 14, 1991. I had spent almost three weeks in a country intoxicated with its liberation. It was a powerful experience. The seven-month nightmare transformed the Kuwaitis I met. This nation of rich, spoiled, feuding individuals had become something grander during the occupation. They had survived. They displayed great courage. They talked of the future with a resoluteness that was impressive. They said they would demand change from the ruling family. It was hard to imagine that Kuwait could go back to the old ways in those first weeks of liberation. The Kuwaitis who lived through the occupation paid so much and believed their cause was so just and their solutions so obvious that nothing could stop them from transforming the country.

I had seen the evidence of Iraqi atrocities. There were the torture houses and the cold mutilated nameless Kuwaitis in the hospital morgues. In every neighborhood of the city the residents could point to a wall and say, "There, where the brown blood stains are, that's where it happened." I listened to the witnesses of the savagery, who told their stories in the flat tone of people who had yet to have the Iraqis return in their dreams.

The destruction in Kuwait City was both wanton and selective. It seemed to me that the Iraqi army sacked the city like a band of reckless teenage drunks. They bulldozed restaurants, looted and then torched the major hotels, the car dealerships, the banks, the fishing marina, and all of its boats. At the Al Ahadat police station, a place that had been used as a prison, the Iraqi soldiers had defecated in every room. They spray-painted "Long Live Saddam" on the walls of the city's radio station after smashing 2000 record albums.

The plunder of Kuwait City was on an unprecedented scale. Soldiers hauled away priceless Islamic artifacts, Persian carpets, and seats from the national football stadium. The occupation unleashed a fever of greed. Iraqis dismantled the country piece by piece. Iraqi university professors had shown up at the city's teaching hospital, Mubarek Al-Katib, and stolen the medical library. At Kuwait University, the school's mainframe computer had been hauled away. At Kuwait's television station, Iraqi television producers packed up a million dollars' worth of equipment plus the master video tapes of "Sesame Street"—*Abu Sim Sim* in Arabic—for shipment to Baghdad.

Saddam's parting gesture was perhaps his biggest crime because it was so pointless. From the window of the Kuwaiti airliner I could see the oil lakes that marked the desert floor with greasy sludge. Plumes of thick black smoke reached up to touch the jetliner. Saddam created a hell in the Kuwait desert where billowing clouds doled out black rain.

The stories of unspeakable cruelty were mixed with touching humanity. A population that had grown used to great wealth and leisure learned the lessons of self-reliance and courage. A Kuwait lawyer, Salah, my translator and guide in the first week of liberation, was proud of the fact that he had mastered cooking and car bomb construction in the seven months of occupation. The long months of fear bonded families as they hid in their homes for survival. The occupation changed them. These Kuwaitis were different from the refugees in Saudi Arabia who had spent the days and nights watching CNN in the lobbies of Saudi five-star hotels. More than 100,000 Kuwaitis had stayed.

Before the invasion, Kuwait was known as a country that had rated its citizens. Kuwaitis joked that it was easier to get into heaven than to get citizenship. The Naturalization Decree of 1959 designated first-class citizens as those who had lived in the country before 1920. The second-class citizens had to show they'd been in the country in 1945. The list continued through the sixth degree. After the invasion, there were two categories that cleaved the country more fundamentally than any grade the government could devise. The fault line divided those who stayed in Kuwait during the occupation and those who left Kuwait for safe haven.

The invasion and the liberation of the city state was an epic endeavor.

It had been portrayed as a fight between good and evil. The invasion and the occupation had been one long vast crime. In the months after liberation, new chapters were added to the story to blur the sharp distinctions between good and evil.

The relief of the liberation was mixed with concern over the ugly stories of revenge. The Kuwaitis had taken a page from their Iraqi masters. There were summary executions of Palestinians suspected of collaboration. Iraqi dissidents harbored before the invasion were dumped on the other side of the Kuwaiti border, left to an uncertain fate.

There were other scandals. There was the case of the Kuwaiti soldiers who had fought the Iraqis on August 2 and had been captured as prisoners of war. They chose to fight rather than run away, but the nation for which they fought had heartlessly refused to take them back. Many had been released from Iraqi jails in the Shiite uprising that had followed the end of the war. They got as far as the Kuwaiti border where they were interned in a camp at Abdaly guarded by the very Kuwaiti soldiers who had fled the country in the first hours of the invasion. They were welcome enough in the Kuwaiti police department and the army, but not quite enough to qualify for Kuwaiti citizenship. They had been trapped in a category known as *bedoon,* meaning "without citizenship."

A week before the ground war, President Bush said, "We have no argument with the people of Iraq. Our differences are with that brutal dictator in Baghdad." Yet Saddam's awful regime had survived. His people were struggling with sickness and starvation as a result of the war while Saddam proclaimed that he had won a "great historic duel." The Iraqi people, the Shiites and Kurds, had tried to destroy Saddam, but their rebellion had come too late to be useful to the Americans and their allies. It was one of the most sobering lessons of the war. "If Saddam can survive after this kind of beating, what hope do we have to get rid of the other dictators in the region," an Arab banker said in London. The new world order looked like the status quo in the Middle East.

The ruling family in Kuwait had been restored to power just as the allies had promised. It seemed they had learned little in the seven months spent in exile in the Saudi resort town of Taif except how to hold on to power. The U.S. Corps of Engineers, contracted by the government to help rebuild Kuwait, had also been assigned to fit new gold fixtures in the emir's bathroom.

The Kuwait airliner door opened on a bright summer morning in a country that had cleaned itself up and was starting again. The only evidence of the terrible violence that seized this nation for seven months was the broken glass in one of the waiting lounges.

The long lines at airport immigration told one of the stories of the new Kuwait. The Sri Lanka ladies had disappeared, taken by bus into the city to start rebuilding. Behind me in line were Egyptians. They stood impatiently in grimy white gallabeyyas and dingy turbans watching furtively for a way to buck the queue.

The Sri Lankans were still at the bottom of the worker hierarchy. The Kuwaitis saw these gentle people as excellent candidates for jobs as housemaids and nannies. The Egyptians had moved up a few rungs. Their government's participation in the coalition had ensured their employment in the new Kuwait. The evidence at the airport suggested that Egyptian workers were already pouring into the country just as the Palestinians were pouring out.

The Middle East had been on the move since August 2. When Iraqi soldiers moved into Kuwait, Kuwaiti refugees fled to Saudi Arabia. East Asian migrant workers preferred the route to safety through Jordan. Later, Iraqi Kurds sought refuge in Turkey, Iraqi Shiite Muslims in Iran. The great migration had not stopped with the end of the war. It was like a great game of musical chairs.

Before the Iraqi invasion, more than 2 million Egyptians worked in Iraq. They were mostly young men from Egypt's rural poor who had a free education but no land. Some were already returning to Iraq. More were coming to Kuwait. The great game moved them here. When the music had stopped, it was the Palestinians who lost a chair.

Before August 2, the Palestinians were the largest single foreign population in the country. Many had come in the 1950s. More than 200,000 Palestinians left the country during the Iraqi occupation. None of them were allowed to return. The rest of the community lived in fear of arbitrary arrests. The Kuwaiti government's unofficial policy was to reduce the Palestinian population in Kuwait to less than 100,000.

My first stop in the new Kuwait was in the diplomatic quarter to meet an old friend. It was a surprise visit. This European diplomat had a fine eye for the way the country worked. He stayed on in the first few weeks after the invasion and returned as soon as it was possible after the liberation. "This society is governed by those who fled and then came back," he said. "Anyone who stayed here during the occupation is viewed as suspicious."

In the mosques that theme had been underlined by the prayer leaders. Those who fled were glorified and compared to the followers of
Prophet Mohammed who had fled Mecca for the safety of Medina.
Those who stayed in Kuwait were compared with the Meccans who
had rejected Mohammed's message. My friend explained:

> I was here in August. I couldn't believe what I was witnessing.
> There were such acts of human bravery. The Kuwaitis here ran
> enormous risks. There is one big family here headed by Mohammed
> Jafer. He had his son work as a truck driver to bring food for the
> community. He did it because any of the regular drivers could be
> killed. It was too dangerous for them.
>
> This was a shared experience. I saw well-known families chatting
> with construction workers. It was new and different and better, and
> it had to be crushed. It was so big that one of the two groups had
> to prevail. This is not a gentler society.

In the first weeks after the liberation there was much talk about a
more democratic, self-reliant Kuwait. There had been much anger too.
Most of it was directed at a government that had failed to anticipate
the war and was unprepared for the peace. The crown prince and the
emir had come home to rule over sullen subjects who were used to
doing for themselves. An explosion seemed inevitable. Yet Kuwait
had not exploded. Over the summer there had been a rush to get back
home for the 400,000 who had spent the occupation outside. My friend
said:

> It's the difference between outside the wall and inside the wall.
> In the old days, when Kuwait City was a walled city, there were two
> categories of people: the fish eaters and the meat eaters. The fish
> eaters lived inside the city. They made their living from the pearl
> business and they ate fish. The meat eaters were the bedouin outside
> the walls. Those who fled were the meat eaters and those who stayed
> were the fish eaters.
>
> It's the traditional loyalties and attachments. The traditional be-
> douin, he follows the sheikh wherever he goes. Those are his values.
> It's so clear which group fled and which group stayed. It had nothing
> to do with courage or fear. It was a matter of those outside the wall
> and those inside the wall.

Twwack. It was the sound of a staple gun pinning another photograph
on a wooden board covered in green felt. *Twwack.* The pictures were

passed up through the crowd of silent black-clad women. An unseen reader recited the Koran over a loudspeaker. More than a thousand people had gathered at the white stone Husseiniyyah, the religious center for Shiite Muslims. The men were shoulder to shoulder inside the mosque. The crowd had spilled down the stone steps and the assembly had separated into two groups. The men stood on the right side of the front lawn, the women on the left. *Twwack*.

Jassim Mohammed. Dia'a al Sayigh. Abdul Rahman Mohammed. Hadi Mohammed Hussein. Four more pictures were passed up through the crowd of women. Five green boards filled with the faces of young men, hand-lettered names tacked under each one. The photographs were family keepsakes taken from places of honor. Wedding pictures, high school graduation shots, young men in military uniforms removed from the tops of television sets and living room walls.

When the display board was complete the women broke their silence. A low moan rose over the reading of the Koran. Thick grieving fingers reached out to touch the pictures, tracing the outline of a familiar face. Two keening women held up a third one near the green board. Further back in the crowd the wailing grew louder as the early evening heat rose up from the pavement. A small boy was winding his way through the swaying black cloaks to scatter rose water from a metal spray can. The smell of roses drifted in. The sweet scent rose thick as smog and settled on the mourners.

"This is the first memorial day of the martyrs," said the man with the staple gun. "We did more, but many forgot."

Kuwait's Muslims were classified along Islam's traditional divide. The historical and religious arguments over the rightful successor of Prophet Mohammed led to the first and only great division in Islam. When the successive tides of the Ummayad and Abbasid empires receded in the land that was to become Kuwait, the religious boundaries were set. There were the Sunnis, or the people of the Sunnah, who were the great majority, and the Shia, or partisans of Ali, who in modern Kuwait comprised 30 percent of the population.

In Kuwait more modern arguments deepened the divide. The Shiite Revolution in neighboring Iran and the Iran-Iraq War exaggerated the tensions between the two religious communities. Assassination attempts against the emir and a series of hijacking and terrorist attacks inside the country led the Sunni majority to question the loyalty of Shiite citizens. The government began to exclude Kuwaiti Shiites from sensitive posts in the military and the foreign ministry.

In 1987, sixteen home-grown terrorists were jailed for attempts to disrupt an Islamic Conference Organization. They planted bombs at the Shuaiba oil refinery. They were all Kuwaiti Shiites. The most prominent member of the group was Fuad Ashur, a famous footballer who played sports for twenty years and then worked as a government clerk. The incident and the trial was a great strain on the country.

A wealthy Shiite businessman, Saleh Selman al Attar, wrote an open letter to a local newspaper pledging his loyalty to the emir and apologizing for his community when he discovered that a member of his family had been killed trying to detonate a car bomb outside the Air France office in Kuwait City: "If this accident was aimed at Kuwait and its people, then they have been judged by God. And if they were misled by some elements or factions that want to harm Kuwait, then we declare our support for all our people and for our emir and his crown prince and the Kuwaiti people."

There was no doubt that the Shiite Muslims of Kuwait were the fish eaters. There were Shiite families who had become wealthy from trade and commerce. Their sons followed in business or joined the military and spoke at home of resentments over their second-class status.

The Iraqis had undone the damage of the Iranian revolution. The occupation erased the Sunni/Shiite divide. For seven months Saddam's army ended the religious distinctions. In the torture houses, Saddam's professionals did not asked if the victims were Sunni or Shiite but whether they were Kuwaiti. The Kuwaiti resistance organized mostly along confessional lines, but there was cooperation between the groups. When food was delivered from underground organizations, Shiites took the same risks as Sunnis. The Shiite community stayed and defended the "homeland." They organized their communities for survival. Their sons and daughters had formed the backbone of the resistance. They believed that no one could question their loyalty again.

This commemoration service was meant to be something far deeper than a rite for the dead. The Shiite community had sacrificed for the nation. Those who were murdered died as Kuwaiti patriots. They were here to call in the debt.

Ahmed Qopazar was the symbol of their sacrifice. His story of service, betrayal, and death was an epic tale that rivaled the great Shiite passion plays. Ahmed Qopazar's brother Salman was brought forward to recount the story. He had a picture of his brother pinned on his navy sports shirt. The other men wore the same badge. A hundred Ahmed Qopazars smiled out from the crowd. He had been a handsome man. The picture showed Ahmed in a military uniform. The face was open, with a slight smile under a large clipped mustache. The two brothers looked remarkably alike except for the eyes. Ahmed had the eyes of a young man. Salman's eyes were old and angry.

"He was on holiday in Beirut," said Salman. Kuwaitis are great travelers in the month of August when the temperatures soar well above the hundred mark and the Shamal winds from Iraq stir the dust and sand. "He got a call through from Beirut on August 2. My mother and father told him not to come home because the Iraqis are searching for officers."

The Qopazars had two sons in the military. Salman was a naval officer and Ahmed was in the police force assigned as a special guard for the emir. Ahmed Qopazar ignored the advice from his parents. He flew with his wife and children to Bahrain. He bought them a car and a house, wrote out his will, and crossed from Saudi Arabia into Kuwait.

"They arrested him as soon as he crossed the border. They picked him up in al Wafra. He said he was a farmer and they let him go," said Salman.

In the first weeks of the occupation, resistance groups formed in every Kuwaiti neighborhood. In those early days the occupation was a chaotic affair. In some neighborhoods the Iraqis had set up check-points while in other neighborhoods the soldiers only came at the end of August. In the early weeks the Iraqi army seemed more interested in setting up gun emplacements on the beach and defensive operations in the south of the country. The complete occupation of Kuwait City would take three weeks.

Ahmed had come home to fight the occupation. He won a reprieve in his first encounter with the Iraqis and like many Kuwaitis he or-ganized a group of young men for battle. There were early victories for the resistance. There were sniper attacks, car bombs, and shoot-outs in the streets, but by the end of August the Iraqi military went about crushing the resistance.

"They managed to kill some Iraqi with a car bomb," said Salman. "But there was a spy in the group. He told the Iraqis about my brother. On September 4 at 7:30 A.M. they surrounded our house."

Ahmed was tortured for fourteen days. On the morning of Septem-ber 18, a car parked in front of the Qopazar's family home. The house was empty, but Ahmed's youngest brother was hiding in the house next door. He watched as Iraqi officers dragged his older brother from the car. A figure that he hardly recognized was dumped at the front of the house. Salman explained:

They used an electric drill on his shoulders. They had gouged out one of his eyes, taken out his finger nails. Before they killed him they showed him some documents, some pictures of others in the resistance. He said he didn't know them. They shot him in the face four times. Then they looted and burned the house. My younger brother didn't recognize him. But then he saw the tattoo on his hand. That convinced him it was his brother.

I looked at Ahmed Qopazar's face smiling from his brother's chest. Had he imagined how it would end? Was there anything in his experience that had prepared him for this brutality? Did he know he'd been betrayed? Kuwaitis had never been exposed to the brutality Saddam handed out to his own population. The television coverage in the years that Kuwait supported Iraq showed Saddam in Baghdad walking among his loyal followers. Ahmed was thirty-three years old when he died, a father with three young children. His picture beamed out from a hundred shoulders. He had died a terrible death and the community had transformed his murder into a tale of a superpatriot.

This episode in Kuwaiti history closed an interesting circle in the political narrative of the country. According to the men at the Husseiniyyah, Ahmed Qopazar's group had been in contact with the Kuwaiti Shiites, including Fuad Ashur, who had been arrested in 1987 for bombing attacks in Kuwait City and had been released on the first day of the invasion. They instructed those new to the art of subversion in the science of car bombs and other explosives.

Fuad Ashur's career had come full circle. He was a national hero in his days as a famous football star. His disillusionment over Kuwait's support for Iraq during the Iran-Iraq War had led him to Tehran where he trained in building bombs. He spent three years in a Kuwaiti jail under sentence of death for planting bombs at a Kuwaiti refinery. When the Iraqis opened the jails on the first day of the invasion, Fuad Ashur joined the Kuwaiti resistance. He would become a national hero again.

According to the men here, in the early days of the occupation the Iranian officials at the embassy in Kuwait City were issuing false identity papers to any Kuwaiti Shiite military officer who wanted a way out of the country. Many had escaped to Iran and waited out the occupation in Qom and Tehran.

The Iranians weren't the only party willing to offer protection. I had heard other stories. One concerned the longtime Palestine Liberation Organization's representative in the Gulf, Ahmed Zanoon. According to a number of people in Kuwait, Zanoon had fled the country after he refused an order from Baghdad to organize a demonstration of Palestinians in support of Saddam. Another Palestinian official, Awny Batach, had forged Palestinian identity cards so Kuwaitis could escape the country through Iraq. It was said that he organized the escape of a high official in the Kuwaiti Ministry of Foreign Affairs. He had fled the country when the Iraqis learned of his underground railroad.

Salman learned of his brother's fate later than the rest of the family. He spent the occupation as a prisoner of war in a camp in Ba'quba. He was captured at a naval base.

"The Iraqis put us on a bus. The windows were blacked out. There was no light, no air. They didn't give us any water or food at first. We went from Basra to Baghdad and then to Ba'quba. The Red Cross got us out on March 3," said Salman.

Kuwait's Defense Minister Sheikh Nawaf al Ahmad al Jaber al Sabah ordered Kuwaiti tanks not to fire on the advancing Iraqi troops. It was one of his last orders before he fled the country to exile in Saudi Arabia. It took the Iraqi troops just twelve hours to capture the airport, the central bank, the radio and television station, and all key government offices. Salman said:

> My brother died for something. He put his hand on the Koran and pledged to fight and die for the country. I can't work with the military people who ran. Some people are saying that Jaber and Saad [the emir and the crown prince] went out. There's a difference. These officers, they worked and studied for twenty years. August 2 was the time to show what they had learned.
>
> There will be no Palestinians in the country within a year. These Palestinians, they helped the Iraqis. They were blind when they first came here, but the Palestinians opened their eyes. The Sunnis and the Shiites will be like the fingers on one hand and we'll build this country without the foreigners.

Salman had no firsthand knowledge about the behavior of the Palestinian community during the occupation. He had been a prisoner of war for seven months. His anger against the officers of the Kuwaiti military made sense. Their betrayal and flight had cost him more than seven months of his life in an Iraqi prisoner-of-war camp. It was true that some Palestinians had collaborated with the Iraqis, but some had joined the Kuwaiti resistance. The majority of the Palestinians simply tried to survive the occupation in conditions that in many cases were little better than those of Kuwaitis. What all Kuwaitis remembered, however, was Arafat's embrace of Saddam.

Hassan Jamawi slid three brown clay bowls across the white table. "This is the best Palestinian food you'll ever eat," he said and smiled. The room of tables and chairs was crowded with men hunched over similar bowls scooping the contents out with small pieces of hot bread. The diners' faces were framed in the red and white checkered head scarfs, the Arab man's common headdress. Hassan disappeared down the narrow staircase. The Led/Ramla Restaurant was a popular eatery in Hawali, Kuwait City's predominantly Palestinian neighborhood. The restaurant had opened in 1953 to cater to the first wave of Palestinians who came to Kuwait for work. A picture of Jerusalem showed the gold dome of Al Asqa Mosque pointing to the blue sky. At the take-out window downstairs, hands stretched out for the spit-cooked chicken wrapped in paper bags.

Hassan bounded back up the stairs two at a time with three more bowls of food balanced on his forearms. "I forget my English language dealing with all this hommos and foul," he said, straddling the back of a chair when all the customers were served.

"I used to be an English teacher, but now I'm a waiter, passing the time until I leave," he said. Hassan had graduated with a B.A. in English from the West Bank University of Bir Zeit in 1985. He moved in with his uncle's family in Kuwait when the job to teach English came through. It was a good job. The pay was well above what he could have earned in his village of Tulkarim in Israeli-occupied territory. There, the salary for an English teacher was 200 Jordanian dinars, a little more than 400 dollars a month. In Kuwait, the pay for teaching English was 600 Kuwaiti dinars, a salary almost six times as much. For Hassan, the move to Kuwait had meant leaving his family and his hometown, but it also meant that he could send money home for a family of nine brothers and three sisters, of which Hassan was the oldest. Part of his salary paid for his brother's medical school tuition in Italy.

The Iraqi army reopened the schools in Kuwait after the first few weeks of occupation. Many Palestinian teachers went back to work in what the Iraqis had called the nineteenth province. They instructed their students to sing the Iraqi national anthem at the start of school. They added Saddam Hussein's speeches as part of the curriculum.

Hassan decided to stay out of the classroom and took a job as a waiter instead. The Led/Ramla Restaurant reopened two weeks after the invasion to a changed clientele. The Kuwaiti customers disappeared. For seven months, Hassan served brown clay bowls of hoummos and foul to Iraqi officers.

After the liberation, Hassan tried to reclaim his teaching job. Kuwait's Ministry of Education announced that any Palestinians who taught during the occupation were fired. Hassan was a waiter. It didn't matter to the Kuwaiti authorities. He was out of a job. "I have Kuwaiti friends," he said. "They say this is temporary. They are nice. They are also naive."

Hassan bolted down the stairs once more and returned with bowls of food and hot bread. Before he sat down he surveyed the room of silent diners. Hassan waited tables as if he were the host of a large dinner party at home. The sheer weight of his hospitality kept me in my seat among the all-male clientele and their curious stares. It was pointless to try to pay for this feast. I learned long ago that when embraced by Palestinian hospitality there is no other course than to submit.

Kuwait's hospitality had run out for these Palestinians. They had been judged as a community. There was no distinction between collaboration with the Iraqis and acts taken merely to survive. The elaborate money distribution scheme that brought 200 million dollars into the country for bribes and food during the occupation served only the Kuwaitis. Individual acts of bravery or sacrifice hardly mattered to a government interested in casting suspicion on anyone who stayed in Kuwait during the occupation.

There were fewer reports of outright revenge murders against Palestinians that had been common in the free-for-all of the first days of liberation. Then Kuwaiti police and military officers joined vigilante groups and members of the resistance to hunt down Palestinians who had collaboratd with the Iraqis. The innocent were swept up with the guilty. It was unclear how many had died. The Palestine Liberation Organization said there were 400 murders, but even Kuwaiti officials admitted that number was low.

The first wave of lethal revenge was replaced by another kind of squeeze. Most Palestinians were fired from their jobs. Kuwaiti landlords were demanding back rent for the seven months of the occupation. The privileges of free medical care and public schooling were withdrawn for the Palestinian community. Private schools were available but prohibitively expensive.

Leaving was as difficult as staying. About 30,000 Palestinians held Egyptian travel documents. The Egyptian government made it clear that Palestinians were not welcome there. Jordan was the most obvious haven, but Saudi Arabia refused overland transit to Amman. At first the Kuwaiti government banned Palestinians from buying seats on the national carrier, Kuwait Air. When they reversed the decision, tickets became prohibitively expensive. The Kuwaiti government took to dumping Palestinians on the Iraqi border.

"For five days, we have lost our uncle," said Hassan. "We had decided that we would all leave for Jordan. He went to get our departure stamps. We found his car in Sweikh, near the Ministry of Interior. We went there to ask about him, but they wouldn't let us in. We can't leave without my uncle," Hassan wailed. He looked up at the diners in an instinctive gesture of caution that had been honed during seven months of occupation.

In many ways Kuwait's "Palestinian policy" had made no sense. Except for about 2000 Palestinians needed in the Ministries of Health and Education and Water, the rest of the 170,000 remaining Palestinians had been fired from their government jobs. The majority of the country's civil servants were gone. One out of three teachers in Kuwait had been a Palestinian. The Kuwaitis had no one to replace them.

Hassan and his uncle wanted to leave the country. Now the family was frozen in place as they searched for a family member who had disappeared. Hassan appealed to the Red Cross for help, but they were swamped with more than a hundred such cases. There was nothing to do but wait. His sixty-two-year-old uncle might suddenly reappear. Or he might just call from Jordan. One of Hassan's neighbors had gone out one night to buy a pack of cigarettes. He left the house dressed in pajamas. He'd been picked up by Kuwaitis and dumped on the Iraqi border. It took him five days to make his way to Amman where he called the family in Kuwait. He was still dressed in his pajamas.

Officially, the Kuwaiti government denied it was driving out the Palestinians. Only Kuwait's ambassador to Washington made reference to international concerns. "If people pose a security threat, as a sovereign country, we have the right to exclude anyone we don't want," Nasser al Sabah had said. "If you in the United States are so concerned about human rights and leaving hundreds of thousands of Palestinians in Kuwait, we'll be more than happy to airlift them to you free of charge, and you can give them American citizenship."

There was no doubt that this was the end of a political era in the Gulf. The open door to stateless Palestinians was closing fast. Kuwait had once been the home of one of the largest Palestinian communities outside of Israel's occupied territories. Yasser Arafat, the PLO chairman, had made his fortune in Kuwait. The Palestineans had been the perfect candidates for building Kuwait in the first years of independence. They were Arab, educated, often English-speaking, and not too demanding. The nationalist Palestinian writer, Gassan Kanafani, had fictionalized the great migration of the 1950s in his short story "Men in the Sun."

It was a sad tale about three Palestinian workers who paid to smuggle themselves into Kuwait to find work. When the truck driver stops for a chat with some lazy border guards, the three Palestinians quietly suffocate in the inferno of rust and metal, victims of their own silence. Kuwait did not take in Palestinian refugees; rather they received immigrants who came in search of a better life. In one of history's sad ironies, Ghassan Kanafani was assassinated in the 1970s for his moderate views. The Kuwaiti government gave his son one of the few Kuwaiti passports granted to a Palestinian.

"I thought paradise had opened for me when I first came to Kuwait," said Hassan as he set two glasses of hot sugared tea on the table. "This is the fault of all of us, all of the Arabs. They are a crazy people," he said shaking his head. "They are either busy making money or killing each other. They all forgot about the Palestinians. We are like sheep here."

Hassan was luckier than most. He had someplace to go. Many in Kuwait's Palestinian community were born here. It was the only place they knew. Some were on their way to Jordan to start a new life there. Hassan had plans to return to Tulkarmin in Israeli-occupied territory.

"Now I feel Israel is paradise. I love the Israelis now. I know they treat us like humans. The West Bank is better. At least before the Israelis arrest you, they bring you a paper," said Hassan exhausted by the evening of talk. He slumped in the chair in dark despair.

"I hate the people who left," said Salah Zamir as he rolled up the smoked windows of his family's four-wheel-drive to shut out some of the heat of an August afternoon. He kept his eyes on the road. Zamir's black hair curled out of the back of an American baseball cap. He was a fragile young man of twenty-seven with nervous energy. He was a walking political statement. His black T-shirt showed a caricature of Arabs clutching weapons first running forward and then backward. "Holy War" was printed under the first picture. "Holy Shit" was printed under the second. His statement about the outsiders was like a newspaper headline that had been cut by the censors who had closed the first newspaper published by the "insiders" after the liberation. The editors of the *February 26th* newspaper printed six issues from a media center in an abandoned kindergarten before the government closed them down.

The one-year anniversary of the Iraqi invasion was being observed in a number of ways. Salah wanted me to see a play called "Desert Storm" that was in rehearsal, but it was another dramatic offering that was on his mind. Kuwaiti television was broadcasting a television play that glorified the role of the "outsiders" during the occupation.

The plot was simple soap opera. The main characters were a husband and wife who had been on vacation when the invasion began. To show their support for Kuwait they had arranged an art exhibit in an unnamed Gulf country. A few hours before the exhibition opened, there was a telephone call threatening violence. The caller had an Iraqi accent.

The couple ignored the threat and appeared at the exhibition. Then a bouquet of flowers was delivered with a ticking clock. The last scene showed an explosion and then the couple lying on the floor with paintings of Sheikh Jaber and Sheikh Saad, the emir and the prime minister, lying on top of the victims.

The plot revealed most by what it left out. The violence was almost laughable compared to the reality of the occupation. This was a play about lifestyle! The television play portrayed the Iraqis as northern barbarians hunting down superior Kuwaiti culture. It was bad art and bad taste.

Salah recounted the television drama without comment. He was organizing a tour in his head and we had come to the place he wanted to show me. It was the place where the Iraqis had their checkpoints in what was now a busy shopping mall. "This is where they stopped my cousin and me," he said.

It was the first time Salah had been animated and I began to suspect that he longed for some aspects of the occupation. He had not been a member of any resistance groups. Salah had simply lived through the occupation and the liberation of his country. The changes that seemed so inevitable in the weeks following liberation slowed to almost a halt. Salah's energy was a gauge of the torpor that was taking over the country. In the early days of the liberation, he organized tours for journalists. He arranged a rummage sale to raise money for a home for handicapped children. But Salah was running out of energy just like the democracy movement in the country. The torpor settled like the black clouds from the oil fields that made day into night. The opposition movement didn't know what it wanted.

The al Sabahs had stolen their thunder. The emir's first act after liberation was to forgive all consumer debts, a gift of about 1.2 billion dollars that applied only to Kuwaiti citizens. The calls for a new election for parliament was blunted by the appointment of a hand-picked national council that could question policy but not legislate.

Seven opposition groups formed in the aftermath of the invasion, but they had been robbed of their preinvasion platforms. The pan-Arab ideology was snuffed out when the first Iraqi tanks crossed the Kuwait border. The anti-American rhetoric that had fueled political debates in pre-invasion Kuwait was unthinkable now that President George Bush was considered a saint in liberated Kuwait. The Soviets? It was no use criticizing Soviet policy anymore. Even the Muslim fundamentalists of the opposition had a problem. Muslim groups in Egypt, Algeria, Jordan, and Syria had stood against them and stood up for Saddam.

The most vocal newspaper in the country, *Al Qubbas,* had printed a list of the country's problems: newspapers without freedom, officials without accountability, citizens without nationality, laws without implementation, banks without checkbooks, men without women, banks with no transfers.

It was one thing to list the country's problems in the newspaper. It was quite another for the opposition groups to agree on common solutions. The only common ground they could find was on the National Assembly. They all agreed it was an illegitimate body despite the fact that Kuwaiti citizens already saw the National Assembly as an address for their complaints.

It was hard to take any democracy movement seriously in a country where less than 10 percent of the population could vote. The franchise is limited to a Kuwaiti male who can trace his roots back to before 1920. The voters number about 65,000 class A male citizens. Only the emir was talking seriously about extending voting rights, a move that could work toward the al Sabahs' advantage.

A Western diplomat had explained the arguments over extending the franchise to women. "It's meddling in the chosenness factor," he said. "Kuwaitis point out that a woman can marry a class A citizen without being one herself. She might follow what her father tells her instead of her husband. They say the women would dilute the elite."

So much for Kuwait kicking off a wave of democracy in the Gulf. The struggle between the opposition groups and the ruling family was simply a power struggle inside the oligarchy. The invasion had done nothing to upset the traditional triangle of power in the country: the al Sabahs, the merchant families, and everybody else.

It was this equation that kept the country operating and it resumed almost as soon as the al Sabahs crossed the border into liberated Kuwait. It was a system established in the days before oil when the mansions in Kuwait were made out of mud and Kuwaitis escaped the unbearable summer heat by sleeping on the roof to catch the breeze. Three large families founded the country in the late 1700s. Two of the families continued as merchants; the third family, the al Sabahs, were charged with running the place and protecting the women and children when the wooden sailing ships sailed off for foreign ports. The merchant princes made their fortunes from pearls and international trading. With the al Sabahs in place, the merchants could get on with making money.

It was a cozy and workable arrangement with the al Sabahs running the country for the merchants and buying the loyalty of the bedouin tribes. The system changed unexpectedly when the Japanese discovered cultured pearls in the 1930s. The new, cheaper pearls had a devastating effect on Kuwait trade. Kuwait's economic system was ruined. The discovery of oil saved the country and revised the power triangle.

It was the state that controlled the oil, not the merchant families, and for the first time the al Sabahs were the wealthiest of all. This could have been the end of the story for the merchant families, but the al Sabahs decided to keep them alive. They instituted the idea of sponsorship. Anyone who wanted to sell a car in Kuwait, or a computer, or designer dresses, or open a hotel had to have a Kuwaiti sponsor. By law, a foreigner doing business in Kuwait must deal with a Kuwaiti agent. It was a way to make money. The merchant class became a social client of the ruling class. The private sector of Kuwait generates nothing much of value. There are no factories of note; there is just the oil and trade.

In both pre- and postinvasion Kuwait, the democratic opposition was a product of the merchant families. While their politics might run from Arab nationalism to Muslim fundamentalism, they're all from the same stock. They all have the same interests and the al Sabahs reinstituted the sponsorship system as soon as they returned. All of the foreign companies hired for the reconstruction had to have a Kuwaiti sponsor.

The resistance was a different matter. Almost all groups in Kuwaiti society were represented in the resistance: the merchant families, the Sunnis, the Shiites, the Palestinians, the Bedoon. Perhaps if the resistance had seized the initiative on February 26 in the first chaotic days of the liberation, the story might have been different. The resistance worked as an unofficial government during the occupation. By all accounts they had operated a fairly smooth operation. Food was delivered, garbage collected.

An underground banking system kept Iraqi and Kuwaiti dinars in circulation in a distribution scheme that serviced almost the entire Kuwaiti population who stayed during the occupation. The al Sabahs disbanded the resistance as soon as they got back to Kuwait. The resistance organized to survive the occupation, not to challenge the al Sabahs, and they complied with the order. The organization had been loose to keep them alive, but it meant that the resistance had no formal structures to transform into a political movement once the occupation was over.

Abdul Aziz al Musalem, a twenty-five-year-old theater director, had lived through the nightmare of the Iraqi occupation. He was shouting directions at a cast of actors on a half-lit stage. The Dasma theater was a testament to Kuwait's civilization. The wide wooden stage faced rows of well-padded comfortable red velvet seats. There was evidence that the occupation had passed through this drama house. The red flocked wallpaper was peeled back to reveal a concrete wall. The dark carpet was stained in places; in other places it had been ripped off the floor. The actors and the director had worked since April to remake the theater for the first theatrical performance in "free" Kuwait.

Abdul Aziz al Musalem paced in front of the stage. He was dresssed in black trousers and gray sneakers. The cast was also in Western dress. Al Musalem's actors were reading their lines under the glare of a spotlight over a simple set. One table and two chairs were placed in front of a large video screen. A spider's web made out of black rope dangled from the ceiling.

Abdul Aziz's play, called "Desert Storm," went to the heart of Kuwait's darkest dreams. The theme was this: No matter what government rules in Iraq, the Iraqis would be back. "Even if another government comes, they might do it again if they need the money," said Abdul Aziz.

The play opened with a video. It was a black and white documentary about the events of 1961. The Iraqi president had his own radio station. He broadcast from his palace in Baghdad. He made a claim on Kuwait. He said he needed the money. Then the British protected Kuwaiti interests. The play cuts to a scene in 1990. This time there were no British to protect Kuwait. A resistance was organized. Abdul Aziz said:

I wanted to show the story of the resistance, too. I want to show the outsiders what we did. How the resistance used satellite phones, how we slept, how we ate, how the air war was. If all the Kuwaitis left, there would have been no Kuwait. We ran the country as if the government wasn't here. We organized the gas stations, the food delivery. It's what made the Iraqis so mad. I want to show the outsiders the suffering we had.

The "insiders" have been shocked because we thought the government would treat us in a better way. I've read in the papers that the government says we should stop talking about ourselves. They say shame on you for talking about yourself. They accuse us of not being for the Sabahs. They say we're not attached to the Sabahs. Of course, they insinuate that we stayed because we liked Saddam.

The key scene in the play is in a Ba'th party meeting. Saddam Hussein is presiding. The Saddam character struts into the middle of the stage and orders one of his colleagues to execute himself. The officer tries to comply but then reminds Saddam that there are no bullets in his gun. Saddam hands him his weapon, but instead of turning the gun on himself, the officer points the weapon at Saddam. The others in the room join the rebellion. They tear the pictures of Saddam off the wall and begin to plan what they will do once he is dead. They all agree that Kuwait must remain the nineteenth province.

"The gun has no bullets," said Abdul Aziz. "So Saddam is smart, but the others have the same ideas about Kuwait."

The actor who portrays Saddam jumped off the stage and stood next to Abdul Aziz. Up close I noticed that he is no more than twenty-five years old. He looked nothing like the Iraqi dictator, but he had learned to mimic the high-pitched emotional radio harangues. It was a voice the Kuwaitis knew well. The actor launched into his favorite routine where Saddam was questioned by a French reporter about advanced technology and in particular about the Stealth jet fighter. "The shepherds would see it and tell us," he said in a high-pitched squeal. The rest of the crew laugh too loud.

Kuwaitis had developed a whole repertoire of jokes about the Iraqis. There was a fifteen-minute daily radio program that recounted the tales of Iraqi stupidity. There was the story about the Iraqi soldier who watched a Kuwaiti withdraw money from a voice-activated automatic teller. The soldier pointed his gun at the teller machine and demanded his share. There was another story about Iraqi troops who stole a computer screen thinking it was a television and then wondered why

LOTUS 123 never came on the air. I heard the same jokes told by Lebanese about the Syrians. Palestinians told them about the Israelis. It was a way of taming the demons of power.

"The whole thing is a joke," said Abdul Aziz. "We thought after liberation we would get our rights. Now everything went back to August 1. We've been through a catastrophe, but we're all paralyzed."

The nature of the commemorations on August 2, 1991, was a clue to the tensions in the country. There were the "outsiders" who tended to see August 2 as the occasion for a party. They were on the streets honking car horns, or attending picture exhibitions, or were at home watching the dozen or more bootlegged video tapes of "Desert Storm" that were on the market. As far as I could tell, Kuwait had the most complete set of quickie video productions on the war in the Gulf. The "insiders" had spent seven months living through the occupation and had no desire to watch it.

There was another sign of the unrest. A call to turn in weapons went unheeded despite the promise of a fifteen-year prison sentence for harboring guns. The government said it was punishable to have weapons, but they did not search house-to-house. There were men in Kuwait who had anti-aircraft guns in their basement. If it happened again they would be ready.

The Gulf Air representative recommended that I arrive at the airport five hours before flight time. "It's because of the baggage," he said. It was a succinct explanation and yet restrained. The Gulf Air flight's destination was Amman, Jordan, and the passengers were almost all Palestinians. The security checks were rigorous as Palestinian families packed up their household goods for their last exit from Kuwait.

As we filed out to the plane, a poster caught my eye. It showed a picure of Kuwait's most famous landmark, the tall blue bulbous towers on Gulf Boulevard. A rainbow framed the symbols. The words "Help Rebuild Kuwait" boldly proclaimed the intentions of the advertisement for a trade fair. This time the Palestinians need not apply. They had done the building and the rebuilding was in the hands of other foreigners. This time it would be the Americans, the British, and the French who got the contracts with their Kuwaiti sponsors. The Americans and the British would provide Kuwait with protection against external threats.

The Kuwaitis were known before the invasion to have the most sophisticated foreign policy in the region. They learned better than any of their neighbors to play the most delicate game of balancing the superpowers. That time was over. Part of the reason was the collapse of the Soviet Union. Another part of the story was here in the waiting lounge of the airport. The Palestinian community of Kuwait had an influence on the politics of the Kuwaiti state. The government had always taken a tough line on the Arab-Israeli conflict and that meant a certain distance from the United States. That had ended when Arafat sided with Saddam.

I stood next to a Kuwaiti businessman who was on his way to Jordan. "I have to go there to see my business partner," he said. "He can't come back here and I have to get the papers for our company from him."

Behind him was a Palestinian woman in a loose black shift and a white gauze headscarf. She was struggling to control the energy of a small boy while large tears rolled down the deep crevices of her face. Families spread out across the isles of seats.

In my row, fifteen-year-old Layla struggled into her seat. She was a handsome teenager in jeans and a T-shirt armed with a walkman for the long flight. Layla had been born in Kuwait. It was the only country she knew. She and her family were moving to Jordan. For how long she didn't know.

"At least the weather is better," she said with a short laugh, accepting with stoicism if not good grace a fate she was unable to alter. Layla fitted on her headphones for the rock and roll that would lead her into a new life.

I settled into my seat. Khalid, a young Kuwaiti, took the last seat on the aisle. He was also going to Jordan to meet with some Palestinian business associates. This was his first trip out of Kuwait since the invasion, occupation, and liberation and he was eager to talk to pass the time.

With an ironic grin he told me that he had spent fourteen years away from Kuwait studying and then working in Ireland. His English had the melody of that green island. He had come home for a short visit last winter but extended his stay until the Iraqis made leaving impossible. He had been trapped by the invasion along with his father.

"He was an important man in state security," said Khalid. "It was too dangerous to try to get him out of the country, so we hid him at the neighbor's house next door. We didn't organize any resistance for the first few days. I really thought the Iraqis would withdraw. Then they announced the annexation of Kuwait and we knew they were going to stay for a while."

Like many young Kuwaitis, Khalid said he wanted to join one of the

resistance groups that was organizing to hit back at the Iraqis. He
decided against joining. The risk was too great. The Iraqi formula for
retaliation usually meant a search of the neighborhood. Khalid's father
might be discovered and the arrest of a high official in the security
service would have been a great coup for an Iraqi commander. Khalid
explained:

> We formed a loyalist group. We were worried that Kuwait was a
> no-man's land. We were worried about the political movements that
> were forming. Everybody was angry at the Sabahs.
>
> Late in September, we started to get reports of secret meetings
> in the Shiite cemeteries. The minister of interior had opened the
> jail on August 2 and the ones who'd been jailed for bombing in
> 1987 were let out. They were organizing to take control of the
> country. The Iranians had given them false papers so they could
> escape from Kuwait when they needed to. The Iranians had tried
> to make sure that the Shiites had a home in Kuwait.

The stewardesses finished serving dinner. The passengers settled
into the lethargy that passed for sleep on a long dark flight. A few
small children wandered up and down the aisle propelled by the nervous energy of excitement. Their mothers succumbed to the emotional
toll of another exodus.

"By October, the resistance movements were locked into a political
struggle," Khalid said. "There were about twenty groups and everyone
knew the implications. We started sending faxes to the emir in Taif.
It was mostly political information. We gave him a list of who had the
guns."

According to Khalid's account, the Iraqis had unleashed a revolution
inside Kuwait. In those first weeks of the occupation no one had been
sure that the al Sabahs would ever be back. By the end of the occupation
some of the groups did not want the al Sabahs to come back.

Khalid's version of events explained why the al Sabahs had been so
quick to disband the resistance groups. In the first few days of the
liberation, the government had dismissed the offer to use food distribution networks already in place during the occupation. Their own
initial clumsy efforts had angered a population that already saw them
as inept.

The al Sabah family had not been a part of the resistance. The older
generation fled to Saudi Arabia in the first hours of the invasion, leaving
the nation to deal with its fate. The sons of the al Sabahs had fled as

well when it was clear that the Iraqis were intent on hunting them down.

There was one exception to the al Sabahs' record. The emir's half brother, Fahd al Ahmad al Sabah, died defending Dasman Palace on the first day of the invasion. Sheikh Fahd was a popular extrovert. He was the manger of the national football team and the head of Kuwait's olympic committee. He had honed his fighting skills in Beirut. Sheikh Fahd fought for the Palestinians in the 1982 Israeli invasion of Lebanon.

One of the resistance groups had taken his name. But there was a persistent rumor in Kuwait that Sheikh Fahd died because he was too drunk to get out of the country and the rest of the family had left him behind. The rumor was retold despite the fact that an Iraqi soldier interviewed in Turkey said he'd been an eyewitness to the siege of Dasman Palace and talked of the bravery of the Kuwaiti royal.

E I G H T

ANOTHER KIND
OF PEACE

"It may be that you dislike a thing which is good for you and it
may also be that you prefer a thing and it may be the worst for
you. God knows all and you know not." (al Baqara 216)
—King Hussein of Jordan, March 1, 1991

AMMAN, 1991

It was a relief to be out of a country where you could taste the air.
The air in Amman was cool and dry; the soft breeze was like an old
friend. This city, with its seven hills, had been my home for three and
a half years. It was my first trip back after the political upheavals of
the Gulf War.

Unlike other Arab cities, Amman was not so good at keeping its
secrets. It couldn't hide behind its great Arab history, like Cairo or
Damascus. Amman was not closed and frightened, like Baghdad. The
Jordanian capital could not inspire in the way that Mecca or Jerusalem
did. Amman took its colors from the surrounding stone and its character from the successive waves of immigrants fleeing from the region's
troubles.

Amman was the most westernized of Arab capitals. It was more than
just the Pizza Huts, the designer jeans, and the art galleries downtown.

It was a city that prided itself on tolerance and the country's king was a "man of the West" among the Arabs.

More than half of the country's 3.1 million residents were Palestinian by origin, refugees of the Arab-Israeli wars. King Hussein had given them a passport and an education. Jordan could boast a literacy rate that matched Sweden's. The country had raised its citizens like crops and exported their talents to the Gulf states. Remittances, the money made abroad, accounted for a large part of the country's wealth. The country's politics were dictated by geography rather than by wealth or military strength. Jordan was a country poor in resources that was surrounded by the region's military, political, and financial power-houses: Iraq, Syria, Saudi Arabia, and Israel.

There were Lebanese in Jordan. There were blue-eyed Arabs of Crusader descent, Armenians, Palestinians, and Iraqis. They were all ingredients in Amman's urban stew, mixed with the country's oldest citizens, bedouins and Circassians who had come from the Caucasus. The Gulf crisis had added tens of thousands more. Jordan had been the first stop for Indians, Egyptians, Sri Lankans, Filipinos, and all the other nationalities who had worked in the Gulf and fled in staggering numbers from the Iraqi invasion.

I had followed the events in Jordan with a growing unease. The country had wrapped its arms around the Iraqi dictator like a survivor on a saint. Saddam Hussein's face smiled from posters in every taxi cab and on every restaurant wall in Amman. Jordanians shouted his name at demonstrations and vowed, "O Saddam, we are willing to die for you." Even businessmen who had been educated in the West and did business there felt they had no choice but to follow the strongman of Iraq. Retired military generals had given speeches at the Royal Cultural Center assuring Jordanians that Saddam could not be beat. The word *invasion* had been missing from Jordanian press accounts on the first days of August 1990.

Saddam's offer to tie withdrawal from Kuwait with Israeli withdrawal from the occupied territories had electrified the Palestinian population of Jordan. His proposal gave dignity and political meaning to a hit-and-grab occupation. When he wrapped his conquest in Islam's green banner, he won over another volatile segment of Jordan's political culture.

Saddam played on Muslims' deepest emotions by introducing *infidel* and *jihad* to his political vocabulary. This secular tyrant tacked the slogan "Allahu Akbar" ("God Is Greatest") to his nation's flag to flaunt his newfound piety. The man who made his political fortune claiming that religion and politics are not mixed had done just that. He played on the latent suspicions in the Islamic world. Saddam was broadcasting on the Islamic wavelength and his message was received loud and clear in Amman. It was a message that bypassed logic and went straight for the heart. He linked Israel's hold on Jerusalem with the American presence near Islam's holy cities of Mecca and Medina. Jordan's political Muslims portrayed Saddam as a Muslim hero in a struggle that pitted "the infidel leaders and the Prophet of Islam."

Jordan's Muslim brotherhood called on Muslims "to purge the holy land of Palestine and Najd and Hijaz from the Zionists and imperialists." Sheikh Abd al-Munim Abu Zant, a popular member of Jordan's parliament and an outspoken member of the Muslim brotherhood, depicted the crisis as a religious war:

> Why is Iraq the focus? Because the Zionists and American enemies don't wish to see the Arabs or Muslims possess any power that can stand against Israel. . . . The Saudis have lost their credentials as Muslims by allowing foreign forces to come to our holy land, which only God can protect! They have brought the Americans, and what the Americans have brought to the holy land is VD and AIDS.

There were voices of dissent in Jordan. There were those who saw the dangers to Jordanian and Palestinian interests in a close stand with Iraq. Their views had been drowned out by the emotions of the street. Jordan's recent experiment in a limited form of democracy gave people a new say in the direction of the country. The elections in November 1989, the first in twenty-two years and the first in which women could vote, had nonetheless won the Islamic movement an unexpected thirty-four seats in Jordan's eighty-seat parliament.

Their campaign slogan, "Islam Is the Solution" was the response to Jordan's disastrous economic situation, but it had its first political test in the Gulf crisis. The anti-West rhetoric was a standard feature of Muslim brotherhood ideology, but their historical support of Saudi Arabia in exchange for cash rewards and criticism of the secular Ba'thist regime in Iraq were reversed in the crucible of public opinion in Jordan. The Islamic movement members proved to be shrewd politicians during the crisis.

Jordan's Islamic movement joined in an unusual coalition with Jordan's secularists and nationalists and organized anti-American and anti-Western demonstrations. The mosques became a center for political speeches and Friday prayers were a ready platform for organization. In the early days of the crisis, King Hussein tried to play a mediating role while the country's elected parliament and newspapers urged him to openly side with Saddam. In the new democratic atmosphere, Jordan's newspapers had a relatively free hand to express popular sentiment.

Jordan's fledgling democracy had failed in one respect. There was no tolerance for dissent. The government censors, so prevalent in the "pre-democracy" days, were replaced during the crisis by newspaper owners and editors who had little patience for alternative views.

King Hussein recognized the perils of the situation and spent the seven months of the crisis dancing on the lid of a boiling pot. The king cajoled and pleaded. He demanded and questioned. He spoke out against Washington's policy. He was slow to institute the United Nations sanctions against Iraq. The king even grew a beard in what was widely perceived as an expression of his confusion and despair.

King Hussein considered domestic politics rather than Washington's wishes. In Amman, the unsettled Palestinian question was the threat to stability rather than the Iraqi invasion of Kuwait. Therefore, he joined in a tacit coalition with the Islamic movement in a country that had prided itself on its tolerance and pluralism. It cost Hussein the enmity of Riyadh and Washington. He sacrificed crucial aid from both capitals. However, the reward was an all-time high in popularity at home.

The Jordanian monarch promised his people a more open country at a time when the country's economy was falling apart. He kept government censors out of the news rooms at the height of the crisis. He did not interfere when Jordan's parliament "saluted Iraq's refusal to go along with American demands and asked it to play its historic role in resisting the great Satan who is threatening every Arab country and belief." He kept his promise to move toward democracy and he kept his throne.

There were no pictures of Saddam in my taxi in the summer of 1991. Saddam had disappeared from the shop windows of Amman. The U.S. president said that real peace in the region must be based on United Nations Resolutions 242 and 338 that called for trading land for peace with Israel. While Jordanians doubted the U.S. president's sincerity, his was the only game in town, and King Hussein appeared eager for a role in the postwar Middle East.

The high fever of support for the Iraqi dictator had burned itself down and had been replaced by a dull headache. The war was not really over in Amman. In a way, it was just beginning. The Palestinian passengers on my flight had been testament to that fact.

There were two parts to Jordan's disaster: A quarter of a million Palestinians were home from Kuwait and the remittances, the lavish salaries of the Gulf, had dried up. The *Jordan Times,* Amman's English-language daily, kept tabs on the numbers. On my first day in the country, a Reuters' story, in a small box above the headline, gave the latest details.

Amman (r) More than a quarter of a million Jordanians have fled to Amman from Kuwait since the start of the Gulf crisis, a senior official said Saturday. He said 269,744 arrived between Iraq's invasion on Aug 2 and July 15, putting a huge strain on Jordan's already limited resources and stagnating economy. "For the country this is a catastrophe of the highest level but you cannot stop citizens from returning. We still expect thousands of others to come from Kuwait after they collect their money and settle their affairs, because life there has become impossible for them." The Palestinian mission in Kuwait says the Palestinian community has shrunk to 90,000 from 350,000 before the invasion. Many if not most are Jordan passport-holders. Kuwait has terminated the contracts of tens of thousands of Palestinian civil servants. Officials often refer to the recent flood as the "third wave of immigration" to Jordan following the mass arrivals after the Arab-Israel wars of 1948 and 1967.

The numbers were overwhelming. The latest Palestinian exodus was equal to the number of Soviet Jews who had come to Israel in 1990. For Jordan, there would be no international sympathy for the strain on its domestic resources. There would be no offers of loan guarantees from Washington or large aid packages from Europe. Jordan would be expected to absorb its additional citizens as best as it could.

The latest wave of newcomers choked the highway as I drove into Shemsani, one of Amman's trendy suburbs. The license plates gave them away. The white and black plates of Iraq's nineteenth province were like a name tag on the bumper. These cars had been driven overland from Kuwait. The Kuwaitis had destroyed these metal symbols of Iraqi repression in the first hours of the liberation. The Palestinians were tagged by their cooperation with the occupation government.

The procession of cars circled around the well-lit shopping streets of Shemsani. It was the kind of sport popular in Kuwait. The procession passed the red and white awning of the Kentucky Fried Chicken shop. The Colonel smiled down welcoming the newcomers. The procession passed Ata Ali, the Arabic sweet shop on the corner with mounds of diamond-shaped honeyed dough piled into sweet mountains in the window. The parade passed the Pizza Hut and Tom and Jerry's hamburgers. The street itself was full of people strolling in the night air. Young men walked hand in hand in the uniform of the young: tight jeans, T-shirts, and sneakers. Families ambled arm in arm. Shemsani had the look of a hotel lobby where the tourists shuttled aimlessly getting their bearings. Except these were not tourists, but Jordan's newest residents.

The Italian yogurt shop had already been designated the teenage hangout. Young men and women shyly eyed each other over paper cups filled with swirls of apricot- and melon-colored confections. I stopped to listen to a sound I had heard earlier in the night. It was a faint melody that was barely there over the low hum of conversations. I had heard it before in the hotel lobbies of Saudi Arabia, Cairo, and Dubai. One of the young men was humming in a low whisper. The tune was the Kuwaiti national anthem.

Zaki Rezeq introduced himself as an ex-banker from Kuwait. The definition made his sad face darken. He lit another cigarette and sucked in the smoke for energy. "There's no possibility of going back to Kuwait now," he said. "But we hope. While we were there we were treated like Jordanians and now that we're here we're treated like Kuwaitis."

Rezeq had worked at the Gulf Bank in Kuwait City. His story was a familiar one. He was born in a village near the West Bank town of Ramallah. He had moved to Kuwait in 1973 and made a good living as a bank clerk. His three children were born in Kuwait City. It was the only country they knew.

Rezeq had arrived in Jordan two months after the invasion. The Gulf Bank had closed in the first weeks of the Iraqi occupation. Out of a job and out of food, Rezeq moved his family to Jordan to wait out the madness. He locked the door of his apartment in Kuwait, expecting to return. He was a slight man with a clipped mustache. A stateless Palestinian with a Jordanian passport. His eyes wrinkled behind his bankers' glasses:

I left on October 15. What is the bad thing that I did? I left when Iraq came. I've been several times at the Kuwait Embassy in Amman. Should they treat us like this? I was working in a bank! They said I

was a traitor. There are guilty people here. There were direct collaborators. But President Saddam didn't consult me when he invaded!

Rezeq lit another cigarette. He wore the crisp white shirt and gray
trousers of a banker, but he was not a banker now. It was unlikely
he'd ever be a banker again. The unemployment rate for Palestinians
returning from the Gulf was almost 90 percent. Rezeq savings were
enough to support his family for a year. He was lucky. Many Palestinians had returned from Kuwait with nothing but the clothes on their
backs. Some were sleeping in cars, or under bridges, or with relatives.
Rezeq put his considerable energies into the Committee of Jordanians and Palestinians returning from Kuwait. He organized the private
committee, solicited donations, and doled out 50 Jordanian dinars, or
about 75 dollars, to desperate families. It was at best a two-day reprieve
for the destitute. Church groups in Amman were distributing food
packages and clothing. The government's social service budget had
been exhausted by the refugees who had streamed across Jordan's
border in the first months of the crisis.
It was in Jordan, among the Palestinians from Kuwait, where the
most vocal criticism of the policies of the Palestine Liberation Organization could be heard. Zaki Rezeq was particularly bitter. His wife's
cousin, Saleh Khalaf, known as Abu Iyad, had been murdered in Tunis
the day before the allied air attacks began in Iraq and Kuwait. Rezeq
was convinced Abu Iyad died because he disputed the PLO chairman's
policy of siding with Baghdad:

> The war was against the Palestinians. It cost them their good life.
> Ninety-five percent of those who lived in Kuwait don't like Arafat.
> He only represents himself. What's the difference between him and
> Saddam? I graduated from politics and law from Baghdad University
> so I know about Saddam. It's not a country; it's a ghetto filled with
> deception and corruption.

Zaki Rezeq was like many Palestinians who had washed up in Jordan.
His head was in Jordan, but his heart was still in Kuwait. He could
tune in to Kuwaiti radio broadcasts from Cairo. He kept up with the
news of a country that had turned him out. He argued with his new
neighbors about their support from Iraq.
"My children were all born in Kuwait. Before the liberation my son
felt isolated here. One day before the liberation he was in school. His
teacher said that Kuwait would not be liberated. It filled him with

despair. He got in fights with his school friends. He challenged his teacher, but then he was happy when Kuwait was free."

"God damn it, why did we do it?" said a member of Jordan's Palestinian elite. He had asked me not to use his name, although his opinions seemed to match the general mood in Amman following the war.

"There was no way to talk against Saddam. The only option was to shut up. I knew what a laser was. I said you can't compete with people who add and subtract on their hands."

He settled back in his chair. Palestinian politics had cost a lot. The Gulf states had cut off the more than 2 million dollars of annual aid to the Palestine Liberation Organization. It couldn't have come at a worse time for the Palestinians in Israeli-occupied territories. They had lost jobs during the three-year-old Palestinian uprising—the Intifadah—and money from the PLO had kept them going.

The money that paid for school tuitions, supported widows, kept businesses running, had dried up. The institutions that the Palestinians built to serve the population under occupation depended on the goodwill of Arab friends.

One example was Bir Zeit University in Israeli-occupied territories. The school of commerce had been built with a 3-million-dollar donation from the Gulf. The engineering school had been built with one donation from a Palestinian businessman living in Saudi Arabia. The 2-million-dollar library had been constructed from a donation from a Kuwaiti. The money had simply dried up.

Jordan's economy was particularly hard hit. The United Nations embargo effectively halted operation of Jordan's factories. The Iraqi businessmen who bought Jordanian pharmaceuticals, detergents, wheat, corn, and clothing were broke. Kuwait stopped buying Jordanian exports and the Saudis had ended oil shipments through the tapline and closed the border to Jordanian products. Jordan's tourist industry was shattered.

The country was in shock from economic devastation, its citizens from geographic dislocation, and the country's leadership was scrambling to find a direction for the future. The Gulf War had been a demonstration of power. The superiority of Western technology over the Soviet brand that equipped Iraq and Damascus was almost total. However, the defeat of Iraq had other implications. The price of the Arab-Israeli conflict was simply too high.

"The competition is killing us," said a Palestinian. "It's like, we open a grocery, and the Israelis open one but stay open for twenty-four hours. The Israelis are crazy and we're part of the same stock. If we do get a state, we have to reduce the level of nationalism . . . and that flag! Every song we have is related to war. We've all wasted our lives. We are all shaped by this misery."

This speech was now a monologue and when I reviewed my notes of the conversation later I realized this was the internal debate going on throughout the Palestinian community. It was part self-criticism and part coming to terms with reality. It was a different political outlook than the one that had existed before the war:

> The Gulf War made it easier to be articulate in the Arab world against us. They don't like the Palestinians. We make them feel shame. We take their money and we're not grateful. It's true we have some ego—we built the Gulf states!
>
> The Arabs of the coalition don't want to appear to be against the United States. The United States came to defend them and now it's time to pay back. And, there's no domestic pressure about the Palestinian issue. It means the king [Hussein] is going to have to give Israel some tangible concession and try to sell it to the people. I'm not sure how easy it's going to be for him.

The news of Saddam's overwhelming defeat had devastated Jordanians. As Saddam turned his guns against the Iraqi Kurds in the north and the Iraqi Shiites in the south, the value of supporting him depreciated. The Jordanian newspapers were slow in reporting the extent of the beating, but Jordanians could watch the Arab service of Israel television, or listen to the Voice of America or the British Broadcasting Corporation for the full details.

Jordan's King Hussein had tacked his traditionally pro-Western regime toward Baghdad in the hot winds of public opinion. Dependent on America for vital economic and military assistance, King Hussein moved back toward Washington when the war was over. The king had gotten his country through the war and now he would have to get them through the peace.

The swing in Jordanian politics could be charted by two speeches given by the king. On February 6, one week after allied bombs hit Jordanian truck drivers in eastern Jordan, he lashed out at the allied coalition. It was his most emotional speech and it reflected the high mark of Jordanian public opinion:

The armies of the biggest and most powerful nations have gathered and unleashed their modern and dangerous weapons on the land, in the sea, and in the sky. These weapons had originally been arrayed by the present international military alliance against an opposing alliance led by another superpower. They are all now arrayed against the Baghdad of Haroun al Rashid, the Basra of Islamic studies and poetry, the Kufa of Ali, may God's peace be upon him, the holy Najaf, Karbala, Al Diwaniyeh, Mosul, Kirkuk, and every Iraqi city and village.

The king's Islamic imagery was the equivalent of marking the destruction of Jerusalem, the shrines in Bethlehem and Nazareth, and the Vatican. Baghdad had been the Muslim capital in the golden age of Islam. The city was rich with the history of Arabic poetry, the first large library, and the first geographical dictionary. Baghdad was the site of the writings of Avicenna, whose principles of medicine remained a model in Europe until the fifteenth century. Within weeks, Saddam's own army would have less respect for Islam's holy sites as they fought to quell rebellion in the ancient cities of Karbala and Najaf.

The Jordanian monarch paid dearly for his role as Saddam's supporter. After the king offered a "salute to Iraq" and "its heroic army, its steadfast people, its glorious women, its brave children, and its aged, confronting with faith, the bombers, the battleships, and tons of explosives," the U.S. Congress reviewed American aid to Jordan and froze 57 million dollars in funds.

Within thirty days, King Hussein's tone changed to one of conciliation. In a speech to mark the anniversary ot the "Arabization" of Jordan's army, he staked out Jordan's postwar position:

I realize that many of us in Jordan and in the Arab Muslim world will carry with them, as they look forward to a new tomorrow, painful memories which can be transformed into hatred and rancor if they are allowed to grow and fester. But vibrant peole are those that can overcome their pain and grievance, and contribute lessons from which they themselves learn as they strive for their future, their hope, and their aspirations.

The King's remarks came less than a month apart, but the words reveal a long and painful excursion. Jordanians had supported Saddam, but after the war the king had been one of the first political leaders in the region to sign on to the American-sponsored peace process with the Israelis. What happened in those thirty days?

I came to see the Jordanian journey as the "Big Bang" approach to peace. All other options had been destroyed. The change began with the exodus of Palestinians from Kuwait. Many of the Palestinians had arrived before the end of the war. The Iraqi defeat had stranded them in Jordan.

Kuwaiti's Palestinian community was once the most adamant in rejecting any compromise with Israel. However, the Gulf War had repeated a bitter lesson: A lifetime of service in Kuwait did not guarantee security. Whenever there was a crisis in the Arab world, the Palestinians were shown the door. The Kuwaiti martial law courts named Jordanians, mostly Palestinians with Jordanian passports, as collaborators to Saddam's regime. They had been sentenced to life imprisonment, or death. There was no state entity, or government, or leader who could protect them.

A few weeks after the guns were silent in Baghdad, Iraqis began pouring into Amman. By the end of the 1991 summer, more than 100,000 Iraqis had come to Amman. These were the heroic men, women, and children that King Hussein had saluted in his February 1 speech. He had commended them for their faith in facing the bombs and battleships of the allied coalition—except these Iraqis did not come to say thank you to the Jordanian people for their support during the war. These Iraqis came to Amman to escape a brutal dictatorship that had silenced them in Iraq while Jordanians were free to support Saddam.

Jordanians could see hundreds of Iraquis lined up in front of Western embassies or the offices of the United Nations. Jordanians could talk to them as they shopped in Amman with Iraqi dinars worth practically nothing. They told their bleak stories of life in Iraq and argued with Jordanians for supporting Saddam.

The third element in the "Big Bang" theory of peace came with the realization that the military option against Israel was over. Jordanians and Palestinians had seen enough of American weaponry to understand the implications of a war with Israel. Iraq's military capability had been practically destroyed; Syria sided with the American-led coalition. The dream of a military resolution to the Arab-Israel confrontation disappeared with the first cruise missile that had slammed into Baghdad.

The Muslim brotherhood in Amman had promised that God was on Saddam's side. Faced with the choice of believing that God had cheated or the Muslim brotherhood were wrong, many Jordanians took the latter option. The slogan "Islam is the solution" had an appeal during the height of the crisis, but the Islamic movement offered no coherent political vision to solve Jordan's postwar predicament.

Many of the homes in the neighborhood of Webdeh are chiseled out of rock. Three sets of concrete stairs led to Abu Khalid's beige, chipped, iron front door, open to let in the breeze and the sweet smell from the grape orchard. Three generations of Abu Khalid's family were now living in the three-room house with its concrete floor. Abu Khalid's daughter returned from Kuwait in July with her five children. Her husband had been fired from his job at a government school in Kuwait. Her passport was stamped "canceled" by Kuwaiti officials.

Umm Khalid, Abu's wife and the matriarch of the family, served tea and coffee, and when that was done she brought a fat watermelon cut up in thick slices. The tiny kitchen was a few steps away from the small living room. The family was not eager to talk to an American. There could be trouble. Abu Khalid's son-in-law was still in Kuwait. He had applied for severance pay and was trying to get the family's furniture out of Kuwait. "No names," said the patriarch as he offered another plate of melon.

"The space here is not very much, it's not much bigger than the refugee camps in the occupied territories. All in all we're in misery up to our bones," said Abu Khalid. "So what Saddam did, well, he can't do anything more to us. When you are in deep desperation, to sit and cheer can harm no one."

Abu Khalid's face was framed by a checkered keffiya. He chuckled with an old man's laugh. His gray face was deeply lined, aged beyond his fifty years. His wife, in a formless shift and white scarf, collected the plates and maneuvered over the children playing on the floor. When Abu Khalid's daughter said she knew the Iraqis would lose when the allies entered the war, he sharply interrupted her.

"Saddam didn't lose; he faced more than thirty countries. He's still in power! Iraq is in victory. We paid the price." Abu Khalid's voice rose with the passion of his belief. Abu Khalid had supported Saddam. He cheered when the scuds had fallen on Israel. Saddam stood up against the world and he had won. In Abu Khalid's eyes, Saddam was a hero. "But Saddam has caused the Palestinians great harm," I said. "He has killed more Arabs than the Israelis."

"Emotionally, he took some of the pain from us. For the first time we saw the Israelis afraid. They couldn't just feel no harm would ever come to them. They never thought they would see that."

• • •

DAMASCUS, 1991

Cab drivers are a good barometer for politics in most countries. In May, on a ride from the center of Damascus to one of the city's concrete government buildings, my driver turned to me and said with a broad smile, "American, Syria, no." He then turned back to driving, satisfied that he had described the political landscape for a visiting American.

At the Ministry of Information I related this shorthand course in political science to Zuhaire Genan, a ministry official. Jennan's small eyes had squinted through his thick glasses. He was the most cautious government official I had ever met, and in keeping with his nature, he weighed his answer carefully. His face darkened with an exaggerated sadness. "It is hard," he explained, "to undo twenty years of propaganda."

The answer caught me off guard and I fought an overwhelming urge to laugh. Jennan's meaty face was set in a slight scowl. He had not meant to be funny. His answer was a serious statement about Syrian policy, an efficient way of articulating Hafez al Asad's turn toward the West.

It had been a good war for Hafez al Asad. Syria's regional and international isolation had ended. The political fortunes of the Syrian leader were looking better. Iraq's victory in the Iran-Iraq War, Asad's record in the West for harboring "terrorists," the decision of the Palestine National Council to adopt a two-state solution and renounce terror had all worked against Damascus. Those accounts had been more than balanced by the spectacular victory in the Iraqi desert.

Syria's diplomatic ties with Britain had been restored. The economic sanctions imposed by the European community had been lifted. An agreement for technical, economic, and trade cooperation between Syria and the United Arab Emirates had been signed. The Gulf Cooperation Council worked out an economic development plan that was worth more than 10 billion dollars. The peace was proving to be more difficult.

If the Jordanians had moved closer to Washington, the Syrians were acting like a shy debutante at her first dance. Syria was unsure of the postwar role that put the country in the American camp. Damascus spent the summer after the war considering signing on to the American proposals for a peace process, but there were lots of questions about where this was leading. The ruling Ba'th party had taken pains to explain the about-face on entering a peace process in meetings with party members and military officers. It turned out that Syria's Ba'thist ideology, "one Arab nation, with a sacred mission," had room to bet on a second term for George Bush. Al Asad dropped two long-held pillars of Syrian policy that could have blocked American efforts: a demand that the United Nations was the proper institution to negotiate peace, and a pledge that Syria would not sit at the table until Israel returned all the territories won in the 1967 war. Asad had sided with the angels in the peace process, and won gratitude in Washington.

How was the new arrangement with Washington playing on the streets of Damascus? There are no polls in the country, no way to gauge the popular mood. It was possible to spend an entire reporting trip in Damascus without seeing any Syrian officials. There was no guarantee that the granting of a journalist visa obligated the officials at the Information Ministry to arrange interviews. I decided to crash the season's opening of the pool at the Cham Palace Hotel.

The mirrored elevator at the Cham Palace opened onto a wonderful party on the third floor. The band, at one corner of the blue-white light of the pool, gave the party an unusual dignity. A constellation of hotel waiters in white jackets orbited with glasses of white wine. The well-dressed crowd was thick at the food tables. The roar of small talk, a mixture of Arabic and French, drifted off the water into the night air.

This was the Damascus elite: Ba'thist party members and government officials. This was a world away from the battered buses spewing blue smoke, the tiny Fiats that clogged the city streets, and the grimy office buildings of downtown Damascus.

There was no hint here of the thousands of Iranian tourists who came to Syria to visit the tomb of Zeinab, the Prophet's granddaughter. There were no scowling Iranian mullahs in their brown cloaks and turbans sipping wine with the Ba'thists. There were no large portraits of Hafez al Asad.

I maneuverd my way around the food tables hoping that some one would strike up a conversation. No one did. I plucked up my courage and asked a plump man in a suit who all these people were. "We all work for the government," he said, responding to my English. "Who are you?" I told him I was an American journalist and to my surprise he gave me a warm smile and pumped my hand. Hamed worked in the Ministry of Economics and he had just received an invitation from the U.S. State Department for a month-long visit to the United States.

"Please, come to my house for lunch, come to my house for dinner, or come to my office tomorrow and we will talk," he said, eager to get back to the table of free food. I had what I had come for—an interview with a Syrian official. Happy with my victory, I wandered back to my room and watched CNN until I fell asleep.

The Ministry of Economics was working toward Syria's version of a free-market economy. The economics minister, Mohammed Fahdi, an American-educated economist, was a strong supporter of free markets. The country was moving away from close economic ties with the Soviet Union. Hamed was part of the team of economists at the ministry working to open up the economy.

At the beginning of our interview he gave me a copy of the country's new investment law. It was designed to promote the private sector and there was some speculation among foreign diplomats that Syria was going to drop its tax rates from a high of 92 percent. The success of the experiment depended on the politics of the region.

About 60 percent of the citizens of Syria are under twenty and their prospects for employment are dim. The government already provides jobs for more than 40 percent of the work force. Asad's Syria is faced with a growing number of young people who see emigration as the only way to find a job. Many who stay in the country and are alienated by the nature of the regime look to the mosque for answers. Some join underground Muslim fundamentalist groups, a particular threat to the regime after an armed rebellion in Hama in 1982 where Syrian forces killed more than 15,000 people. The struggle against Israel is the official reason given for Syria's economic chaos, but Syrian officials recognize that the economy is the country's weak spot. Hamed, like every Syrian, was concerned about the peace process.

He leaned across the desk and asked:

Let us just be citizens of the world, not American or Syrian.

Why is Israel not happy for peace? Why is Israel using so many no's? They say no to Europe, no to the United Nations, even though the U.N created Israel. They just want a ceremony instead of a peace process, which is nonsense.

I soon realized that Hamed's definition of citizen of the world only applied to him. My answers were brushed aside and he continued on his tirade against Israel and the peace process. He explained that Syria wanted peace. He explained that Syria must have the Golan Heights back, the piece of rich farmland lost in the 1967 war. He explained that the Americans had to pressure the Israelis.

If there was one issue that galvanized Syrians and was the under-pinning to Hafez al Asad's regime, it was the idea that Israel was the enemy. There was agreement from the leading intellectuals to the poorest cab drivers that Zionism was the root of all evil. The Syrians were obsessed with the topic in ways that other Arabs were not.

At the end of the first face-to-face meeting between Syrian and Israeli officials, in Madrid, Spain, Syria's foreign minister had said, "The Israeli government is more hard line than its people, while the Syrian government wants peace more than its population." It was probably closer to the truth than any official pronouncement issued by the Syrian government in the entire four-day conference. But that was far in the future.

The "Big Bang" theory of a peace conference was also operating in Damascus. The old options had been blown away with the opening of the ground war. Asad sided with the American-led coalition because it had been in his interest to do so. He gained a free hand in Lebanon. He ensured a steady stream of Arab aid and a role in the postwar Arab order. He lost one superpower patron and gained another. But, as Zuhair Gewan said, it was hard to undo twenty years of propaganda.

The government-controlled Syrian press stopped using the "Zionist entity" to define Israel. "So called" was dropped from newspaper reports on Israeli political developments. It was a small step in a process that was just beginning.

I tried to imagine Hamed's model for a successful peace conference. It would go something like this: The Arab delegates would gather in a conference hall and announce that Israeli policies had been unfair for forty years. An Arab spokesman would read out the relevant United Nations resolutions that contained the formula for "land for peace."

At some moment, the Israeli delegation would announce that it had all gone terribly wrong. They had seen the error of their ways and were now prepared to hand over the Golan Heights, the highlands overlooking Israeli cities, that had been captured in the 1967 war. The Israelis would then offer to return the occupied west bank and the Gaza Strip. This was only right, considering that the United Nations resolutions had set out the terms of a peace treaty. The Americans and the Europeans would have already weighed in with their pronouncements on the justness of the Arab cause.

A casual browse through the English-language *Syrian Times* was a lesson in Damascus politics. In an article entitled "President Asad's Statement on the Israeli Obstacle Pivot of Attention," the Syrian news agency reported that the Italian newspaper *Al-Messagero* had reported the Syrian president's remarks: "Israel's behavior is disobedience to international legitimacy and disrespect to U.N. resolutions." The *Syr-*

ian Times reported that another Gulf news agency had taken the topic further based on the Syrian president's statements. "The just and comprehensive basis [for peace] is known to all and is explicitly expressed in U.N. resolutions which represent the international legitimacy. If the concerned superpowers have a true intention to resolve the conflict comprehensively and justly, thus guaranteeing peace and security, then the path is as clear as the sun."

In the midsection of the newspaper, a book review offered the Syrian view on international terrorism. The book titled *The International Terrorism*, written by Dr. Muhammad Aziz Shukri, a law professor at Damascus University, included a black and white picture that showed an Israeli soldier standing over a Palestinian teenager who was lying on the ground. The review's title, "Israel: Real Incarnation of Systematic Terrorism," left no surprises about the author's analysis:

> Terrorist practices in its ugliest forms started from the very dawn of this century by the Zionist settler-colonial gangs which based their strategy on the elimination of Palestinian Arab people from their own homeland to usurp it as a whole constituting a bridge-head to expand more and more until the foundation of "greater Israel from the Nile to the Euphrates."

It was vintage Syrian propaganda, the typical diet of views fed to the Syrian public. Yet, Hafez al Asad had sent his diplomats to Madrid for an unprecedented face-to-face meeting with Israeli negotiators. The linkage, so strongly denied by President Bush during the crisis, was there. Operation Desert Storm had brought the Syrians to the negotiating table. Syrian's realignment in the months following the invasion brought the country closer to the Gulf states, Egypt, and the United States. The neutralization of Iraq and Saddam's support of radical Palestinian actors had been a factor; so was the new posture of Moscow so clearly demonstrated during the crisis.

RIYADH, MAY 1991

Desert storms usually destroy rather than build, but Saudi Arabia, the protector of Islam's holy places, and the possessor of 25 percent of the world's oil reserves, emerged from Operation Desert Storm with few regrets. With remarkable speed the House of Saud put the war behind it, satisfied that an international coalition was called, defeated the Iraqi enemy, and most important, packed up its gear and went home. The victory was so complete that many of the allied armies departed within weeks of the liberation of Kuwait. The House of Saud had survived the most serious challenge in its history at a political price that few would have predicted on August 2, 1990, when Iraqi tanks were right next door. Nevertheless, the financial toll for the protection was enormous. Saudi accounting put the overall cost of the war at 60 billion dollars.

President George Bush's undefined promise of a new world order did not extend to the countries of the Gulf. These traditional and tribal societies seemed remarkably untouched by the most violent chapter in their history. The new world order looked much like the old world order in Riyadh except for one important difference: The kingdom's military and political relationship with the United States could no longer be denied.

After the war Kuwait and Saudi Arabia abandoned the Arab option and openly looked to Washington for their protection. The Damascus agreement on regional defense between the Gulf states with Egypt and Syria was stillborn. The participation of Arab armies in the defeat of Saddam Hussein was politically significant, but it couldn't hide the fact that Washington had provided the power behind the military punch. The American military umbrella was unfurled to protect Saudi Arabia from its external enemies in a region that remained deeply suspicious of Washington's relationship with Israel. The more public relationship makes Saudi participation in talks with the Jewish state a liability if the process collapses because of American weakness in the face of determined Israeli opposition to compromise with the Arabs.

Saudi Arabia's dilemma remained the same as it was before August 2, 1990. The kingdom is a sparsely populated state with no great military power. The consequences of that fact began to play out in domestic and foreign policy in the year after the fighting ended. The military conflict prompted the House of Saud to take an active role in settlement of the region's most intractable dispute: the Arab-Israeli conflict.

Saudi Arabia's new international assertiveness survived the crisis. There were small and large examples that the kingdom was stepping out on the international stage. In August 1991 the Saudis suspended their first loan to the Soviet Union to protest the coup. When a countercoup prevailed, the loan was restored, and in December, Saudi Arabia extended diplomatic recognition to nine former Soviet republics. The kingdom, along with other Arab governments, took part in peace talks with Israel, and the Saudis played a behind-the-scenes role in keeping the Syrians at the table. Saudi Arabia paid the tab in Moscow when the Russians couldn't afford to host the multilateral component of the peace talks. While members of the royal family still spoke with bitterness about Jordan, the border between the two countries was reopened.

Saudi Arabia's relations with the Palestinians was a complicated and contradictory affair in the months following the fighting. Yasser Arafat, the chairman of the Palestine Liberation Organization, was unwelcome in Riyadh. His political pronouncements during the crisis had earned him the enmity of the House of Saud, and no PLO official was extended an invitation to the Saudi capital. The large Palestinian community in the kingdom remained uneasy with the knowledge that its future was uncertain. At the same time the Saudis continued to subsidize HAMAS, the Muslim fundamentalists' group within the Palestinian movement that had a strong following in Israeli-occupied territories. HAMAS posed a direct challenge to the PLO's secular leadership and was adamantly opposed to any negotiations with Israel. Yet, the Saudis promoted the very negotiations that HAMAS was working against.

In the months leading to the military confrontation with Iraq, Saudi Arabia's ambassador to Washington, Prince Bandar ibn Sultan, was a key player as the kingdom abandoned its usually behind-the-scenes diplomacy for the front-line role in the crisis. Prince Bandar lobbied like-minded constituencies in Washington and forged links with American Jewish groups who shared the Saudis' vision of Iraq's threat. Bandar tapped those channels again as the parties deeply involved in the Arab-Israel dispute prepared for their first face-to-face negotiations.

A year after the Iraqi invasion of Kuwait, Joseph Lieberman, a United States senator from Connecticut, was welcomed to Riyadh by the Saudi government. Senator Lieberman was touring the region as the chairman of the Gulf Pollution Task Force. The trip would not have been noteworthy except for two items: Lieberman was a Jew, and when he filled out the visa application form, he stated his religious preference. Lieberman, a strong supporter of Israel, had traveled to the Jewish state and his passport contained an Israeli stamp. The Saudis had chosen an American senator, an observant Jew, to make a political gesture. Bandar made the trip possible.

For years many Arab states denied entrance to Jews to protest Israel's policy of restricting visas to Arabs. The Arab League policy meant that travelers with an Israeli visa in their passports were routinely denied entrance to Arab countries. In March 1991, U.S. senator Frank Lautenberg, a New Jersey Democrat, complained that the Saudis would have denied him entrance if he had an Israeli visa stamp in his passport. But now Saudi Arabia ended the taboo.

Lieberman first met Bandar on Capitol Hill in the office of Senator Bob Dole. The occasion was the congressional vote on the United Nations resolution to use force in the Gulf. "He said to me, 'People say I should get to know you,'" said Lieberman. Bandar invited the junior senator from Connecticut to a farewell dinner at his home for the head of the Central Intelligence Agency, William Webster. "Bandar convinced his people that the policy couldn't be explained after the war. We had cemented a relationship. We went over there to fight. I said I hoped they would change the policy," Lieberman noted. A few months later an eight-member delegation from the American Jewish Congress was invited to the Saudi capital, the first official American Jewish group to come to the country.

In November 1991, Prince Bandar broke another important taboo. At a meeting in New York he spoke for two hours to the Conference of Presidents of Major Jewish Organizations. Bandar had met some of them during the crisis. He shared their concerns about Iraq. He formed private alliances, and he had made friends. On a November morning in Washington, the private relationship became public.

The Saudi prince talked to the group about peace in the Middle East. He shared his vision for the future. It will take time, he told them, but it will happen. "God had to send three messengers to the Middle East," he told them. "If it took God three times, it will take us a little longer."

In Riyadh, the talk focused on Saddam Hussein rather than on the peace process or the war. The images of the conflict faded as private businessmen experienced a postwar boom. The wartime government spending, and the ready cash of the Kuwaiti refugees, brought real advantages to Saudi Arabia's private business community. The quick victory gave Saudis a confidence in the future and they expressed their feelings in a flurry of business activities. On the other hand, the shock of the Iraqi invasion and the response of the House of Saud jolted the extreme polls of political activism in the country, and the opposing camps resumed their confrontations almost as soon as the smoke cleared from the battlefield. In the year that followed the war with Iraq, the House of Saud began to define the limits of political activity in what appeared to be the faintest stirring of political reform.

In the summer of 1991 the forty-seven Saudi women who had mounted a driving protest in the capital were quietly allowed to return to their university posts and collect compensation for the pay they had lost. Their passports were returned. There was no public announcement of King Fahd's decision, but like all important events in the kingdom, the decision was well known. The ban on driving remained firmly in place.

A few months earlier four of the "driving" women had been summoned to a meeting with King Fahd. They were told to bring a letter of apology signed by the forty-seven participants. Late one evening, the four representatives were ushered into the king's palace in Riyadh. They were greeted by the king's wife, who made it clear she was unhappy with their deeds. According to an account of the event, the king's wife chided them for their behavior: "We sent you abroad, and you come home and don't care about the customs here."

They listened in silence as she accused them of contacting CNN just to embarrass the country. The conversation was not what they had expected. However, when King Fahd entered the room he greeted them with a wide smile and shook the hand of each woman.

"Why didn't you come before?" he asked. "I had nothing against you. When a mother speaks harshly to a child she hugs them later."

The four women had spent hours practicing their apologies but King Fahd had other topics on his mind. He talked about Saddam Hussein for the next two hours. He recounted the history of the Gulf War and told them that he had tried to call Saddam on the telephone in the early hours of the invasion. King Fahd had come through the crisis with his popularity at an all-time high. His decision to invite American troops to the kingdom to protect the country had proved to be a wise choice in the minds of his subjects.

"Tell your friends I have nothing against them," said the Saudi king as his bid his servants to show them to the door.

The meeting was a demonstration of classic Saudi domestic policy, the traditional balancing act between the traditional trend and the modernizing one. The king did not address the issue of driving in his meeting with these bold Saudi women. King Fahd was the good cop and the bad cop. He had punished the demonstrators to assuage the anger of the conservatives, and he had taken their punishment away when he felt the moment was right.

In the months following the crisis Saudi Arabia's outspoken liberals renewed their demands for a more open system of government. They delivered a petition to the king that called for democratic reforms, respect for human rights, freedom of expression, the creation of political parties, and the right for women to vote. The liberals, often the Western-educated graduates and technocrats in Saudi Arabia's government bureaucracy, were reminding the king of his commitment to a consultative council, a form of government that would not rival the power of the House of Saud but establish an open forum *for* debate.

The first reply came a few months later, not from the royal family, but from the religious political opposition. This memorandum, distributed in the mosques, contained demands for a restructure of the government, the military, and a religious critique of the country's banking system.

The document defined an alternative to the platform of the Western-educated elite and contained these key points:

> Punishment of all corrupt elements, "whoever they are, wherever they are, without any exception of rank."
>
> Equitable distribution of wealth among all members of the nation.
>
> Total reform of the press: the creation of a strong Islamic media and of propaganda tools to be used in the service of Islam worldwide; closure of the "corrupt" media.
>
> Preservation of the Islamic nation's interests, purity, and unity by "keeping it out of non-Islamic pacts and treaties," complete reform of the kingdom's embassies abroad to bring them into line with the laws and interests of Islam.

Those public documents, from opposite sides of the political spectrum, distributed throughout the kingdom and published in Arab newspapers, would have been unthinkable before the Gulf War. Open domestic political debate was unusual in the kingdom. The royal family preferred to handle issues privately and were only moved to act when a clear majority of public opinion bubbled to the top in the meetings that royals had regularly with small segments of the population. The country was not equipped to handle demands for quick change.

Within weeks of the manifestos the Saudi government made tentative steps to address the discontent of the political activists. In the fall of 1991, King Fahd issued a royal decree that showed he was responding to the political fault lines in the country. On that day the king accepted the resignation of Lieutenant General Khalid bin Sultan, the Saudi commander of the Arab coalition forces.

The forty-two-year-old two-star general had been carefully selected to head the Arab coalition in the war with Iraq. Khalid bin Sultan was the young, Western-educated son of a powerful prince, the minister of defense. He commanded the Arab armies of the coalition with a cocky self-assurance. He served as General Norman Schwarzkopf's counterpart, confidant, and friend in the seven months of American deployment in Saudi Arabia. Prince Khalid represented his king at the cease-fire ceremonies in the desert of southern Iraq. He presided over the departure ceremonies of the foreign armies of the coalition. He had done all that, and planned to preside over Saudi Arabia's post-war expansion of the army.

Part of the reason for his dismissal could be explained by his dealings during the American deployment in Saudi Arabia. The Saudi contribution to the Gulf War was an "in kind" payment, meaning that the Saudi government supplied food, water, housing, and fuel for the American military. In the time-honored tradition of Saudi princes, Khalid spread the contracts for the work to a close circle of family and friends. The war had been good for Saudi Arabia's private sector, especially for the Saudi businessmen who were favored with the lucrative government contracts to supply the foreign forces in the kingdom. The fact that Khalid kept the contracts within a small circle prompted grumbling among those who had been left out. The news of Khalid's political troubles spread quickly within the American military community, who were sad to see him go.

At the same time as the country's activists were making their political demands known, religious zealots were stepping up their profile on the streets of Saudi Arabia's major cities. They had been disturbed by the sudden influx of so many non-Muslims during the American deployment, and the mutawa, the enforcers of Saudi Arabia's strict code of Islamic conduct, stepped up their patrols as the American forces went home. Their targets were women deemed to be immodestly dressed and what they saw as the war-induced drift toward Western influences. The excesses of the mutawa reached such a point that shopkeepers reported a sharp drop in business because Saudi shoppers chose to stay home rather than face the harassment.

Saudi Arabia's Muslim extremists railed against almost every aspect of the kingdom's policies, agitating in mosques and on cassette tapes circulated throughout the country. In a particularly reckless gesture, the extremists labeled female relatives of powerful members of the Saudi royal family prostitutes. A new petition, signed by twenty theologians and jurists, was addressed to the country's supreme religious leader, the grand mufti. This was another brand of political activism, targeted against Saudi Arabia's participation in the November 1991 Middle East peace conference in Madrid. The petition pointed out that the peace talks amounted to a capitulation and that those who wanted peace with the Jewish state were not Muslims.

In a defining moment in Saudi Arabian politics, the country's religious establishment turned against the zealots. The grand mufti, Bin

Baz, said the zealots were working "against the teaching of Allah" and denounced the "lies and false rumors of tapes" from those who "whisper secretly in their meetings and record their poison on cassettes distributed to the people." The fissure between the older generation of Saudi Arabia's political establishment and the younger, aggressive religous extremists who used the language of Islam to challenge the House of Saud was established. The limits of political protest were taking shape. The House of Saud was setting the stage for the country's first consultative council, a political reform that had been promised in the months of upheaval caused by the Iraqi invasion.

On March 1, 1990, the Custodian of The Two Holy Mosques addressed his desert kingdom. The ordinariness of the televised performance belied the importance of the message. King Fahd peered out from his heavy black rimmed glasses as he read from a document that described unprecedented political reform. In part, it was the fulfillment of a promise made by his father, Abd al-Aziz ibn Saud, almost forty years earlier.

The reforms were small steps by western standards. The King outlined a plan for a sixty member Majlis Al-Shura (Conservative Council) appointed by him, rather than elected for a four-year term. The members of the Majlis would propose but not approve legislation and the King maintained his power to arbitrate disputes between the Saudi cabinet, a bastion of royal family power, and the Majlis. This was not democracy but a cautious process of liberalization that institutionalized popular participation in government.

King Fahd outlined a new "Basic Law" that amounted to the country's first constitution with guarantees of personal freedoms and civil liberties. Saudi citizens were told that the state is to "ensure security for all its citizens and residents. No person can be arrested, or jailed, or have his actions restricted except under the law." The message appeared to be aimed at the excesses of the religious police who had become enforcers of conservative cultural customs rather than Islamic rulings on behavior.

The House of Saud's power remained intact but it appeared that the beneficiaries of the package of reforms were Saudi Arabia's highly educated corp of government bureaucrats, academics, and businessmen. For the first time, the House of Saud was reaching out beyond the conservative religious establishment to this new class of modern Saudis.

The king cited "momentous events in the recent pass" that had made the reforms necessary. It was the first public admission that the Gulf crisis had fundamentally changed this insular desert nation. Desert Storm, with its deployment of more than a half a million foreign troops on Saudi soil, had excelerated a political as well as a religious debate over the future direction of the country. The crisis had sharpened a taste for the political freedoms enjoyed in the other parts of the world.

INDEX

Kuwaiti
  in Dubai, 88–90
  in Saudi Arabia, 106
Palestinian
  from Kuwait, 178–79
  in Jordan, 193–97
Representative government
  in Kuwait, 182
  in Saudi Arabia, 124–25, 210–11
Reservists, U.S., callup of, 96–97
Resistance, Kuwaiti, 173–75
  broadcasts by, 89
  effectiveness of, 183–84
  formation of, 75–76
  intelligence reports by, 18
  al Sabah family and, 20, 188–89
Rezeq, Zaki, 195–97
Rodeeni, Col. Khalid, 20
"Romads," 30
Rushdie, Salman, 14

al Sabah, Fahd al Amad, 189
al Sabah family
  democratic government and, 90–91
  loyalty checks on Kuwaiti soldiers, 20
  origins of, 183
  policy in postwar Kuwait, 181–82
  resistance and, 17, 188–89
  return to Kuwait, 169, 171
al Sabah, Nawaf al Ahmad al Jaber, Sheikh, 176
al-Sabah, Saad, at Cairo summit, 84
Sager, Staff Sgt. Mike, 30
Salman bin Abd al-Aziz, Prince, 120
  women drivers and, 123, 126–27
Sanctions, against Iraq, Kurdish massacres (1988) and, 59–60
Sarin, 114
Saud, House of, modernizers versus traditionalists in, 126–27
Saudi Arabia
  American cultural influences, 98–99
  at Cairo summit, 83
  challenges from Arab left to, 47
  changing male-female relations in, 132–33
  hawks versus doves in, 104–7
  Iraqi invasion of Kuwait and, 67–68

liberals versus Islamists in, 125
military agreements with U.S., 47, 49
moves for liberalization of government, 124–25
nationalism in, 129–30
non-aggression pact with Iraq (1989), 67
oil boom, 42
political demonstrations in. See Driving, by women
political views in, 100–2
postwar economic situation, 209
postwar policies, 206–14
religious conservatism of, 119
restrictions on women, 117–20
U.S. arms sales to, 140
U.S. relations with, 69
See also Mecca
Saudi military
  chemical weapons equipment and, 114
  in liberation of Kuwait, 22–25
  organizational structure, 113–14
  readiness of, 109–10
  U.S. military education of, 110–11
  U.S. Special Forces and, 94–95
  U.S. training of, 111–13
Saudi National Guard
  American advisors to, 69
  preparedness, 38
Saudi Royal Air Force
  combat experience, 37–38
  See also Air Defense Command
Schroeder, Patricia, 118
Schwartzkopf, Gen. H. Norman, 37, 68
  as head of CENTCOM, 39–40
Scud missiles, Iraqi, 28–29, 160–161
Seigman, Henry, 105–6
Semik, Lt. Col. Martin, 20–21, 30
Sex, in Saudi society, 130–31
Shaheed Brigade (Kuwaiti), 21–22
Shamir, Yitzhak, 86
Al-Shamrani, Capt. Ayed, 115–16
Sharif, Col. Ibrahim, 153–54
Shiites
  in Kuwait, 172–73
  Iraqi invasion and, 76
Shopping malls, in Saudi Arabia, 98–99, 131